David Marshall

CAL/CBT– the great debate

Chartwell-Bratt  Studentlitteratur

© David Marshall and Chartwell-Bratt, 1988

Chartwell-Bratt (Publishing and Training) Ltd
ISBN 0-86238-144-4

Printed in Sweden
Studentlitteratur, Lund

ISBN 91-44-28111-0   1 2 3 4 5 6 7 8 9 10 | 1991 90 89 88

Contents

David V Marshall is a senior lecturer at the North Staffordshire Polytechnic and a visiting lecturer at the University of Keele and at the Management Centre, University of Aston in Birmingham. He has been an active researcher into CAL/CBT for fourteen years, being responsible for the creation of major educational and training software systems, and is author of *'Best Terms – A Guide to Software Acquisition'* and *'The Computer and the Law Teacher'*, as well as articles in *Computers and Law*, *The Computer Law and Security Report* and *University Computing*. He has also developed a significant number of management games, simulations and training exercises and is an active consultant in the management training field.

Dedication

This book is for Lloyd Currey who keeps finding me
good books to read,
and for
Adrian Trivett who literally keeps me on the move.

With special thanks to Bob Ritchie of the North Staffordshire Polytechnic
who was brave enough to read some of the chapters in draft (any remaining
mistakes being the fault of the author), and both Andrew Sherwood and
Chris Griffiths who proved that the PC of one manufacturer can be made to
talk to the mainframe of another.

CHAPTER 1

AN INTRODUCTION

This chapter is a general introduction to the principal theme of the role and function of computers in education. Computer technology has become commonplace in our everyday lives but, in the educational environment, computers may serve one of two purposes. They may either represent the subject matter of tuition, or they may support the tuition itself. But, as a preliminary issue, it is necessary to consider the scope of the function which education performs in our society, and to identify some of the problems which those in education face. Against this background, the potential contribution of the computer can more clearly be seen in later chapters.

1.1   Teaching in a social context

The traditional Socratic form of education is based on the human interaction between a teacher and one or more learners. It is not a science. It is a semi-intuitive process through which the teacher attempts to produce an environment in which each learner may develop in a personal capacity. This development depends upon a dialogue between the teacher and the learner in which there is sufficient flexibility of stimulus and response to cater for most individual needs. But because the process depends upon personal relationships, it is capable of being highly fallible. This will almost inevitably be the case where the temperaments of teacher and learner are not compatible. As a teaching system, it has the

1

virtue that the learner is the primary focus of attention, all information being tailored to that individual's immediate needs. But equally, it is an extremely inefficient use of valuable human resources because the teacher will only see one or two learners at a time. It is therefore a characteristic either of cultures where a leisured class can afford a more personal means of self-development, or of a highly egalitarian society where potentially the most effective form of teaching is made available to all those people likely to benefit from the education process.

Through the passage of time, human society has tended to become more complex. One of the more usual consequences of this complexity is that rigidities begin to appear in most of the major social systems which develop. Indeed, these rigidities represent an instinctive form of social conservatism – a form of self-defence mechanism which is designed to keep all novelty, uncertainty and confusion at bay until it can be safely assimilated into the domain of the known and acceptable. As a part of this gradual development of social understanding, education theorists and psychologists have followed a pattern of scientification, i.e. they have taken observable human actions and reactions, and have defined and described them in increasingly scientific terms. The result is a technical discourse to explain more precisely what occurs during the interactive education process. Yet, at its heart lies the simple proposition that the education process is divisible into the two related functions of teaching and learning, the purpose of teaching being to promote learning.

The teacher's choice of teaching methods inevitably reflects assumptions about the purpose of teaching. Since understanding is not genetically communicated from one generation to the next, knowledge must be learned. This is not to deny the instinctive human drive to acquire knowledge, for information, in the most general sense of that word, may be gained through everyday experiences in a non-structured fashion. Hence, the baby with normal physical and intellectual capacities learns the skills of locomotion and speech through experimentation and observation. Then, as each individual begins to grow up, parents, friends and events begin to provide both conscious and subconscious insights into the roles and manners of society. But for the communication of more specialised information, and to provide a degree of control over the socialisation of the young, the education process has moved away from the original Socratic ideals of one-to-one tuition, and has been formalised by grouping professional teachers and the learners in schools, colleges and universities.

There are many justifications for this promotion of education as a communal activity, and among the most important are the desire to give the learners the opportunity to gain a breadth and a depth of experience unlikely or impossible through chance, and the need to acquire economies of scale in the use of skilled teachers. Further, the rapid growth of human knowledge, particularly in the science-based subjects, has made it impossible for a single human being to grasp all the essentials

2

of human knowledge. Thus, both teachers and learners should benefit from the opportunity to pool their knowledge, for even the most gifted of modern polymaths will benefit from exposure to the new ideas and perspectives represented by different people.

The result of this growth in the amount of information available to be learned, and in the number of basic skills necessary for survival in the increasingly complex social environment, is that, for each individual who lives and grows within the contemporary framework of Western urbanised society, the education experience may be a long, and sometimes painful, process. It is frequently characterised by uncertainties, where outcomes are difficult to predict or assess. Yet, where these outcomes take the form of qualifications, they are now cloaked in new significance. Many of the better jobs depend upon the acquisition of an appropriate diploma or degree, so the pressures on the contemporary education system and its students have become increasingly significant.

Indeed, British society has always claimed a desire to establish itself as a true meritocracy, but the progress actually made has tended to produce a potentially inegalitarian structure. This is reflected in the fact that the quality of education to determine apparent merit is so dependent both upon the type of educational opportunities offered by the particular schools and colleges attended, and upon the calibre of the teaching staff who control the particular courses studied. Hence, attendance at certain schools and colleges may predispose some employers to offer employment even though the resulting examination grades are poor. But the converse is not necessarily true, for good examination grades achieved may not in themselves overcome the inhibitions held by some professions against employing individuals who do not have the right social and educational background.

1.1.1 Why do people study, and what effect does this have on the education system?

A further factor of importance in this equation of education and social opportunity, is the diversity of motivation for undertaking study. Initially, attendance at school is compulsory for most people, and this fact alone may induce some resistance to learning. If the physical and spiritual environment in each school cannot overcome this perhaps perverse resistance, and no examination-based qualifications of substance are obtained, the number of employment opportunities available to each individual will be reduced. In practice, much of the teaching at secondary and tertiary levels is non-vocational; it is teaching dictated by administrative requirements, and not by the needs of commerce and industry. As a result, the transition between education and employment is made more difficult. Moreover, even if there was the will to make changes, the usual educational establishment lacks a sufficiently rapid feedback from employers upon which to

3

base corrections for deficiencies. Sadly, these deficiencies are often recognised by the students, and add to the demotivating quality of the environment.

However, regardless of individual reaction, the schools exist to pass on what the experienced feel that the young need to know. In this early context, a more authoritarian and didactic approach can legitimately be taken toward the teaching process. But as the student matures, a greater burden of responsibility for the assimilation of knowledge should fall upon the individual, and the learning process should, within the limitations of good learning practices, be democratised. Sometimes, the student will have a narrow utilitarian motive in terms of career, training or certification, and will not necessarily respond to this apparent responsibility. But other students will be self-motivated and will relish the freedom to make a contribution towards self-improvement. It will also produce much greater intellectual self-reliance which, in turn, should make the student more attractive in the employment market.

However, no matter what the motive or the method, education is now being demanded by a larger percentage of the population. On a more grandiose basis, the state may see the money spent on education, "as an investment in the nation's human talent" (1) where each student becomes the inheritor of, "the funded capital of civilisation". (2) On a more practical level, those going through the system may be see the end-product qualifications as the only way in which to get one of the better jobs. As a result, there are conflicting demands for both greater specialisation and greater general adaptability, i.e. people want more precisely targeted qualifications as against the employment market which needs more portable skills, while changes in the economy give rise to the need for rapid retraining facilities. Indeed, with such large numbers of unemployed, continuing education and retraining may be perceived as useful political mechanisms for keeping the number of registered unemployed down, and in turn create new teaching jobs.

The overall resultant pattern is one of increasing divergence in learner age and background. The British system begins in the pre-school environment of the kindergarten/nursery school, moves through primary and secondary schooling, and emerges into further and higher education. All these opportunities for learning should cover the multiplicity of individual pupil or student needs – from elementary arithmetic to GCSE and A Level courses; from technical engineering training for school-leavers to post-graduate courses in quantum mechanics; and from the Open University degree courses and part-time courses for the mature students, to pre-retirement and similar courses for the older student.

However, it is only outside the realms of compulsory education, where the focus of the program will tend to be the convenience of that institution and its staff, that there are any real pressures to make the courses positively attractive to students. If adults are to be encouraged to join evening classes out of interest, and the viability of these classes is to be determined by student numbers, their willingness to give up their time will be determined by the nature of the course offered. This pressure is encouraged by the ever-increasing number of learners who demand new arrangements for the provision of information and more flexible teachers. Further, the individual must learn more in a shorter time. The status of individuals within employment, or the needs of an individual in seeking employment, create needs for vocational training. With these pressures in the job market, more articulate adults are brought back into the education milieu with resultant potential for criticism if the courses offered are not those of most utility. Indeed, what often makes the criticism effective is that the criteria for judging the competence of staff and the relevance of materials, are those of adults who are usually acknowledged to be the equal of the staff in terms of age and experience.

1.1.2 What are the problems in the education system?

Added to the pressures generated by the general increase in demand, there is an "information explosion". Human knowledge is now expanding at an exponential rate, with more people producing more new ideas at more centres of learning in the world than ever before. Further, there is an increasingly rapid downwards migration of subject matter. Topics that would only be taught at universities twenty years ago, are now considered suitable for secondary schools and sometimes primary schools, e.g. set theory and computer programming. In the more dynamic subject areas at a higher academic level, both teachers and learners must adapt and change together. Even in schools, where the pace of change is slowed by curriculum constraints, staff development is still essential. Thus, at a time when teachers are expected to become more economically efficient, i.e. teach more students more effectively, more research and subject development time is required simply to keep up to date; something which cannot be done effectively if class contact hours are kept high.

Yet teachers do conscientiously overcome many of these problems, and there is significant academic progress and achievement in which Britain may justifiably take some pride. But for all the undoubted success, the problems of truancy and disruptive behaviour are also spreading through the schools system, and are now becoming a problem even at primary school level. Lawrence and Steed (3) recently carried out an extensive survey, and report the strong view that disruptive behaviour, both as individuals and as a group, has particularly begun to affect the youngest age groups during the last ten years. The behaviour most frequently observed consisted in not listening, poor concentration, aggression towards other pupils, disobedience, and bad or abusive lang-

5

uage. This combination of bullying, restlessness and defiance of
teacher authority now significantly disturbs the teaching process
and/or the running of schools, particularly in urban areas, and
the resultant poor learner attitudes inhibit overall levels of
performance.

Even where there are no behavioural problems, difficulties have
been caused by the dramatic falls in the school rolls in some
parts of the country. This has produced a wider range of abilities in any given class or set, and an inefficient use of manpower
in small units. Sadly, the standards of education have suffered
in such contexts, because the right level of staffing and coverage of subjects cannot be justified in economic terms. But there
remains strong opposition to the closure of "local" schools. This
has perpetuated the decline in standards achievable across each
affected Local Education Authority's area at a time when rate
capping forces economies.

1.1.3 What should the goals of the education system be?

As a paper exercise, it would be possible to list all the most
desirable educational outcomes from the education system. But
no matter what the context, achieving the ideal in the real world
is frequently impossible. Consequently, if the aim is more modestly to optimise educational outcomes at all levels of the
education system, both majority and minority groups' interests
need to be canvassed and directed towards agreed and defined
social goals. However, this exercise should not be restricted to
pedestrian practicalities. The primary goal should not merely be
minimum educational standards followed by employment. In this, it
must be acknowledged that, to some extent, one of the explicit
functions of schools and colleges, and of the examination system
which they support, has been to label people as successful or
failures, and consequently, to make jobs more or less available.
But the long term goals should transcend this obvious necessity,
and include the creation of dignity and self-respect for the
individual, and the transmission of enough confidence to be able
to face life's challenges rationally. Moreover, not only the
intellectually gifted deserve a good education. All relevant
classes and groups should be assisted, and the development of
skills should be encouraged at all levels of performance.

In an attempt to realise these goals, all the available technologies should be utilised. But the educational environment has
grown complex. Teachers used to define curriculum elements,
identify relevant books and begin teaching. Today, textbooks are
only a part of the system. In appropriate circumstances, presentational media such as language laboratories, audio-visual aids,
and computers may each have a role to play. Indeed, the very
existence of such a multiplicity of potential communications
media resources requires more careful planning if all the devices

selected are to be effectively used, and integrated into a single course.

Yet, at this time of reappraisal of role and redesign of curricula, departmentalism and large group teaching has the tendency to produce a depersonalisation of teaching methodology by reducing the opportunity for staff to get to know the students. The economic arguments based on the efficient use of a teacher as an expensive resource, mask the fact that even though a great deal of teaching can be aimed at large groups of students, the activity of learning is ultimately performed by individuals. Further, monetary arguments gloss over the real educational difficulty that the larger the group, the greater the range in ability is likely to be. These and other similar problems must be confronted by the teacher.

1.1.4 What does a teacher actually do, and what teaching aids are appropriate?

A good teacher will do far more than merely communicate information – the learner's progress must be monitored, tasks may be set to give practice in the use of new information, side issues can be discussed and evaluated to throw light on the main point from a different perspective, and interest in, and motivation for, the subject in hand should be created and maintained. In seeking to meet these objectives, no teacher can or should rely exclusively on voice or personality. Instead, ways must be found to combat the inherent tendency of the system to depersonalise the educational experience, and to minimise the risk of alienation on the student's part. One such way is to make use of teaching aids. A "teaching aid" may be defined on a self-evident basis as a device which aids the teaching of a topic. The important point of omission in this definition is that it does not do the whole job. "[Teaching] Aids are not activities," (4) they merely permit diversity of activity.

Different aspects of a topic can be taught by different means:-

(a)   through a lecture whereby a teacher aims information at a larger group. This is the least precise instructional vehicle because the teacher cannot easily match the pace and style of presentation to the reaction of individuals. The basis of the judgement is that given effects of the teaching are only probable because student performance is not usually elicited. Lectures are therefore linked to other instructional delivery mechanisms which allow more feedback;

(b)   a discussion group where a smaller number of students, with or without the assistance and guidance of a teacher, interact by confirming or correcting each other's performance. Although time only permits a few students to be actively involved, it is a better guide for the teacher;

(c)   a tutorial where a small group of learners interact with a
      teacher,

(d)   guided reading or other individually-based activities, which
      must be allied to testing mechanisms to allow the teacher
      to monitor progress;

thus providing a possible variety of learning experience which is
important in capturing and holding a student's interest. For the
teacher, the smaller the group, the easier it is to maximise
control over the learning process, and both educational theorists
and practitioners have long had to face the problem of how to
make group teaching more effective on an individual level. Books
were an early attempt to overcome the difficulty, but student
response to written stimulus material may still be too passive.

The problem is therefore to select the most appropriate teaching
aid for each task. "It is intuitively obvious that for certain
kinds of learning objective, certain modes of presentation will
be more appropriate than others." (5) Television and video
sources, voice only or tape-slide preparations, the use of overhead projectors, slide projectors and the still media (viz.
charts, posters, magnetic boards and, even, chalk on blackboards,
rather than the dangerously new fangled felt pen on washable
white boards) may all have a role to play. It is a case of
matching the method with the characteristics of the students, the
subject matter to be taught, and the practical constraints (both
administrative and economic). It is also impossible to ignore the
personal preferences of the teacher who may not feel comfortable
with one particular method. Indeed, many of the long-term studies
have suggested that, whatever the theoretical advantages of any
one device or technique, no real advantage will be derived unless
the device or technique is properly integrated into the teaching.
Manifestly, this will not really occur unless the attitude of the
teachers is at least sympathetic, if not enthusiastic.   This
reflects the fact that teaching is not an engineering discipline
whereby students are manipulated according to preset theories, it
is a personal activity.

1.1.5 How can teachers be motivated to accept particular teaching
aids?

In this, motivation is a psychological phenomenon which cannot
really be trained or taught, but Richard deCharms argues that it
can be enhanced by going beyond the mere learning of facts, and
by introducing the individual to the concept of personal causation. This is something more than mere learning by doing, and is
based upon what happens psychologically when someone does something intentionally to produce a change. (6) The way in which

people originate an action implies freedom of choice on the part of the actor, and a corresponding acceptance of responsibility for the consequences of those actions. Conversely, a lack of choice releases the actor from responsibility. The idea is that people who do things have a sense of ownership in the outcome; they feel that they have something of themselves invested it. Thus, if someone else tries to impose a solution this tends to undermine the respondent's sense of ownership in the action, and may actually provide a disincentive to continue the activity.

One of the reasons that it may be difficult to persuade teachers to adopt any given teaching aid is that they do not own either the concept represented by the given aid nor, in the first instance, the material which is to be used in learning how to exploit the aid. If the teacher is simply supplied with existing teaching materials, and instructed in the use of teaching aids which are not considered acceptable, personal causation is not necessarily invoked, i.e. the teachers do not feel that they are making the qualitative difference in their students' performance. Consequently, unless teacher enthusiasm is engaged through training or actively solicited cooperation, there may be little inherent incentive to use the prepackaged materials. But, once a teacher has developed material which is suitable for pursuing a particular educational strategy, and has invested hard work in planning the implementation of that material, the strategy will tend to be used.

However, this leaves the difficulty that the teacher frequently considers that he or she is, or ought to be, the centre of attention. In some situations, the use of visual aids may extend the teacher's range without being perceived as threatening or damaging to self-esteem. Indeed, if these aids fail for any reason, then they can be blamed and criticised for not fulfilling their supporting role. This mechanical side of education lends itself for use as a scapegoat for the ills of the educational process, and often teachers may be apathetic or unaware of its potential uses. (7) This has proved to be particularly so in the case of the computer.

1.2 No one technology represents a panacea

Technology should not be anthropomorphised nor judged on an emotive basis. All machine innovations and developments are inherently neutral in terms of whether their likely impact on human society is good or bad. Man has always been a maker of tools, but he has also been a social animal and therefore has made tools within the context of the contemporary social organisation. "Innovation means the introduction of new traditions, roles and relationships. It means changing the way things have been done, perhaps for many years." (8) Thus, the development of the motor car led to the replacement of the horse as an everyday means of transportation. Although it was quicker and usually less trouble than the sometimes quirky quadruped, (and given that there were real difficulties in making the equine emission control regulations effective), the car was nevertheless often condemned as dirty, dangerous, etc. Mere efficiency may therefore be seen as not the only criterion of acceptability and, as a result, technological progress is not inevitable. Aesthetic and other intangible considerations may have equal validity in determining the pace and direction of change. Further, the actual results achieved in each case will depend upon the uses which are made of the given new device. If product utilisation occurs in a haphazard fashion and subject only to the public's whim, positive long-term social benefits may actually be achieved, but equally, non-constructive or asocial uses may arise. Thus, the best of glues and solvents may be found to have quite unsuspected side-effects.

1.2.1 Technology is not simply negative

Technology does not merely create new problems, it also offers new routes to the solution of existing problems. On a purely theoretical level, it would therefore take deliberate planning, or a formally interventionist policy, to maximise the opportunities for the most favourable human results. But in practice, it must be acknowledged that even with planning, favourable results cannot be guaranteed. Hence, like all other innovations, one of the problems about the computer is its capacity to change the world, e.g. it may produce a paperless society, which may help to preserve the landscape and to avoid the greenhouse effect by requiring the destruction of fewer trees, but automation may replace people and dispense with jobs.

Significantly, however, a study conducted by the Organisation of Economic Co-operation and Development and the International Tele-communication Union on the impact of telecommunications technology on employment, clearly demonstrates that the introduction of new technologies does not necessarily imply a reduction in industry as a whole, but rather the transfer of jobs from one sector of industry to another. The planners must therefore strive to ensure that society is peopled by the computer-enhanced human being rather than the computer-replaced human being. "There has always been a tendency that the introduction of new technology threatened to, and actually did, replace human labour, and thus employment in one form or another. I could imagine that this question came up during the Stone Age, right after the invention of the wheel and the construction of the first carriage. The stone carriers at that time may have feared unemployment, as one man could now push as many stones in a barrow as, let us say, three men could carry before." (9)

1.3 Why is the computer becoming so important?

Society in the 1980s is undergoing a period of rapid change which is, "perceived by society as accelerated change and somehow different from past change. This transition is reflected in the rapid development and integration of the computer with telecommunications technology and is evolving into what is called the Information Age." (10) Information is now a major sector of the economy which has grown out of the service sector. R.E. Butler estimates that in highly industrialised countries, it represents an average of 35% of their GNP. (11) The contribution of the information sector in the United States of America has been measured at approximately 40% of the gross domestic product, thus making this sector the single most significant sector in the US economy. In the modern information sector are included services such as education, databases, financial services, research and development, publishing, office machines, business activities, and clerical work for which there is not necessarily a physical product at the end of the production process.

The computer is a tool like any other, but the dynamic and continuing impact of the now ubiquitous chips is in part attributable to defence expenditure and the space race where the military necessity for ever better weaponry, code breaking and other intelligence requirements, has stimulated research. The diversification in the application of the new technology was then stimulated by the development of a more entrepreneurial spirit in world moarkets. Because the computer chip is a flexible creation, it is capable of being an expression of the mind, or some of the characteristics of the programmer. The only real limit on applications is the imagination of the designer. To that extent, Marshall McLuhan optimistically describes the computer as an intellectual prosthesis or potential amplifier of intelligence. (12)

Although this would have been an exaggerated claim at the time it was made, hardware and software developments have produced more machine-based capacities which will enhance the user's abilities. Thus, for example, a computer's database can be treated like a surrogate memory which can be accessed and manipulated according to the interrogative skills of the user. The claim may therefore be seen to be true in the same way that the development of the telephone has widened the power of human speech by facilitating conversation between persons who are geographically separated. However, with better interface technology, the longer-term dream (dystopic or otherwise) may be that computers will more directly expand human memory and augment human computational capacities. Thus, just as the development of the telescope and the microscope revolutionised science because, "those instruments broke through the limits imposed by the naked eye; computing has broken through the limits imposed by the naked brain." (13)

If real progress is to be made in this direction, it is suggested that the software itself should implicitly fulfil an educative role. Hence, programming developments should be designed to optimise the way in which people think rather than merely to improve machine function. The dangers are exemplified by the language of BASIC. "The advent of personal computers has pushed BASIC into a more extended role, not because it's easy for the programmer, but because it's easy for the computer!" (14) Thus, software applications and developments do not necessarily lead to improvements. In the business community, for example, it has been customary to view the computer in terms of the existing paper system. It is a matter of record that programs were developed to tackle specific accounting problems such as stock control, payroll and ledgers. The need came from the financial community, but the developments were computer-led. But by simply computerising the existing system, the antiquated or merely traditional methods became entrenched because people had spent time and money doing it. The result has been years of unplanned data-processing development of systems which lacked the necessary flexibility to adapt to the changing needs of business. As business in fact becomes more competitive, management needs more information about more events and in more detail than most systems were designed to provide.

The optimal way to computerise any organisation, commercial or otherwise, would be to make real changes. This is best achieved through an objective top-down study of the real needs of the organisation in terms of its strategy, operations and the systems needed to support its tasks. It demands that those responsible for the management of the organisation should think, for computers will not initiate thought. However, there is now even more to think about because the technology has developed the concept of the network. This is a communication system linking individual work stations which will perform a whole range of activities which previously were done manually, or were undertaken by a distant centralised data-processing department after a long delay. This devolution of computing power to individuals within the organisation has been matched by the development of simple to use, but highly sophisticated, applications packages, and this overall phenomenon is creating a training problem for decision-makers who now have powerful data analysis facilities at their desks, but are not sure what to do with them. However, no matter how sophisticated the hardware and software, it still requires human beings to have the will to change, and this is not always to be found.

1.3.1 To what extent is the computer like a motor car?

In many ways, it is reasonable to compare the computer with a motor car. Both are reasonably robust and reliable pieces of proven technology, but it is not necessary to understand the arcane inner workings of the internal combustion engine to be able to catch a bus or drive on the road. Similarly, it is not necessary to have any technical understanding of hardware design or software programming to be able to run the present generation of more user-friendly packages. With technical skills a car owner can customise the vehicle, undertake routine servicing or effect repairs. Equally, some understanding of the computer's capacities will enable the user to draw up specifications for software which a programmer would be able to implement, or there will be enough understanding to get the best out of complex packages, or to write simple programs. Finally, the expert driver may engage in minority sports like rallying or racing which make heavy demands on equipment, time and money, while the expert programmer can produce sophisticated software and suggest hardware modifications or improvements. After many years of social and economic evaluation, the car was accepted as one of the standard methods of transportion. Similarly, the computer is capable of providing powerful support for the human intellect, and it will do so if society is prepared to accept the consequences of redistribution of function as between human and machine.

1.3.2 What should the Government and industry be doing?

Perhaps sufficient progress has been made in contemporary society towards the general acceptance of computer technology, that the Government ought to acknowledge that the computer may now actually be going to revolutionise society. It is all very well for politicians complacently to mouth the phrase that, "a new information age is imminent". If an upheaval to match the industrial revolution is about to take place, then policy makers should start to plan for the future now. If society is changing, "from a capital-intensive, labour and resource based economy to one based on services... [where] information and human resources are becoming the key strategic resources, even more important than land and capital." (15) then the transition should be as smooth as possible.

In seeking to understand the nature of the possible changes, a clear distinction must be drawn between the computer hardware and the information which it manipulates. Most policy makers now have an opinion of the potential for change arising from the physical equipment, but information is a difficult resource to value. Inaccurate information may be worthless or even dangerous. Good information may be invaluable in the right hands. The ability to appraise and evaluate information is therefore as important as the ability to mechanically manipulate it. Hence, if tomorrow's children are to be able to live in confidence in a world dominated by computer technology, then computer technology must become a more relevant part of a more critically-based education process. If this does not occur, then those who are responsible for determining the nature of education, must be able to justify the omission in terms of the effectiveness of their planning and strategies. The burden of proof will be a heavy one to discharge. The reason for the difficulty is that, in order to be able to plan, the policy-makers must be able to understand and anticipate the consequences of change, and without controlled and co-ordinated research, prediction becomes a intuitive process. Thus, in America, the point of the IBM Secondary School Computer Education Program was research funding of $8m for a pilot project, "to identify and exemplify practices encouraging effective educational use of computers." (16) Although cynics might seek to devalue this effort as a mere sales pitch aimed at gaining a toe hold in the increasing education market, it has proved a useful stimulus to proper planning as a result of the involvement of the Educational Testing Service.

1.3.3 What should the teachers be doing?

It must be said that whatever is taught in the schools may be obsolete by the time the students enter the job market, so rapid is the rate of change in some subject areas. The answer is therefore to move the emphasis from subject matter to process. Students must be taught how to think, analyse and solve problems, rather than concentrating on factual and narrative information. In all education, the policy ought to be to prepare the students to explore ideas that are not doctrinaire. In fact, to help stimulate creativity, it would even be appropriate to encourage the unorthodox. Yet this may not be easy. Education has for many years been moving towards the encouragement of empirical thinking, i.e. many students at all levels of education are now encouraged to plan and execute experiments which will produce data. The ideal is to ease the students into theoretical thinking, which has, for too long, remained the sole province of the teacher, i.e. information has been seen as something to be learned, and not something to be thought about, let alone created.

1.4   How should the curriculum be modified?

Teaching is not an unstructured activity which takes place in a vacuum. A curriculum is required which imposes a structure on the skills and information to be learned. Further, although innovation and creativity are desirable qualities, teachers feel a need to encourage group discipline and to impose a social structure on the learning activity. The alternative, it is said, is anarchy. This can be seen in the practice of safely regimenting children and students into rooms with other children and students. Conceptually, teachers also put ideas into little boxes which are termed specialisations.

The core curriculum subjects have tended to be related to the use of symbols, i.e. in a study of language both native and foreign, mathematics, and factual, i.e. history, science, etc. The traditional teaching method was the rote learning of pre-packaged information. Thought was not encouraged. But it is often the case that an individual who comes to a body of knowledge without any preconceptions as to the categorisation of the various elements subsumed within the whole, can see links and connections that a single disciplinary individual could never identify. This type of insight is valuable, but the difficulty is that all aspects of education which result in flexibility are expensive. So, for example, buildings which permit multiple functioning are more demanding to design and construct. Yet even in this statement is an assumption that may not be justified. Apart from the need to promote the socialisation of the young, what objective justification is there for the retention of conventional school and college buildings? Terminals or stand-alone facilities could be provided at a wide variety of locations, and still provide high quality educational opportunity. Perhaps a simple truth should be recognised: better teaching requires more teachers of a better quality and, if society's best minds are to be attracted to the education service rather than to the City of London or other high technology environments, competitive salaries must be offered.

Teachers exist to service student demand. It is therefore necessary to state the key questions for all educators:

What are the educational needs of the student?

What are the capacities of a student?

How does a student approach problems?

What motivates a student?

By answering these questions, the educators would be specifying what they are trying to accomplish, i.e. that their goal is that learning should occur, and they could positively draw up curriculum strategies for the achievement of that goal.

1.5   Will the potential social changes be well-managed?

At a macro level,   history acknowledges that governments did not plan, nor maintain coherent policies for, the introduction of the internal combustion engine and its dramatic effect on society, so it may be unreasonably optimistic to assume that planning for the introduction of computers will be any more successful. The motor car can now be characterised as the architypical Jekyll and Hyde object - a boon as an individualised form of transport while a bringer of pollution, both real and spiritual, to the urban landscape. The problem is that while the car gives each person the opportunity of personal freedom of mobility, it only does so on roads which can become congested or dangerous. Hence regulation of the design of the motor car itself, and of the reality of traffic flow, is required.

It is not clear how comfortably the computer will be integrated into future society, but it is already possible to observe emerging problems. In the sphere of education at the micro level, the individual teachers and the administrators of schools and colleges, have the day-to-day professional responsibility for interacting with the students, but they have less opportunity to grasp the broader patterns of social change than government officers. This produces an irony in that, although central planners have the opportunity to acquire an overview, the teachers on the ground are often the only real source of knowledge and expertise about the current practice of teaching. They know about the attitudes and the responsiveness of the pupils or students, but the lines of communication between the doers and the planners are so poor, that it is unlikely that central policy making can be influenced by the majority of those who will have the task of implementing that policy.

1.6   The computer as a teaching aid

The role of the computer in education is two-fold: either it is the subject matter of the teaching, and programming and applications are to be taught, or it is the means whereby any subject matter is to be communicated, i.e. it is the difference between teaching about technology, and teaching with technology. For immediate purposes, the latter role will be discussed. Early examples of educational machines were somewhat unimaginatively, if functionally, called "teaching machines" - the first being described by Sydney Pressey in 1926. The device which he described offered a sequence of multiple choice questions, and the student selected an answer by pressing a button. The machine then indicated whether the given answer was correct. (17)

This machine function in education is sometimes referred to as CAI, i.e. Computer Aided Instruction. There is an element of ambiguity inherent in the use of the word 'instruction'. One interpretation would tend to retain emphasis on the activity of teaching rather than learning, i.e. knowledge is directed at the learner, so that the learner may be informed. Yet, according to Gagne, "Instruction is a set of events which affect learners in such a way that learning is facilitated. Normally, we think of these events as being external to the learner – events embodied in the display of printed pages or the talk of a teacher. However, it must also be recognised that the events which make up instruction may be partly internal, when they comprise learner activity called self-instruction." (18)

Gagne's intention is therefore to reflect the totality of the events which may be involved in the learning experience, and not just those which are initiated by a teacher. Whichever interpretation of the word is technically correct, it is suggested that the proper focus of attention in education should always be the learner. Indeed, a rather more cynical and extreme view might be that the teacher is really no more than a learning aid to the pupil or student. However, the more normal expectation in practice would be that teachers expect passivity in the pupils. Many teachers are proud of their reputation as disciplinarians, but discipline is merely another way of describing enforced passivity on the part of the learners.

As against this, in machine terms, the computer has significant interactive qualities and these may be used to produce an inherently active method of learning which is not necessarily reflected in the word 'instruction'. The better educational emphasis is consequently reflected in the term CAL, i.e. Computer Aided Learning, although it must be acknowledged that many writers use the two terms interchangeably.

If there is a real difference between CAL and CAI, it is that CAI sees the computer as an instructional medium like textbooks, video tapes, etc., and the problem is how to use the delivery system to the best advantage; whereas CAL sees the computer as any other tool which the student may use, e.g. slide rule or pocket calculators, microscopes or other laboratory equipment, etc., and the main aim is to see how the students may be induced to use the computer's capacities to make their learning most productive. To reflect this possible distinction, it is sometimes suggested that there are three possible CAI strategies which are, drill and practice, tutorial and socratic, whereas CAL is simulations/games, databases and programming. (19)

However, such artificial and generalised distinctions seem to blur the important issue which is to identify the most effective role for the computer in each educational situation. Given that the membership of the target group of learners is capable of such massive intellectual and motivational diversity, any categorisation or specialisation in computer application to the exclusion of others, is not considered constructive. The only semantic modification that might be considered is that, in a sense, the computer regulates rather than aids learning because it times and patterns the learning experience for the user. Thus, perhaps a better compromise version of the acronyms would be CAL, i.e. Computer Administered Learning with all the ambiguity that the word Administered brings with it. There is also a transatlantic divide in that CAI tends to be preferred in America, while the English preference is for CAL. In this work, the term CAL will be preferred.

Keith Hudson argues that, "CAL is not a teaching aid: it is a total teaching system. A true CAL program once loaded into a microcomputer, will take the student from one definable skill level to another without any help or intervention from a teacher or other adult." (20) To some extent, this is a function of the multi-media qualities of a computer. Books can supply the written word and pictures, slide projectors and video recorders can supply high quality pictures, and tape recorders can supply sound, but only a computer-based system can combine all these teaching aids into a single form. Although Hudson does go on to qualify this by agreeing that CAL is not suitable for some types of learning and some types of subject matter, it is not clear that such a use is necessarily desirable even if it does become possible. Indeed, Rushby takes a firm view, "we should not use it [CAL] unthinkingly to emulate the lecturer – such mimicry can easily become a parody." (21)

moved ③

1.7 Why has interest in Computer-Aided Learning grown?

At least three factors may be identified as contributing to the growth of CAL:

(a) interest in the concept and practice of programmed learning following the work of Skinner (22) which focussed the attention of teachers upon the individual student rather than the group;

(b) the growth in the availability and cheapness of hardware which makes research into the use of computers as an educational resource economically feasible; in fact, the actual manipulative capacities of the computer have changed little, it is merely our ability to access those capacities that has changed. Indeed, better equipment does not necessarily mean better learning; and

(c)   the degree to which computers have become integrated into
       our society which makes it at least difficult, if not impos-
       sible, for teachers to ignore both the fact of their exist-
       ence, and the results of their social impact.

In recent years, there has been a significant increase in the
number of articles and books on the use of computers in education. This is a somewhat artificial phenomenon – separating out
computers for special treatment simply because they are new.
Hence, no-one today would consider writing an article on the
educational utility of chalk and blackboards.   It is tempting to
think that this literary output has been matched by rapid progress in the field. There is however, a truth which must be
acknowledged:

       Invention is worthless unless followed by implementation!

Inventors and innovators are always over–optimistic. The computer
may be an impressive machine with increasingly magnificent data
storage and manipulative abilities, but without the work to
produce the software, and the enthusiasm to integrate that software into teaching methodologies, it remains no more than a good
prospect. All technology is merely a means to an end, the most
usual effect of any act of automation being to produce the non-
human performance of tasks previously performed by humans. J.
Aaron Hoko poses the question, "Does automation immediately conn-
ote qualitative improvement? Or does it merely carry with it the
propensity for such improvement?" (23)

In this instance, the computer is simply one more way in which
the basic teaching materials can be presented to would–be learners. It may be that the materials can be better presented by
using the technology, but the technology on its own cannot improve the quality of the teaching. Many of the technological
innovations of this century have simply been used to re–implement
the existing curriculum and teaching methods, and therefore any
improvements have been marginal. Indeed, in the first instance
CAL must relate to the actual school and college classroom environment, and in schools, this tends to mean one teacher in charge
of about thirty pupils. Given current timetabling practices, each
class will receive about two hours of tuition per week in each
subject within the curriculum and, in many instances, there will
only be one machine or terminal to which the class may have
access. Most colleges and universities have better staff–student
ratios, and will usually have better computing facilities, but no
matter what the particular constraints or advantages of the
teaching environment, there is no automatic correlation between
the quality of teaching and the quality of student learning. The
quality control of teaching will always be the responsibility of
the teacher and/or programmer, while the responsibilty of learning will always be on the student. Further, "There is every sign
that the headlong rush into micros is causing a reversal to

techniques and philosophies which had been discredited in computer-assisted learning many years ago." (24)

Too often the myth that because it is computerised it must therefore be better, is uncritically accepted. The reason for this mistaken faith in the computer is that it is believed that in order to program, the information must be restructured and made more specific so that it may be programmed into, say, an authoring system. However, any teaching material developed without clear educational objectives is likely to be bad. Indeed, "Designing computer applications for education might be called cognitive engineering, for its objective is to shape children's minds. That lofty goal must carry with it a commitment to cognitive science, the study of how knowledge functions and changes in the mind." (25) At this point a further problem becomes apparent in that what may be new technology to the teacher is quite likely to be old technology to the real computer specialist. Thus, the aim is to introduce the technology to a group where the performance possibilities are unknown, and the learning effort required is substantial.

"The prospect of change implies criticism, for if the reason for change is to improve learning it follows that what already exists is less than ideal." (26) Some would say that computers should be used where existing approaches to the teaching of the given material can be improved and those techniques now considered obsolete can be removed. But by what criteria does one judge obsolescence? Others would argue for the basis of change on the basis that computers are a new and desirable method of teaching. But, however it is worded, it has emotive overtones which may cause unthinking rejection. This is sad because, in an environment where the pursuit of academic excellence is the declared goal, the contribution which CAL can make should be objectively weighed.

One possible conclusion from an objection evaluation exercise may be the likelihood that the results of any genuinely successful implementation of CAL would be a more efficient use of resources, but without co-operation from the teachers, proper funding and a series of incentives to change, the present apathy and indifference are likely to continue. Yet, because the influence of the computer is becoming so widespread within education, its threatened introduction has brought into clearer focus some of the issues and problems which previously were only vaguely visible. Thus, for example, it may be proper to consider whether education should only take place in the formal setting of the school, college or university system, or whether it could more properly be considered a community or home-based system. On this point, the Government has announced MSC funding for a scheme known as TAPS (Training Access Points), which are computer terminals with VDUs mounted in public places, and which give information about training opportunities available both locally and nationally. The locations will include libraries, colleges, shops, bus and railway stations, etc. This will supplement data held on NERIS (the National Education Resource Information Service) and ECCTIS (the Education Counselling and Credit Transfer Information Service).

1.8 Will CAL lead to more distance learning?

At a policy level, there is increasing commitment to the concept of distance learning. Self-evidently, this takes place when the learner is physically distant from his or her teacher. It began with the correspondence course which, today, may be supplemented by radio or television broadcasts, e.g. the Open University. The point of the technique is to open up scholarship to the public at large. There are three levels at which a judgement should be made. Culturally, study and research should not be considered the exclusive domain of the formal academic, it should be open to all who can demonstrate their interest and competence. The concept and practice of only admitting an elite to higher educational levels should be forcefully attacked. Politically, the more people who become interested participants, the more funding the overall educational activity should warrant and deserve. Academically, much valuable research data may be forthcoming from the supposedly amateur sources which will enrich human knowledge. On the other hand, it may be argued that face-to-face contact is an expensive use of resources on an individual or small group basis, so the privilege of individualised human teaching should be reserved for those who have shown that their abilities warrant it.

One of the design problems in the distance learning field is that written and support materials must be prepared in advance and, to gain the maximum return on investment, must have the maximum life span. This can make it difficult to change support materials without amending the written information, or vice versa. Material is easy to change within a computer system and, in dynamic subject areas, this can be a positive advantage. The core written materials would therefore only deal with unchanging principles, while the student would be expected to take the detail of the course from the regularly updated computer. With the improvement in telephone technology, the student could connect with a remote computer facility and receive audio-based, computer-controlled tutorials, the student entering responses by using the telephone key pad. Alternatively, a modem interface to suitable hardware gives access to CAL software and written materials using standard keyboard facilities.

A difficulty must be acknowledged in the first contact situation, where a student may find the experience of contacting the computer daunting, no matter how clearly the introductory documentation has been prepared. This problem will remain until such time as the use of home-based terminals for routine transactions becomes the norm, and can only be mitigated with visits by personal tutors. A further difficulty arises from the natural desire to economise. Hence, the student will tend to use the telephone in the evenings when the scale of charges is lower. In turn, this will tend to lead to a disproportionate loading of resources and, in some mainframe systems, to very poor response times which counters the savings of the cheap rate charge bands, and leads to user-frustration. Similarly, telephone conferencing could lead to home-based tutorials, but the general educational use of the telephone system would have to be formally recognised as socially desirable by British Telecom or the Government, and subsidised. Given that the boom in the video market has placed a cinema in every home and made the future of the communal activity more expensive and less viable, that banking, buying goods, and most other ordinary transactions could now be carried out in the home through the use of modems and a modified television set, it should not be an unreasonable step to encourage learning at home.

1.8.1 What is the American experience in the distance learning field?

In America, the TICCIT project (Time-shared Interactive Computer Controlled Information Television) was developed by the Mitre Corporation as a part of their cable television system. (27) The approach is that the effectiveness of the learning strategy is independent of the subject matter, so students are given information and examples, and then tested on their understanding of the information thus supplied. Both visual and audio messages may be given, with user communication either by keyboard or light pen. Significantly, the project has not been a success as far as student course completion rates are concerned. The reason for the high drop-out rate may simply be that students are not always able to cope with self-directed study, or it might be that the courses were not properly supported by the human tutors. But other data seems to suggest that it was an effective way of teaching, with TICCIT students producing higher test scores than non-TICCIT students.

Despite this apparent academic success, the TICCIT system is not widely used in America. "The TICCIT system and its learner controlled instruction paradigm suffers from two drawbacks. First, it is limited to adult populations who are expected to make reasonable decisions about what to do next within the learner-controlled environment. Second, it restricts instruction primarily to a strictly expository approach, which precludes simulations, games and other creative uses of the computer." (28) Given the fact that it has had a measure of success, despite the fact that the actual educational approach is tedious and sterile, with an improvement in CAL design, it seems likely that this type of delivery system could be successful at all levels of student endeavour.

1.8.2 Why should distance learning be considered a serious alternative to conventional schools and colleges?

Distance learning facilities, whether CAL-based or not, are particularly important where the subject is not popular enough to justify local teachers in every school or college. With greater capital input, the more sophisticated facsimile document systems could transmit teaching materials, while satellite and cable television systems, and video tape and disc systems, offer unlimited potential for education on both a national and an international basis. In this, local cable systems are particularly important because of the interactive capacity which they can support. However, networking is a mixed blessing. While it offers the attraction of access to a world of learning, computers sometimes fail and students will find it frustrating when they cannot gain access. There may also be difficulties in communication arising from noise on non-digital telephone lines which may distort the signal or cause a sudden disconnection. It is to be hoped that such problems will be reduced or eliminated as new telephone equipment is installed.

1.8.3 Is the ideal answer a compromise between the conventional and distance learning opportunities?

All students could be given a portable IT capacity as in the Strathclyde QL project. Each student has his or her own QL which can be taken home, and the expectation is that it will be at least be used for report writing as well as for programming exercises, etc. The QLs interface with the VAX mainframe where a lecture note browser facility exists whereby the student can load relevant notes and add his or her own footnotes. (29) The success of this venture is now reflected at a national level by the recent announcement by the Department of Trade and Industry giving support to the Open University. The Government is to give £2.5m to the Open University for the purchase of up to 4,500 micros which will form a pool of machines available for rental by students. This is in support of an OU initiative to ensure that all students on their information technology related courses gain extensive hands-on experience of computers. Quite apart from promoting the use of computers in students' homes, the scheme will provide a test-bed for new approaches to computer-based learning for students studying at home.

Similarly, the Open Tech project in Computer Aided Engineering based at Warley College of Technology, gives the students books, documentation and a low-cost, computer graphics work station called Hektor which can be linked into the mainframe facility at Warley by telephone. So far, eleven computer-based modules are available which simulate real-world skills, the students being able to access CNC engineering machines at any one of twenty centres set up around the county to see the results of their programming on genuine machine tools. By pooling equipment in this way, very cost-effective education in capital expensive skills can be achieved.

But no matter how inexpensive the terminals or micros, at today's prices, it is still significantly cheaper to give students access to books, or to distribute written materials. While this will always be a suitable strategy for describing purely academic information, it is less satisfactory where practical skills are to be communicated or updated as the success of the Warley Open Tech project demonstrates. Education planners must therefore make decisions which, among other things, will seek to balance manual library development against the acquisition of new information resources. Such decisions are often taken on an piecemeal basis by people who have not fully grasped the implications of the new technology, and who naively wonder whether the new technology is outdistancing either the human capacity or willingness to keep up with the change.

It must, however, be acknowledged that the decision-making is made more difficult because of the costs involved in hardware acquisition and software development. Schools and colleges can be given a reasonable discretion to purchase capital equipment, but given the larger sums of money involved in setting up a computing installation from scratch, less individual discretion is allowed to individual schools and colleges. This leaves more centralised decision-making in the hands of those who can only compromise in the reconciliation of each diverse claim for resources, and thereby leave all claimants less than fully satisfied.

1.8.4 Can the teachers benefit from the networking of computers?

The practicality of future developments which will support more significant information exchanging at a higher academic level also deserves serious consideration. Thus, in particular areas such as the shared specialism, computers are helpful to a team that is trying to formulate a theory that covers the separate ideals of the group. It enhances the technology of thinking because all may enter the files, read and add their thoughts. The activity of team writing is based upon co-operative revision and criticism. But if communal writing is to be based on a paper system, the endless revisions make the process cumbersome and slow, and the costs, both real and social, of retyping are frequently prohibitive. Yet the networked computer facilitates the exchange of text with revision, distance and time no problem.

24

More generally, the act of consulting colleagues is also reassuring and confidence-building, and is a fertile ground for the exchange of ideas. This form of development is considered by Gary M Boyd and, with reservations as to the timescale necessary to develop computer systems sophisticated enough to support the activity, he concludes, "that the transparent system advocated is intended as a means of bringing together people who are well enough matched to be capable of making valuable contributions to each others' work, without introducing excess noise and without wasting valuable time." (30)

1.9   How can computers enhance the education process?

At the lowest and least creative level, "Computers are sometimes being used to provide light relief to the serious business of teaching and learning. Sometimes they are seen as a useful alternative means of keeping the dull and the disruptive occupied." (31) However, even in this dismissive approach there is implicit recognition of a more fundamental truth, namely that no student needs to be rejected, for a way of educating that student can always be found. "...the computer can contribute by being responsive even to limited skills. It immediately expands the range of accessible and interesting activities, and that, in turn provides a student with more to think and communicate about." (32) In a conventional course, the normal expectation may be that a few will do well, the majority will perform in an average fashion, and an unfortunate few will fail to achieve the performance goals.

The individualisation of tuition achievable through CAL could change performance expectations if a full range of presentational packages is available. Each person's abilities are identified and can be catered for. If Student A is shown to be a slow performer who performs best with a wide variety of different stimuli to help in maintaining interest, a detailed programme of learning can be provided for that student which should maximise achievement within the known intellectual limits. What finally distinguishes between students is their ability to understand and apply concepts. If the optimum route to understanding is identified for each student, all may perform to a higher standard. This is sometimes referred to as CAMOL (Computer-Assisted Management of Learning). If everyone is proceeding at their own speed, it needs the computer to keep track of everyone's progress, and to tell the teacher which students have studied which CAL units, and with what degree of success. One of the problems in this approach is that if there are testing mechanisms which may make reference to a parallel face-to-face remedial or explanatory tutorials, great care must be taken to set the right standards, or to build in filters. If everyone failed the tests, then all would seek to appear at the designated tutorial hour. Thus, the computer must keep track of the number of those referred to given time slots to minimise the risk of chaos.

This leads to a further distinction. Some courses are based upon independent study where the student can make decisions on the speed of learning and the sequence of study. Indeed, a student's assumption of responsibility for his or her own learning is capable of being highly motivational. But it may just as easily be demoralising, hence the need in appropriate cases, for guided study and a high degree of teacher control. Here the teacher will identify the possible avenues of study and investigation and, after discussion between teacher and student, guide the student from one unit of knowledge to the next. Overall, the pace of study may be determined by a lecture course which introduces each unit of knowledge, but the long term object would normally be to gradually ween the students into acceptance of more responsibility. Naturally, the overall character of each course will be determined by the learning objectives specified in the curriculum, balanced against the need to provide a suitably motivating environment for all the learners.

1.10 Can CAL promote learning among the young and disabled?

One of the more interesting aspects of the use of computers in the learning environment is that many computers require accuracy of typing or in the use of a mouse, if either any programming is to be achieved, or some of the applications packages are to be activated. The communication constraints of the computer therefore force motivated students to pay attention to detail; "...computer use seems to lead to dramatic improvement in pupil's visual attentiveness." (33) Student impulsiveness and guesswork is unthinkingly penalised by the computer. Any failure to properly obey instructions will prevent progress, and motivated students will quickly learn to check their input to avoid disappointment. "The computer is also an excellent medium through which children can become aware of and understand their own thinking processes. It is in developing thinking–problem–solving and a sense of competence and autonomy in children that computers hold the greatest promise in education." (34)

This is particularly important for the disabled student where deafness, blindness, and emotional or behavioural disabilities may inhibit normal classroom delivery systems. Thus, reading screened materials may help those with hearing difficulties; computer-based voice synthesiser reading systems which scan and then read aloud any printed matter, may help those with restricted vision; and the computer may offer those with emotional or behavioural difficulties a learning opportunity with a degree of privacy to minimise embarrassment, because no-one in the class is going to think the pupil slow or stupid if the wrong answer is given. Confidence may therefore be built up. This is particularly important where the Local Education Authority is pursuing a policy of integrating disabled students into the ordinary school environment. The computer as a machine is value free. Any student can be embarrassed to ask a human teacher for a public explanation of a point known to be elementary and, thus, basic points may never be grasped. Machines allow students essential privacy, and can enable a student to maintain both self-esteem and peer group respect.

Computer exercises can be made more simple than standard school lessons which may be too dependent upon communication fluency. The vocabulary range and sentence structuring of everyday speech, with its implicit cultural overtones, can be daunting to those who are disabled, or where English is a second language. The computer can always be programmed to display and accept text of a consistently straightforward nature. Obviously, the pupil has to be able to read but, with good graphics and an intelligent approach, there is no reason why pupils cannot be encouraged to pick up basic language. In playing adventure games like dungeons and dragons, many "children often become fascinated with the very fact that there are words that they know which the machine does not." (35) This type of game gives invaluable practice in reading short pieces of textual material and gives the incentive of fun or excitement. Excelling in such exercises can significantly enhance overall performance. However, it should be emphasised that the software itself is not the key. The students' self-esteem is enhanced simply by using the computer successfully.

Further, the function of the computer can be to normalise the teacher's perception of the child. It is odd to note that a person who has to wear glasses to correct a weakness in eyesight is not perceived as disabled, yet a person with a hearing aid is considered handicapped. With improved performance possible through the computer, the teacher is able to gain a more objective view of each student. Thus, one who might be diagnosed as dyslexic in a school requiring written work, might be considered indistinguishable from any other child if access to a word processor and spelling checker was normal procedure. However, it must be noted that, say, a screen display with enlarged letters for those with sight difficulties would not be suitable for ordinarily sighted students. The software should always be matched to the particular students, and their individual abilities or disabilities. Software diversity actually enhances the selective and control function of the teacher. Computer messaging and mail facilities also assist the disabled to make friends and contacts that might otherwise not be possible. But CAL can be more tiring than conventional lectures because the individualisation of tuition requires more intensive effort on the part of the student. The concept of the school/college day may therefore have

to be significantly revised to allow for rest periods. But overall, the student can be freed from the tyranny of the fixed time-
table, and can find genuine scope for the optimisation of innate
abilities.

1.11 Women and IT Technology

Women are not seen as active participants in the technological
arena, hence the promotional effort by the Equal Opportunities
Commission (EOC) in 1984. This campaign used the acronym WISE
(Women Into Science and Engineering). The aim was to encourage
more women to gain suitable qualifications which, in turn, would
enable them to compete more effectively in the new employment
environment. The DES reported in 1981 (36) that only 28% of O
Levels, and 20% of A Levels, in Computer Science were passed by
girls in 1981. In 1984, the UGC reported (37) that only 9.2% of
those graduating in engineering and technology subjects were
women. To some extent, this is attributable to a differentiated
school curriculum, partly because of the poor careers advice for
young women, and partly because of role stereotype expectations
and the discriminations which they represent. However, for all
the time and money invested by the EOC, Bruce and Kirkup report
that the WISE effort was largely ignored by LEAs, the WEA and
University extramural departments in their courses to cater for
the adult woman. (38)

In 1983, the EOC had reported (39) that the response of girls to
computers in schools made out a good case for single sex classes.
In the mixed class environment, girls lacked the confidence to
volunteer answers to questions and feared ridicule. Further, they
were often faced by a number of immovable boys who monopolised
the equipment (40). The girls who do trespass into the domain are
also met by many male teachers who help female students in a way
that encourages their dependence and acquiescence. (41) A further
problem is the lack of women teachers as role models for their
students. In teaching style, women teachers are likely to encourage greater self-reliance and confidence and, in running
single sex classes, they also tend to produce a more supportive
and relaxed atmosphere where a more co-operative approach to
learning tends to arise. In confirmation of objective ability, a
study of female students at Keele found no sex differences in
learning about information technology. (42)

Many investigators have now confirmed that women and minority
groupings are often under-represented on computer-based courses.
(43) These groups show less interest in the subject, and evince a
fear of technology. The justifications commonly advanced for this
technophobic response are the perception of computing as being a

28

mathematically-based discipline and therefore too difficult, or simple avoidance of what is perceived to be an excessively white male dominated domain. Anything which improves gender and racial balance is to be encouraged, given that employment opportunities may be dependent upon academic courses and qualifications. Thus, computers should not be linked exclusively to science or mathematically-based disciplines, and there should be no specific qualifications required as a precondition of using computers, with computing clearly being made available to all with equal encouragement given.

1.12 Conclusions

From the earliest days of computerisation, there have been reports of improvement in student performance, e.g. following research at Stanford in 1968. (44) In part, these results are obtained because the drill and practice sessions, and tutorial sessions which are computerised, exactly mirror teaching practice. The reason for their greater success rate probably lies in the degree of individualisation possible. But Hoko asserts that, in general, automated and human teaching are qualitatively different, and argues that it is not possible to say which is the better method. He further suggests that the primary research emphasis should not aim to declare a winner between as between the computer and the human, but should be to identify how and why any given presentational medium is effective, and to build upon the strengths of such media. (45)

The IBM Secondary School Computer Education Program report significantly more learning taking place among the above average students. This is hardly surprising because such students tend to receive preferential access to computer resources. Better learning was also reported in the average ability class, with more students overall achieving performance levels consistent with their abilities. The general level of student enthusiasm was high with over 51% working much more successfully on their own. (46)

With such evidence to support it, perhaps CAL ought to be more widespread. But it has to be admitted that, for all the encouragement from both Government and the academic publishers, CAL is only making slow progress. A part of the reason for this is the time taken to produce good software. Perhaps the programming effort should therefore be concentrated on the more uncommon subject matter. Regardless of the size of any given educational unit, it is not economically feasible to have teachers for every possible subject discipline. Existing books and teaching aids usually require some form of teacher support for learning to be effective, since most books are written without self-teaching aids such as comprehension exercises, reinforcement tests, etc.; and even if such elements are present, the answers are not often supplied. If it is assumed that teachers will always be provided in core curriculum subjects, CAL can bridge the gaps in the less common areas to give diversity of opportunity which is not made available with current staffing arrangements, even where peripatetic staff are provided. Work is even being done on a music course, (47) or systems to permit the study or composition of music. Such developments would be short term measures, allowing time to re-evaluate the concept of the school and the college, to determine whether computer-supported learning in the community should represent the future.

References

(1) Education: A Framework for Expansion. HMSO 1972.

(2) The Philosophy of Education. J.Dewey. Littlefield. 1971

(3) Primary School Perception of Disruptive Behaviour. Jean Lawrence and David Steed. (1986) Vol.12, No.2 Educational Studies. pp.147/57. For a more general survey see Disruptive Behaviour in Schools. Holman and Coghill. Chartwell-Bratt.

(4) Computers, Education and Special Needs. p.84.

(5) Styles of computer-based learning and training. D.M.Laurillard. collected in Computer-Based Learning. A State of the Art Report. pp.103/110 at p.104.

(6) Motivation Enhancement in Educational Settings. Richard de Charms. collected in Research on Motivation in Education. pp.275/310 at pp.276/7.

(7) The Self-Teaching Process in Higher Education. P.J.Hills. Croom Helm, London. 1976. p.42.

(8) Computer-Based Training. A Guide to Selection and Implementation. p.123.

(9) Information Technology: Policies for Industry and Growth. (1987-88) 2 CLSR p.8.

(10) The Sociopsychological Impact of Computer Technology on Knowledge Workers. Charlotte L. Neuhauser. collected in Capitolizing on Computers in Education. p.369.

(11) R.E.Butler is Secretary General of the International Telecommunication Union and is interviewed in (1987-88) 2 CLSR pp.6/8.

(12) Understanding Media. M.McLuhan. McGraw-Hill, New York. 1964.

(13) Modern Computing: A Force for Diversity or Conformity? Edward E.David Jnr. collected in Cohabiting with Computers. p.64.

(14) Why LOGO? Brian Harvey. collected in New Horizons in Educational Computing. pp.21/39 at p.37.

(15) Perspectives on a High-Tech Society. William F.Miller. collected in Cohabiting with Computers. p.10.

(16) The Electronic Schoolhouse. Hugh F. Cline et al. p.4.

(17) A Simple Apparatus Which Gives Tests and Scores - and Teaches. (1926) 23 School and Society 373/6.

(18) Principles of Instructional Design. Robert M. Gagne and Leslie J. Briggs. Holt, Rinehart and Winston, New York. 1979. p.3

(19) Computer-Based Training. A Guide to Selection & Implementation. p.30. The distinction between the terms "tutorial" and "Socratic" is that the former is textual presentation with some comprehension questions whereas the latter is more of a dialogue based on Artificial Intelligence systems.

(20) Introducing CAL. Keith Hudson. p.8.

(21) Some problems in education and training. collected in Computer-Based Learning. A State of the Art Report. pp. 163/73 at p.172.

(22) The Science of Learning and the Art of Teaching. B.F.Skinner. (1954) 24 Harvard Educational Review. pp.86-97. Teaching Machines B.F.Skinner. (1958) 128 Science. 969/77.

(23) What is the scientific value of comparing automated and human instruction? J.Aaron Hoko. Educational Technology. February 1986. p.16.

(24) Learning and Teaching with Computers. Tim O'Shea and John Self. p.3.

(25) Designing computer-based microworlds. Bob Lawler. collected in New Horizons in Educational Computing. pp.40/53 at 40.

(26) Educational Innovation and Computer-Based Learning. Nick Rushby. collected in Selected Readings in Computer-Based Learning. p.13/29 at p.20.

(27) described in Learning and Teaching with Computers. Tim O'Shea and John Self. pp.86/93.

(28) Computer-Based Instruction. Methods and Development. p.273.

(29) Computer Centres - The Next Decade. J.L.Alty. collected in Proceedings of the Management Conference. Inter-University Committee on Computing. Edited R.F.Smith. University of Durham. 1986. p.7.

(30) The Importance and Feasibility of 'Transparent' Universities. Gary M Boyd. collected in Selected Readings in Computer-Based Learning. pp.113/8 at p.117.

(31) CAL in the teaching-learning process. P.M.Bradshaw. collected in Teachers, Computers and the Classroom. pp.8/24 at pp.9/10.

(32) Computers, Education and Special Needs. p.46.

(33) The Computer in the Reading Clinic. G.E.Mason. (1983) 36 The Reading Teacher 504/7.

(34) Literacy is Not Enough: The Computer as a Bridge Between Psychological Research and Educational Practice. Jean M.Barton. collected in Capitol-izing on Computers in Education. p.200.

(35) ibid p.70.

(36) Statistics of School Leavers, CSE and GCE England 1981.

(37) University Statistics 1983, Vol 1, University Statistical Board, Cheltenham.

(38) Post-experience Courses in Technology for Women. M. Bruce and G. Kirkup. (1985) Adult Education 40/50.

(39) Information Technology in Schools, EOC Manchester.

(40) Infotech and Gender: an Overview. 1985. EOC Manchester.

(41) Sponsoring and Stereotyping in School. C.Boswell collected in World Yearbook of Education 1984: Women and Education. C.Aker, J.Megarry, S.Nisbet and E.Hoyle (ed) Kogan Page, London.

(42) Sex Differences in Learning about Information Technology. Jack McArdle, Stephen Bostock and Roger Seifert. collected in Microcomputers in Adult Education.

(43) Sex Equality: Increasing girl's use of computers. Why is there less interest among women? M.E.Lockhead & S.B.Frakt (April 1984) The Computing Teacher 11(9) 16-8.

(44) see the research report of R.C.Atkinson. (1968) 23 Amer. Psychol. 225.

(45) supra at p.18.

(46) The Electronic Schoolhouse. p.121.

(47) A Computer-Assisted Music Course and Its Implementation. and
A Computer Project in Music Analysis. Dorothy Gross. collected in
Computing in the Humanities. edited by Peter C Patton and Renee A
Holoien. Gower, London. 1981. p.287/313.

CHAPTER 2

THEORIES OF LEARNING AND OF MOTIVATION

This chapter represents a series of outlines of the most commonly acknowledged theories of learning, and of the main theories of motivation and mastery. It is impossible to consider how best to design educational software, or to configure hardware in such a way as to optimise learning outcomes, unless there is some under-standing of these theoretical issues, but it is acknowledged that the coverage of complex theoretical ideas in this chapter is highly superficial, and represents no more than sign posts to later more detailed explanations.

2.1   Introduction

From a lay person's stand-point, the primary characteristic which is said to distinguish the human being from the animal world, is the capacity for thought. "Thinking" is, however, one of the more elusive activities since it cannot really be directly observed. The observer tends only to see the end product of thought in the shape of words or actions. Thus, the words used in this book are not "thinking" per se, but rather a vehicle for the expression of thought. In a non-technical sense, therefore, the term "thinking" is a vague generalisation for many different functions including memory, understanding, imagination, guessing, opinion, judgement and, even, day-dreaming. However, the yardstick which is most usually applied to determine whether what is said or done is the product of responsible intelligence, is to look at the quality of purpose. Intelligence selects goals and develops strategies to achieve those goals. "Thus in the usual way, a rational person is thought to have a coherent set of preferences between the options open to him. He ranks these options according to how well they further his purposes." (1)

Preferences arise from the way in which creatures relate to their environment. Both animals and humans may learn that some situations produce consequences which are pleasing, and some consequences which are displeasing. In the world of instinct, drives which actuate conduct may be rooted in basic needs. Thus, to eat is to relieve hunger; to fear is to respond to danger. But neither of these responses is necessarily characterised by conscious thought. In the world of intelligence, where basic and otherwise animal drives are glossed by the veneer of thought, two questions are raised. The first is as to the way in which people come to understand the essential cause and effect which underpins the human perception of reality. The second concerns the nature of rationality, and seeks to define the basis upon which people actually process the information which they possess as to that causality in such a way as to make meaningful decisions.

Both questions are vital to educators. The first question asks about learning as an activity. The second asks about the way in which the human animal applies knowledge which has been acquired. However, a further refinement is necessary. People tend to live in a haphazard fashion, and within a context of experiences often outside direct control. Most of what is learned is only partially directed, and often coloured by complex motivations, prejudices and cultural intangibles. Whereas, in the controlled environment of formal education, teachers are invited to communicate a body of structured information, there is no justification for the automatic corollary that the students will learn it. Thus, one of the continuing debates in the world of professional education has come to be the nature of the information to be communicated, and the way in which educators should seek to measure or assess whether this information has been learned. It is inevitably to be acknowledged that not everything which is presented for learning will be understood; that not everything that is understood will be remembered; and that, even if it is remembered, there is no guarantee that it will ever be applied outside the classroom.

2.2   Is it possible to define "learning" and "teaching"?

In practice, it is not possible to determine whether the communication process which is termed teaching, has been a success unless some resultant action or behaviour can be observed on the

part of the recipient. To that extent, therefore, it is legitimate to describe learning as an observable change in behaviour
or a capacity for new behaviour, and to recognise that it can
only be measured by inviting the learner to exhibit the newly
acquired behavioural characteristics.

The essence of a good teaching approach may be seen in the
communication of information. This must be followed by the opportunity for the learner to recall the information, and to practice
the desired response under the supervision of a tutor. The
function of the tutor is to supply an evaluation of the response
thus demonstrated. Although this essentially artificial process
takes place within a formal environment, the hope or expectation
is that the learner will see sufficient merit in the material
learned to repeat the learned response in a non-classroom situation. Thus, if one teaches the art of replacing a carburettor jet
to a student in a motor vehicle apprentices' class, it is hoped
that the apprentice will be able to repeat this process in a
garage for an employer offering a service to a customer.

2.3   When is teaching and/or learning effective?

It is difficult to define the criteria against which to measure
the effectiveness of the educational process, since education
often involves a wide range of objectives, not all of which can
be formally measured. In many courses, the aims have a social as
well as an intellectual form, and the impact or effect of attending school or college may be the enhancement of personality or
the development of motivations, hopes, aspirations and other
equally intangible values, as well as the acquisition of academic
qualifications.

All students in higher or further education potentially have
greater maturity than those in schools, but the way in which each
individual studies, will reflect his or her own perception of
what must be done to fulfil the course requirements and to respond to peer group pressure. As a Chinese proverb puts it,
"Teachers open the door. You enter by yourself." However, in the
present system, moving from school to Further or Higher Education
can cause considerable anxiety for many students, and school-
based study skills may actually prove to be inadequate for the
assimilation of the new factual and conceptual approaches to be
undertaken in colleges. Thus, students frequently need to achieve
more independence of thought, and to refine study skills such as
note-taking and faster reading. But, to some extent, this presupposes that there will be no major changes in presentational
methodology in Further or Higher Education. If CAL were to become
the norm throughout the education system, the progress of the

student between the different tiers of the system could be more smoothly managed, as the same basic study skills would be required throughout.

Today, short-term effectiveness of learning might be claimed in that a student is seen to get good grades in course work, tests or assignments, but the evidential quality of formal examinations, say held at the end of a course, may be dubious. The way in which the traditional essay-based examination is framed, the differences in the forms of answer produced by examinees, and the manner of its assessment by the examiner, make the process difficult to rely upon as the provider of objective yardsticks for student evaluation. Yet examinations, both internal and external, often dominate Further and Higher Education courses.

One of the issues to be considered later must therefore be whether the computerisation of the examination system could produce an improvement in student attitude or performance. The examination may or may not be an effective method of measuring cognitive development, but it is almost certainly ineffective in measuring the development of attitudes, character and values. That the area of student, staff and course evaluation, and thereby the measure of educational effectiveness, is difficult, but important and worthwhile, may now be judged from the efforts of both the staff themselves, and of outside bodies like the Department of Education and Science, to produce improvements and reform in the curriculum, and to encourage staff development in both the schools and the colleges.

2.4   What are the main theories of education?

Many formal theories have been developed to explain the phenomenon of learning. One of the earliest is Behaviourism, which is based on a concept in psychology which sees its essence in the examination and analysis of that which is publicly observable and measurable. The emphasis is on the teacher to provide for, and to promote, the desired response to the given stimuli. But the early work of writers and experimenters like Pavlov, Watson and Guthrie (2) is largely criticised as crude and mechanical, and is said to be of little interest to contemporary educationalists. The reason for this dismissal is that much of the work was performed under controlled laboratory conditions and involved the use of animals. Generalisations were then made from the behaviour of animals to humans. The standard, and somewhat pejoratively emotive, response to this type of generalisation is that it is hard to accept that, say, the behaviour of a rat in pressing a lever to obtain food, is meaningful in human terms.

However, even in rejection, the ideas which the Behaviourists advanced, have formed useful stepping stones to a better understanding of the general processes involved. Thus, while Tolman (3) rejects the simplistic stimulus and response model, he develops the concept by adding purpose and goals. He argued that, in thinking about anything, a person uses a 'cognitive map', i.e. that each individual builds up a general appreciation of the relationships which exist among different stimuli, and so devises a set of expectancies about the meaning of those relationships. Further, the expectations which an individual may form about goals are important in motivating activity. Learning, according to Tolman, is gaining an understanding of causal relationships, discriminating between internal drives, developing goals and making choices about behaviour. In short, he may be characterised as a Purposive Behaviourist.

At the most fundamental and mechanical level, the neo-Behaviourist psychologist, Professor B.F.Skinner (4), describes learning as a predictable response to a given stimulus. He is famous for the range of animal experiments which he performed, and was the developer of the so-called Skinner box. To that extent, he follows in the experimental traditions of the classical Behaviourists. Indeed, he asserts that the more predictable the response, the more effective the learning process can be said to have been. His main concern has been the functional analysis of behaviour and, in this, he discriminates between two types of response, viz. the elicited and the emitted. Responses are elicited by known stimuli, whereas they are emitted to operate on the environment to produce a consequence. Thus, learning may be seen as a response to emitted behaviour on the part of teachers, and learning is evidenced by elicited responses on the part of the learners. In order to induce the most consistent responses from the student, he emphasises the need for reinforcement, and has suggested a schedule of reinforcement to systematically confirm the desired responses and deny the unwanted responses. The teacher's task is therefore to shape behaviour, a task which requires a detailed awareness of learning objectives, and a good grasp of the various techniques of attainment.

Although this may be interpreted as inducing an almost Pavlovian, physical response, Skinner's ideas have gained some currency in the education world, and have formed the basic philosophy underlying linear teaching methods. The idea is to supply the learner with small bits of information which sequentially build up more complex ideas. Such an approach is seen by some to be an ideal way of using the computer, which can patiently take a student through a topic one step at a time. However, there is little or no flexibility allowed in this approach. Moreover, each piece of information is reduced to its most simple form, but while they may be easily digested, they cannot really be taken out of sequence. Linear sequences, whether computerised or not, may therefore be perfectly suitable for learning facts, and for practising routine processes. But they are not so effective when trying to grasp an argument or to 'discover' concepts. Such distinctions will be seen as vital in design terms, when it comes to designing the most effective computerised delivery system for the given subject matter.

An alternative theoretical approach which may assist in the design of software to present more subtle material, is to be found in Gestalt Psychology. The proponents of this school see a student as striving towards an understanding of the general form or shape of a problem, before a constructive response can be made to the detail of that problem. Here, there is less stress on practice. The teacher (human or automated) is to aim to give insights into the problem or concept and, instead of providing information in a wholly structured way, should allow the student to move around the topic a little, gaining experience until the concept is grasped or the problem solved.

In this respect, the term "insight" is being used in a specific sense. It is said to emerge when the learner suddenly becomes aware of the relevance of his or her behaviour to some objective, and is the result of a sudden reorganisation by the learner of his or her field of experience. It does not result from separate responses to a series of separate stimuli, but is a complex reaction to a situation in its entirety. The basic laws of the Gestaltists arise from the view that perception is governed by organisation, i.e. a human being imposes a gestalt on his or her environment. This involves perceiving patterns in relationships, and grouping or classifying those relationships according to the degree of similarity or disimilarity which they display as between themselves. Learning is therefore seen as a dynamic process, and not merely constituted by a mechanical concatenation of discrete stimulus-response events. Thus, once the entirety of a group of relationships is grasped, the learner may organise and reorganise the whole to produce a variety of insights. This is not "learning by doing", it is the achieving of awareness.

The advantage of this approach may be seen in problem-solving terms, where the best strategy is not blindly to apply rote-learned solutions which may or may not be relevant, in the hope that one may do the trick. Instead, the would-be solver should seek to understand the structure of the problem so that the solution may be discovered. This is the process of creative thinking. Thus, the Gestaltists advocate that teachers should avoid drilling students in compartmentalised techniques. (cf. the Cognitive School where, as Bruner (5) puts it, what students should be learning is not "particular performances", but "competence"). Teachers are instead to be encouraged to plan their lessons and to arrange problem situations so that it leads to the learner's discovery of the solutions, and of the route to those solutions. It is believed that the retention and transfer of skills becomes easier when overall relationships are perceived. Learning is therefore seen in organic terms, rather than in the autonomic terms of the stimulus-response behaviourist school. As can be appreciated, this would have profound implications for the presentational style of a CAL system.

Similarly, the Cognitive Psychologists assume that, in the interactions of an organism and its environment, not only is there a
change in the overt behaviour of the organism, there is a change
in its knowledge of the environment. It is assumed that the
learner's behaviour is based on cognition, i.e. acts of knowing
or thinking about the situations in which behaviour occurs. Any
changes in cognition will affect present responses and future
attitudes to the environment. Learning is therefore seen as a
process of interaction whereby the student attains fresh insights
(cognitive structures) or sheds or modifies old ones, and develops cognitive strategies, i.e. the capacity to select and modul-
ate thought and perception. It is therefore the task of the
teacher to assist the student to restructure his or her insights.

To that extent, Dewey (6) argues that learning involves the
exercise of intelligence. The learner is to be guided towards the
proper use of the powers of reflective thinking. This should
encourage the development of inductive and deductive powers of
reasoning, a process which will be enhanced if mere imitation and
mechanical drill are avoided. Dewey is important because he makes
the pupil the centre of attention. The teacher's responsibility
is therefore to encourage reflective thinking in the students
which, if the students' interest is aroused, should lead to the
exploration, selection and verification of hypothetical solutions
to problems. In a way, the student is to be encouraged to build
mental bridges between the stimulus and the response, and not
simply to provide the response to the stimulus. This approach
therefore represents a significant refinement to the Behaviourist
approach, and it has real importance in that it encourages the
practice of discovery teaching rather than expository teaching.
Taba (7) suggests a refinement to this development of problem-
solving skills by arguing that students should first be given a
grounding in specifics, and then confronted by problems that
cause bafflement. By encouraging the students to explore the
problems, opportunities naturally arise to apply the previously-
acquired knowledge. This should stimulate an analysis of the
structures of the problems and lead to discovery of the solutions. The students should then analyse the combination of problems and solutions to derive the organising principles.

To some extent all these schools of thought come together in the
ideas of Robert Gagne (8) who suggests that there is a hierarchy
of learning from very simple conditioned responses, up to complex
learning such as may be required in problem-solving. He acknowledges that the learner will start with simple rules which can
then be classified by type. By being able to discriminate between, or to group together such simple rules, the learner can
progress and construct higher order rules. The more sophisticated
these rules become, the more effective the learner will be in
problem-solving. He lists five major categories of capability
that can be considered outcomes of learning. The student will be
able to express information verbally; to demonstrate intellectual
skills by performing various tasks; to formulate cognitive strat-

egies to guide his or her own learning and thinking; to develop attitudes which influence the choice of personal action; and to refine motor skills making physical performance accurate and precise.

Gagne also lists the tasks which a teacher should perform, viz. to identify and channel the student's motivation by identifying educational goals; to direct the student's attention so that the learner is ready to receive information; to present the information and to stimulate retention through repetition, practice, tests and feedback; to stimulate recall by requiring the student to apply what has been learned in novel situations; to induce a generalisation of acquired-knowledge through both lateral and vertical transfer, i.e. to problems of equal and greater complexity; to elicit appropriate performance reflecting the newly-acquired knowledge; and to give feedback, indicating the level of the student's overall performance. It will later be suggested that, in this overview, lies a series of helpful guidelines for the educational software designer.

2.5   What is the best way to motivate a student?

Quite independently of the need to study how people learn, it is necessary to form a view of why people learn, for unless prospective students are motivated to engage in the activity, the theories of education would be worthless. In trying to decide what motivates a student, the full spectrum of the so-called cognitive processes should be considered, viz. attention, memory, search and retrieval mechanisms, classification, judgement and decision-making. This is based on the proposition that all human behaviour is intended to fulfil the function of assisting the actor to achieve identified goals, and that all the cognitions serve a similar adaptive function in allowing the actor to aspire towards a desired state.

Initially, each person should be considered as an individual. For these purposes, individualism implies an independence of goals, i.e. that the rewards which one person desires are not to be considered dependent upon another's, and where the individual relies more on self-evaluation than comparison with peers. However, it cannot be denied that all persons, to a greater or lesser extent, do seek to maintain self-esteem in relation to perceived social norms. In a classroom environment, the most usual ways of measuring or attributing success and failure are through social comparisons, formal and informal testing, and the use of examinations. Sometimes, those involved, whether as teachers or learners, may consciously formulate strategies to deal with the anxieties and pressures that students may experience, and thereby realistic goals are maintained and rational decisions are made. On other occasions, the learner may be personally deluded as to the levels of performance which are required or achievable, and expectations can become sadly irrational.

Moreover, in trying to understand the motivations of those engaged in the learning activity, it must also be recognised that such people have a life outside the classroom, and are subject to non-school or college influences. Here, longer-term aspirations may be linked to educational and occupational features, and may be coloured by religious, racial, cultural and other intangible values. Further, in class terms, higher socioeconomic status can be associated with a stronger need to succeed, while middle and lower status groups are not necessarily so strongly motivated to succeed.

In a sense, the nature of the learning experience is simply the students' search for understanding, both as to the subject matter of the given course, and as to their own performance levels. It is a natural response to any evaluation exercise, whether formal or informal, to attempt an explanation of all the aspects of relevant causation. This will be particularly the case when there has been an unexpected failure. Knowing why something has happened assists the student either in replicating that successful result, or in avoiding similar embarrassment in the future. In order to help understand why the particular consequence has arisen, the student may adopt a dialectical approach by logically grouping causes, and seeking any apparent contradictions in the hope that this will allow an insight into the overall processes involved. Equally, such an analysis may lead merely to a more honest reappraisal of expectations. Whatever the outcome, some of the contributory factors that will be taken into account are stable, e.g. personality, and both physical and intellectual aptitudes; others are unstable, e.g. luck, the amount of effort invested, or temporary illness. Inevitably, the resultant classification of causes will affect future judgement of likely outcome. In this, the student will assess the degree of stability in each contributing cause, and this will affect the expectancy of future results. It is a simple formula. The more stable the combination of causes is perceived to be, the more predictable the given result.

If the learner decides to produce changes in outcome, the decisions which are made will directly affect the intensity, quality and persistence of goal-directed behaviour, i.e. the student will either work longer and harder, or not work at all. The problem is to understand what motivates a student in such situations. If a student fails through lack of effort, this may not be considered so serious, and motivation will be maintained because the student believes that, when more effort is expended, success will follow. But should the failure be attributable to a fundamental lack of aptitude, this is more disheartening because innate ability is outside conscious control. Objective results must also be seen in their proper human context. Different results are associated with different emotions - feelings of satisfaction and pride are linked with success, while sadness, guilt, anger and humiliation march with failure; there may be gratitude if assistance has been given by others, and surprise or resignation if luck has played a part. If it is possible to plan for particular results through actions controllable by the actor, then emotions can be powerful motivators.

One mechanism for assessing the rationality of any indivudal's behaviour, is to subjectively assess that person's goals. Once these goals have been established, the observer simply predicts the behaviour on the basis that it will be a rational or economic way of achieving those goals. Such judgements do not necessarily mean that a person always formulates explicit goals, or acts in a subjectively intentional way. However, the usual approach in the education environment is for the teachers to draw up a curriculum which specifies the achievement criteria by which competence is to be assessed. It is therefore reasonable to assume that willing learners will wish to demonstrate the appropriate competence reactions. This raises the question of how an individual assesses competence.

This is usually achieved through a conception of ability. Ability is usually defined both by refering to the performance of others, and by measuring innate capacity. Generally, young children do not judge their own ability either by objective performance norms or by more subjective social comparisons. There are two reasons for this. First, they lack the necessary experience and powers of discrimination, and second, they largely make judgements about themselves. On the other hand, older students can become more disheartened, even in success, if they perceive that their level of mastery is not as profound as that of their colleagues, or that success was achieved only after intense effort which was not the case in their peers. At this point, the attitude of the teacher can assume an ironic significance. If a student performs badly in an activity requiring low skill levels, this can invite sympathy and helpful reactions from the teacher. Unfortunately, these are behavioural cues which tend to confirm the learner's poor self-image and, with increasingly low levels of confidence, performance is likely to spiral downwards. Hence, if one of the primary lines of communication between the teacher and the student is the computer, the reactions of the computer must always be discreet.

It is true that if someone is prepared to invest effort in an activity, this can nearly always improve ability. But if people are to be motivated to maintain that effort, they usually require support in the form of belief in the likelihood of ultimate success. Then, actually achieving the desired competence can be extremely satisfying, and therefore motivating when facing the next challenge. To determine likely outcomes, each person seeks to evaluate their own performance levels, and judges the performance of others in a comparable situation. However, people aspire towards competence for a variety of different reasons. Hence,

John G. Nicholls (9) postulates that a distinction should be made between task-involvement, which is the innate satisfaction in developing mastery of a given task, and ego-involvement which is the demonstration of that mastery to others or to oneself.

How well or badly each person performs will often be a function of the purpose in seeking to achieve the mastery. From the earlier definitions, it should be recalled that the nature of the task of learning is to demonstrate consequential ability, i.e. learning or mastery should be an end in itself. Thus, if the ego is involved, the primary desire of the learner is probably to demonstrate superior abilities. To that extent, the learning activity will be merely a means to that end, and the learner will feel more constrained by the process. But if the actor is task-involved, learning will be attempted if there is a suitable opportunity and the actor wants to do so. In such a situation, the learner will tend to feel more free and less under pressure. The move from task to ego-involvement is likely to occur when concerns are raised about the methods for measuring the standard of performance, and the scale of measurement is made inter-personal. Hence, in a classroom situation, if the teacher announces a test, it implies that an important topic or ability is to be evaluated. The more the test is stressed and the more publicly comparisons are to be made with others, the more a learner may become concerned about ability and therefore ego-involved.

At a simplistic level, learners tend to see a simple progression whereby more effort leads to more learning which, in the long term, amounts to more ability. But not all learners will accept this rationale as the sole justification for undertaking certain tasks. Thus, if a task is thought to be moderately difficult, i.e. it requires high effort, but nevertheless a degree of effort which is within perceived existing or foreseeable performance levels, then if success is achieved, it will imply high ability. People can experience strong feelings of satisfaction if they succeed in such challenging situations, and the emotional over-tone may supplement the existing motivation. But if the task is perceived as being trivial, it will not be thought to contribute towards learning. Equally, if no amount of effort appears likely to produce success, the task will not be considered suitable for demonstrating ability, except and in so far as it may be instruc-tive to see how much progress can actually be made. In such situations, effort for effort's sake will not be so readily forthcoming.

However, when the ego is involved, each individual's perceptions of difficulty are not the sole standard. If others can perform the given task easily, then success does not necessarily prove high ability and failure will confirm low ability. Alternatively, if the majority cannot perform the given task, failure does not prove low ability and success will confirm high ability. Thus, each person's expectancy of being able to demonstrate ability will depend upon the perceived level of normative difficulty. But regardless of actual difficulty, many students become disheart-ened because they believe that their best is not good enough.

They therefore adopt the strategy of avoiding the demonstration of low ability and opt out. As an adult, it may be considered fruitless to continue the course, and the student will simply withdraw. However, this is not always a straight forward option. Where grant or comparable financial constraints would impose penalties for early withdrawal, the student must attend and show some degree of commitment. In such situations, only tasks which are perceived to be easy will be attempted. As a young person within compulsory education, physical withdrawal may result in legal sanctions against parents or guardians, and so the student seeks whatever compromise is possible as between the demonstration of indifference, the coercive powers of the school authorities, and the possible recriminations of affected parents.

Where the student decides to hide within the system, but cannot choose the tasks to be attempted, any difficulty may be considered threatening because basic inadequacies cannot easily be hidden. Thus, even realistic challenges may not be attempted or, if attempted, the student may adopt the rational strategy deliberately doing badly. The rationality in this strategy lies in the fact that the student may legitimately fear that any success may bring more difficult challenges, and that these, in turn, will uncover the perceived lack of capacity. Anxiety therefore substantially colours decision-making.

Aronson and Carlsmith found that following an unexpected success, the students in the study produced a failure, presumably in an attempt to minimise the extent of their initial success. (10) This was explained on the basis of a cognitive consistency theory where incongruent outcomes are reacted against to maintain a consistent conception of self. The problem with this model is that, in the real world, people who have been deprived of success over a period of time, can desire it more intensely than normal and, thus, the self-enhancing properties of a success are likely to outweigh the need to maintain consistency. The way in which a person reacts will, in part, be determined by the level of their self-esteem, and by the degree of certainty in that estimation. An individual who is wholly or partially uncertain as to the validity of their low ability estimation, may be motivated to seek self-enhancement. This might be because any prospect of improvement may be considered desirable in its own right, or because it may also provide a means for reducing uncertainty in a desirable direction. It should also be said that someone who is certain of low ability would not be affected by an unexpected and transient success because it would be irrelevant to self-assessment. Equally, a success which is attributable to pure luck would be disregarded because it is not self-determined.

The later research team of Marecek and Mettee (11) therefore proposed an experiment to test the validity of these predictions. A number of American college-age students were asked to complete a questionnaire which was actually designed to determine their level of self-esteem and the degree of certainty in that perception. Subsequently, a random selection of students with either high or low esteem levels, was asked to perform a task in which the result was either obtained through their own efforts, or through chance. Half way through the task, and regardless as to actual performance levels, all the students were told that their performance to that point was highly successful. The second half performances were then carefully monitored.

The results show that students for whom success is inconsistent, will only reject or minimise success if they are certain of their low-esteem assessment, and the manner of their success is self-determined, i.e. such students showed no improvement in the second half. But, where the students were uncertain of their low-esteem assessment, and where luck was apparently the determining element, the low ability group's performance improved in the second half. "Perhaps the most important finding was the great improvement shown by the low self-esteem/certain subjects in the luck condition. Here first half success gave great impetus to actual second half performance, indicating that if success is not self-produced, even persons with deeply rooted chronic low self-esteem will enthusiastically embrace a successful outcome. Apparently, a success that does not implicate the person as causal agent is irrelevant and immaterial to the person's self-appraisal." (12) Thus, even a poor driver cannot be at fault if the car is damaged while properly parked and in the driver's absence. So if luck is the causal factor, a good performance has nothing to do with the person's actual abilities. This leaves persons with low self-esteem free to react to success without worrying about their self-appraisal. Should the 'luck' persist, the person may take some credit for the successful outcomes and gently raise self-esteem, thus breaking the vicious circle of low self-esteem leading to avoidance of evaluation and confirmation of negative self-assessment.

Where there is stronger self-esteem and the ego is involved, with some confidence in ability, the student may choose to expend effort only if a challenge is recognised. This is because many better performers take the view that it is only in such situations that high ability can be demonstrated. If high effort is in fact expended and the predicted success is achieved, confidence reinforcement will result. Alternatively, given certainty of ability, a failure is likely to be stimulating to future effort and, assuming that it is still considered realistic, the attraction of the challenge will probably be enhanced. Little effort may therefore be expended on low ability level problems, sometimes resulting in poor performances where carelessness produces error. Thus, it is all very well having an ability in CAL systems to match the teaching materials and standards to the individual student. But if the student is not motivated to learn, the very fact that material is presented at a level where the student perceives that it could be understood and implemented, may actually be more threatening. Conversely, if the material is not considered sufficiently challenging, the better student may not be motivated to pay proper attention. Such potentially conflicting demands make CAL design more difficult than most software engineers realise.

Some people who have high abilities are perceived as achieving results with less effort than normal being required, but whatever effort was actually involved, people with high ability are normally expected to try harder. The reason for this expectation is that there is thought to be a positive correlation between a person's ability, motivation and attainment. Yet, people who have high ability, tend not to seek to subjectively assess the level of difficulty which is going to be involved, but instead concentrate on the strategies for task-mastery, i.e. they forget about their capacity, relax more and become more involved in learning. If a high ability individual achieves success as a result of high effort, this may produce the emotions of pride and pleasure, and may lead to the expectation of continued success. Conversely, low effort leading to failure is likely to cause feelings of shame or guilt, feelings that 'we have let ourselves down'. If the person is also ego-involved, he or she may also be embarrassed through failure whether the effort actually made is high or low. Indeed, high effort followed by failure may be more embarrassing to some. However, inputting high effort always enhances the chances of success, and therefore minimises the risks of either guilt or embarrassment. The degree of pride in success, or of shame in failure, depends upon the degree of self-perception of ability. When all goes well, pride reinforces motivation. If failures occur, individuals are likely to abandon the task, particularly where there is an element of self-doubt.

2.6   What is the aim of education?

The aim of education may be for each student to make the most of his or her abilities. This is not to produce an equalisation of educational standards, but represents an effort to ensure that each has an equal opportunity to develop their inate potential. In such an environment, a high degree of ego-involvement on the part of the learners is bound to maximise the inequality of motivation. The most likely result would then be the production of inequality, if only because those who are perceived as having low ability are more likely to become demotivated. However, where task-involvement teaching strategies are used, equal and optimum motivation are more likely to be maintained.

Alternatively, the aim of education may be to prepare individuals to play an active part in the social and economic life of the community. Thus, ego-involvement and competition in the classroom would be a model for the real world, where rewards are often dependent upon capacity and effort rather than need. If students cannot make the adjustment within the comparative safety of the classroom, they are not going to succeed in a meritocracy. However, it must be against the capitalist ethic that a significant proportion of the future working population should become alienated and give up learning before they have learned even the basic skills that they will need in the lowest status employments. All extremes of ego-involvement should therefore be avoided in the classroom unless teachers wish to risk the collapse of the social and economic system, and minimum standards should be communicated, before more competition is allowed into the system.

2.7 Teaching strategies to underpin CAL design

A person's sense of optimism and the willingness to try diminish with age as each individual becomes more status conscious, and as the distinction is made between effort and ability. Everyone has the possibility of feeling competent, but it fades as each person inevitably begins to make comparisons of competence with his or her peers. Indeed, true competition is really only possible when children learn to perceive differences in ability. In a genuinely competitive environment, success is more impressive where only a few succeed. But if teachers approve one person's winning performance, this implies another's incompetence. The problem in this approach is that the adolescent is vulnerable to the fear of appearing stupid because, as personality is forming, it may confirm a more fundamental lack of ability. Worry and self-doubt may substantially interfere with performance. Teachers and CAL designers should therefore aim for more task-involvement, which will minimise the number of situations in which formal comparative judgements will be made, and hopefully enhance self-esteem.

However, current research suggests that teaching styles tend to the opposite pole as the groups age, breeding an atmosphere where success and failure become remote from each other. This mirrors the real world where capitalism and market forces do not encourage an even distribution of ability or reward. So teachers do not question the proposition that the existing socioeconomic status ranking is valid, and that the purpose of schooling is to prepare students for a role in a meritocracy. Students therefore come to believe that they are only as good as their achievements. The real answer is to encourage a proper valuation of effort so that self-criticism in failure becomes linked to a recognition of insufficient effort.

Linking self-esteem to ability is a gamble because perceptions of adequacy are easily threatened by failure. Schools and colleges and the examination system which they support, base their philosophy on the proposition that it is not possible to reward success at all ability levels. An environment is therefore created where, if success is to be achieved, students must compete among themselves for the few rewards. The few succeed at the expense of many. This leads to a greater consensus in the peer group, and among teachers, about ability levels, and this in turn, reinforces the likelihood of demoralisation among those of now more publicly acknowledged weakness. "Losing in competitive settings magnifies negative affect more than winning enhances positive affect. While winning evokes self-aggrandising motives, the findings are strong that failing in competitive structures elicits feelings of nondeservingness and dissatisfaction; and because competition engenders a situation of many losers and few winners, an esteem rating for this structure must necessarily be low." (13) The message is therefore clear. Consensus information in a competitive context tends to emphasise ability criteria. Thus, even in those schools and colleges where each individual has his or her own computer terminal, and a degree of privacy is potentially offered to each learner, learners can still compare notes and establish a pecking order of progress. So only in those environments where task-involvement is the norm, can be more destructive consequences of those comparisons be avoided.

If competition is the norm, many students will struggle to avoid failure rather than struggle for success. As a goal, this is unlikely to maintain good academic progress, but it may preserve some self-esteem. It will, of course, be accepted that one failure is not usually fatal to self-esteem, because there can be so many alternative explanations. It is in repeated failure that acceptance of low ability becomes the only viable explanation for the failure. Repeated failure increases the negative dynamic, and falls in the self-perception of ability become a more positive cause of distress. One of the keys to personal resiliance in the face of failure is the ability to externalise responsibility, to be able to point to causes like illness or lack of good fortune in the examination questions as an excuse. However, if a theory of consistency is adopted along the lines suggested by Aronson and Carlsmith, once the perception of low ability is formed, some students will act in ways consistent with that image. Teachers and CAL designers should always try to counter this tendency by altering the psychological meaning of failure, and one possible strategy would be to increase the number of apparent rewards in the system so that everyone stands a realistic chance of achieving some success.

A failure to consider these issues in the design of teaching materials, is likely to lead to increasingly defensive action by the learners. One strategy to avoid admitting weakness is for the student to set unreasonably high performance goals. If the student then fails at a task that would usually defeat the even most able of students, the failure says little about the particular student. The student will also procrastinate, feigning interest, and perhaps looking as if working too hard to interrupt. If a person appears active or persistent, the teacher may believe him or her to be well motivated. Such a student is in fact a deliberate underachiever, i.e. not trying is no guide to true form and therefore failure causes little shame. Indeed, one of the dangers is that a perverse sense of pride in failure may emerge as a mark of nonconformity. Alternatively, a series of apparently reasonable excuses can deflect the implication of lack of ability. Similarly, the closet worker who claims no work prior to an exam, protects a reputation if failure results, and may actually appear to be unusually clever or just lucky if successful. If all else has failed, and a testing mechanism is about to be used, absenteeism may be tried.

All such manoeuvres are in fact self–defeating mechanisms for maintaining public credibility because, ultimately, they destroy the will to learn as the students come to accept the fact of failure, and cut themselves off from even the possibility of classroom rewards. However, teachers or their computer programs ought to be seen to reward effort as well as mere success. Students would therefore have to decide whether to risk high effort which may prove lack of ability even though there may be compensations in the teacher's direct or indirect approval. What is said, and the way in which it is said, should seek to convince the students that those who try will be rewarded more in success and less in failure than those who do not try.

2.8   What is mastery?

The mastery paradigm involves what may be termed a criterion-referenced grading arrangement, i.e. an arrangement whereby absolute performance standards must be met by each student in order to achieve different grade levels. The very existence of absolute standards may tend to make the students goal–oriented, and what might otherwise be individualism can become self–competition. This is reflected in the fact that any number of students can achieve a given grade so long as their performance meets the criteria. The testing is therefore not directly competitive in intent. Indeed, several testing opportunities may be offered to allow students to reach each given standard, because the declared purpose of the exercise is to encourage self–improvement. One explanation for this is that the existence of absolute standards may offer enough rewards and reduce peer group competition. This is confirmed by research findings that the availability of a large number of success opportunities does not seem to reduce motivation through a lack of scarcity value. Hence, the research of Martin V. Covington (14), amongst other things suggests that even belated success in retesting situations after initial failure, frequently leads to more satisfaction, and tends to reinforce the students' valuation of effort.

In the mastery situation, there is still competition, but it is less peer group competiton, and more a competition against the standards of the curriculum, or of the individual teacher as tester. The classroom emphasis then hopefully shifts from invidious social comparisons to one of task-persistence. However, the number of testing opportunities may create problems for students who suffer from self-doubt, and may therefore only see the possibility of more opportunities to fail. But Covington reports that the decrease in self-esteem was significantly less among low ability students in a mastery situation, and he detects an increasing sense of competency. "In individualised settings, students' achievements are independent of each other and the opportunity for the attainment of rewards is equal across students. A student's task performance becomes a step in a process of learning or achieving mastery... [and] the salience of past performance should be strong... because this information is central to a "process" of achieving." (15)

In a situation which is directly competitive, students are given a chance to win. But, if the pursuit of victory becomes the dominant ethic, many will succumb to temptation, and will both overtly and covertly cheat. The resultant focus is how to win and not necessarily how best to perform the given task. On the other hand, students working alone are simply given an opportunity to do their best; for the spirit of the mastery paradigm relies upon focussing a student's attention upon the continuity of progress, rather than upon the individual component elements of the course of study. In a sense, therefore, a student-centred course which is strongly based on CAL with face-to-face teacher support when necessary, could produce exactly the right non-threatening learning environment where the optimum progress may be achieved.

2.8.1 Are there alternatives to mastery?

One possibility would be a form of equity paradigm which would seek to give all students sufficient reward, irrespective of ability. Thus, some would advocate the negotiation of a semiformal agreement whereby the teacher and the student contract to determine what work is to be achieved before a reward is to be given. Others suggest a co-operative approach whereby the peer group, in consultation with the teacher, set group achievement targets, and allocate work on the basis of individual interests or abilites, with consequent rewards allocated in a mutually acceptable fashion. The group would then be working towards a common goal, and members of the group helping each other should become an increasingly common feature, both because it fosters greater social interdependency, and because shared effort may be seen to enhance the chances of the group fulfilling the goals. This approach would also tend to reduce the excesses of individual stereotyping by teachers, since the teacher's perceptions would tend to focus on the group rather than on individuals, and tend to consider contributions to team effort to be more equal, hence the distribution of rewards.

The difficulty in co-operative situations is that a group failure can be more demoralising, regardless as to how well or how badly each individual member performed. When the group fails, the question of responsibility can suddenly become important, and the weaker performers can be blamed by the other group members. This may be counterbalanced by the norm of interdependency generated during the work towards the goal, whereby each individual should fulfil his or her commitment to the group. The hope would be that it leads to feelings of group solidarity, where the high performers become more protective of the low performers. The teacher or computer coach should encourage this possibility by identifying efforts of each person which might not otherwise have been made to support the group's progress. Such an approach seeks to redefine success by exceeding one's own goals, rather than overtaking the accomplishments of others. It also emphasises the view that only if students accept personal responsibility, will positive effort be forthcoming. All learners ought to come to believe in ability as the primary cause of achievement. The need is therefore to have the right amount of structure in the classroom. Too much is too bad, too little is chaos.

The optimum structure allows students both personal and collective responsibility. This is not encouraged by a laissez faire teacher. The teacher should therefore adopt a pattern of positive and consistent behaviour, with the welfare of the students obvious. However, this should not lead to overdirectiveness, for this will will tend to inhibit the assumption of responsibility by the students. The best strategy is to invite influence from the students rather than to impose influence upon them. However, in order to be able to make a contribution that is perceived as sensible, the students must have some basic information. The task of the teacher must then be to strike a proper balance between the input of seed corn information and helpful supervision, to permit students to achieve greater success sooner, and to become more confident in their ownership of self-originated behaviour.

2.9 What is the function of feedback?

Young children react more to social reinforcement such as praise or criticism, than to objective or normative feedback. This arises for two reasons: firstly, because they are less experienced in relating to adults and look for confidence building signals; and secondly, because adults are expected to know more. Hence, some form of positive reinforcing remark would always be potentially desirable to confirm correct answers, whether from the human teacher or from the computer. However, to always praise the few good young students in open class is to run the risk of demoralising the others, and it is not educationally appropriate to take up too much time if the same type of remarks are to re-appear with boring frequency. It is best to introduce a variety of constructive responses, avoiding humour and, particularly, sarcasm. Many students will not enjoy the teacher's sense of humour, and others whose confidence is already low, will be further disheartened by the sarcasm.

Older students rely on both subjective and objective evidence. The age at which marks or grades become important depends upon when the teacher begins to make approval contingent upon perform-ance. As soon as school becomes more formal and structured, the amount of whole class instruction increases and therewith, the opportunity for public comments where some students are held up as good examples to the others. Grading by ability completes the process. "All children can surpass their own past performance level, but not all children can surpass the performance level of peers. By failing to compare their performance to other children, young children are spared one potential source of information indicating low competence." (16) This helps to explain how young-er children manage to remain optimistic and motivated, and should also help to point the way to using feedback to reinforce the confidence, and to maintain the motivation, of the more mature student.

References

(1) A Theory of Justice. John Rawls. Clarendon Press, Oxford. 1973. p.143.

(2) I.Pavlov (1849–1936), a Russian psycholgist; J.B.Watson (1878–1958) professor of experimental and comparative psychology at John Hopkins University, Maryland; E.R.Guthrie (1886–1959) University of Washington.

(3) E.C.Tolman (1886–1959) University of California.

(4) (1904 –), professor of psychology at Harvard University, see particularly Cumulative Record, Methuen. 1961.

(5) J.S.Bruner (1915 –) professor of psychology at the Univer-sities of Harvard nd Cambridge.

(6) J Dewey (1859–1952) professor of philosophy at the Univer-sities of Chicago and Columbia.

(7) Learning by Discovery. H.Taba. (1963) 3 School Journal.

(8) Gagne (1916 –) professor of psychology at the Universities of Princeton and Florida. See particularly, The Conditions of Learning. Holt, Rinehart, Winston. 1970

(9) Conceptions of Ability. John G. Nicholls. collected in Research on Motivation in Education. pp.39/73 at p.43/4.

(10) Performance expectancy as a determinant of actual performance. E.Aronson and J.M.Carlsmith. (1962) 65 Journal of Abnormal and Social Psychology 178/82.

(11) Avoidance of continued success as a function of self–esteem, level of esteem certainty, and responsibility for success. J.Marecek & D.R.Mettee. (1962) 22 Jo of Personality and Social Psychology 98/107.

(12) ibid at p.105.

(13) Competitive, Cooperative, and Individualistic Goal Structures: A Cognitive–Motivational Analysis. Carole Ames. collected in Research on Motivation in Education. pp.177/207 at pp.179/80.

(14) The Motive for Self–Worth. Martin V Covington. collected in Research on Motivation in Education. pp.77/113 at pp.104/6.

(15) Competitive, Cooperative, and Individualistic Goal Structures: A Cognitive–Motivational Analysis. Carole Ames. collected in Research on Motivation in Education. pp.177/207 at p.184.

(16) The Development of Achievement Motivation. Deborah J Stipek. collected in Research on Motivation in Education. pp.145/74 at p.165.

CHAPTER 3

THE ACTUAL MEANING OF COMPUTING IN THE CURRICULUM

This chapter directly addresses the issue of the role of the computer as the subject matter of courses within the curriculum. In many institutions, including those which make provision for the disabled, the students are exposed to formal computer literacy courses, or are required to learn about the computer in some specific way. This leads to difficult educational decisions as to whether students should be taught how to program and, if so, in which languages, and what should the programs do? Similarly, if students are to be taught the use of standard applications packages, e.g. wordprocessor or spreadsheet systems, what standards of expertise should they be expected to achieve?

3.1 What is computer literacy?

Although many schools and colleges now offer courses which either directly or indirectly purport to teach computer literacy, it is difficult to find any real consistency in the declared content of these courses. The reason for this is that the underlying subject discipline of computer science has not been a part of the school and college curriculum over a long enough period of time for the general process of harmonisation to take place. In order to be able to establish a common denominator computer curriculum which is satisfactory, it ought to be proved in the classroom. The resultant degree of satisfaction would usually be measured by asking whether the course meets the performance criteria laid down in the curriculum. In this situation, however, the difficulty of the chicken–and–egg process is exacerbated through the novelty of the subject matter. Consequently, the initial content of each course tends arbitrarily to be fixed by the level of knowledge and the enthusiasms of the individual staff who will teach it.

Moreover, given the capital and revenue implications for creating and staffing adequate computer facilities, it is inevitable that some educational establishments will be limited in the resources with which to support these courses. In those schools and colleges where the staff are not fully aware of their own limitations, an objectively satisfactory course may not be achieved until supervisory staff are confronted by the reality of outside values. This may be through the failure of students entered in externally marked or assessed examinations, through some peer group validation mechanism, or through unfavourable reports from ex–students and their employers. But even if feedback does suggest the need for some change, the resource allocation mechanism or the attribution of priorities may not have sufficient flexibility to allow the necessary improvements to be made before the next cohort of students enters the course. Even if administrative inertia can be overcome in time, and the necessary hardware and software are acquired, difficulties of staff competence are not so easily resolved, and there is no doubt that many courses are knowingly run on a second–rate basis until new staff can be acquired or existing staff can be more effectively trained.

However, if it is assumed that all the available teaching staff are competent, then within the resource limitations, the staff must constantly compromise between the ideal subject coverage specified in the syllabus, and the practicality of the teaching environment, until an acceptable course emerges. This is a problem which is partly educational and partly political, as within each institution's or authority's budget, the appropriate staff must compete for resources, and argue a case for the continuous improvement and enhancement of existing facilities.

One solution to the problem of hardware constraints is whole class teaching, using a micro which may or may not have multiple screens. Either the teacher enters all the data, using the consensus question–and–answer approach to establish the group's view of the right answer, or the "game show" format is adopted, where star pupils come to the keyboard and make their entries before the admiring (?) eyes of the class and with their encouragement. It might be argued that this latter type of approach can increase motivation, and that it supplies an opportunity (albeit limited) to offer hands–on experience to a scarce resource. However, the performer may actually be fairly passive, entering data at the behest of the teacher or the rest of the class. It can also be demoralising to all those students never given the starring role, or to those who hope to star, but end by demonstrating their incompetence before their peers.

The alternative is group work around the computer. The primary constraint is that everyone needs to be able to see and read the screen. This means that the students will need to sit close together. Even so, the screen may need to be lifted higher than usual, and care should to taken to minimise any reflection on the screen, and to optimise lighting conditions. The keyboard should also be to one side of the screen so that the operator does not block the view of the screen. The use of computers by small groups can make a scarce resource go further, for even the bulk purchase of computers can be a significant drain of capital re- sources, and a ratio of up to three students to one micro or terminal still makes economic sense. But if group sizes of more than three are tried, it will be found difficult to seat everyone so that the screen can be seen, and hard to allow everyone a reasonable opportunity to make a contribution to the discussion, or to the machine. Only if the hardware is developed to permit multiple access through separate keyboards to the same machine, could larger group work become educationally feasible.

In a group context, the computer itself can become much less significant, because the group predominantly learns through per- sonal interaction, with the computer merely acting as a mediator. It is not simply that two heads are better than one. In the first instance, there is increased emotional security in a small group environment, where students will not fear embarrassment to the same degree as in the full classroom, and are therefore better placed to learn. Working in a group also forces the verbalisation of ideas and strategies, and this inevitably improves learning. A further advantage of group discussions is that they mitigate the limited nature of the man/machine discussion until the technology improves to the point where natural language exchanges may take place. But it cannot be emphasised too strongly that none of these advantages should be taken as an excuse for writing poor CAL software in the hope that any inadequacies will be concealed by the work which the group does.

If access to computers is limited by timetabling constraints, this can place unreasonable pressure on the teachers to push the students to complete projects within the limited time available. This can lead to overdirectiveness on the part of the teacher, instead of allowing the learning to proceed at a more relaxed pace. However, an equally valid explanation of the phenomenon of overdirectiveness is that it is sometimes a defensive measure by teachers to retain traditional teacher values and a denial of the possible advantages of CAL. Shepherd comments that, "the teacher sees the computer as his personal preserve, and any access by students is carefully controlled and monitored. Sometimes a teacher is unwilling to allow students any direct access to the computer. This clearly denies students any opportunity of learn- ing by their own experiments." (1) This is using the computer for reinforcement purposes only, and not to promote student-centred learning. In seeking to establish the scale of this abuse of the technology and to take remedial action, the problem most usually encountered is that when researchers enter a classroom to observe, they may not see characteristic behaviour, i.e. the teacher may think that he or she is showing the class and the system off to the best advantage to have a high directorial input. The alternatives of covert observation or student interviewing, involve ethical implications which the teaching profession might find unacceptable.

Regardless as to whether the adequacy of the course is known or subsequently recognised, or whether the actual use of the hardware is effective, the curriculum situation is further confused by the fact that the subject is not static in terms of content. The continuous process of change in the technology and its applications requires a constant updating, both of specific topics in the literacy course itself, and of the hardware and software which supports it. Thus, keyboards may, to some extent, be replaced by mice, touchscreens or light pens; new languages and packages may require a different emphasis in an introduction to applications, and so on. Indeed, it is the very rapidity of change in the technology which makes it so difficult to establish a validated body of knowledge and/or skills which will comprise the domain of the computer literate.

In a perfect educational world, the goals of any computer literacy course should be broadly similar to those to be achieved in a print literacy course. Bostock and Seifert argue that print literacy requires the psychomotor skills necessary to read and write, coupled with some knowledge of the uses of text, an ease in the print milieu, and an absence of the social and intellectual constraints which illiteracy imposes along with undesirable attitudes and anxieties. (2) They reason that whereas the technology of writing and printing had been reserved to special groups in order to maximise their power, the emergence of mass literacy coincided with rapid industrialisation and the political ideals of equality, freedom and democracy. Today, a new post-industrialisation society is emerging with a new technological elite whose existence alienates the mass of computer illiterate. As in the case of the Industral Revolution, where commerce reshaped an essentially agricultural society and produced a new political reality, the information revolution is producing a power imbalance within society as the new information society emerges from the old industrialised society. The mass of citizens are therefore left to seek to redress the balance by whatever means are available. Where the trade unions can offer protection, time for reflection and retraining can be obtained; but many have found themselves replaced by machine-based information systems without the opportunity to aquire suitably portable skills. In all cases, if it is assumed that destructive responses are excluded, the only hope lies in education.

Sadly, basic literacy courses will make no real impact because their primary function is really only to improve access to equipment and little is done to address, let alone mitigate, the more

fundamental social and political effects of information technology. Thus, in the standard computer literacy course, all the
students should:

acquire a general understanding of the nature of computer
hardware and software, and of the associated terminology;

be able to operate the standard key board and other common
interface mechanisms;

be able to use a printer, plotter or other hard copy device;

have some familiarity with the operation of standard applications packages;

have an insight into the both the strengths and the weaknesses of computer technology;

have some basis upon which to assess the worth of software
and hardware;

be aware of the personal and ethical implications of computer technology in society;

understand what career prospects may arise as a result of
the implementation of the technology;

appreciate the computer's role as a tool in industry and
commerce, and as an aid to recreation;

have an appreciation of the general contribution which computers can make to problem solving,

have some understanding of flow charting as a mechanism for
analysis and planning; and,

possibly have some understanding of simple programming.

It is possible to distinguish three quite distinct levels of
knowledge achievable in the computer sciences, viz. computer
literacy, which some would dismiss as complete superficiality;
computer competancy, i.e. the ability to make a sensible use of a
computer within any given specialism, and computer proficiency,
which would be the standard achievable by the professional. Many
course developers seem to take the view that basic computing
skills should be the fourth of the 3Rs; that all should have a
grounding in computers and the new technology which they support.
The usual justification for this view is the cliche that the
young and old alike now have chips with everything from the
mundane toaster to sophisticated cars, from automated banking to
robotics in the manufacturing industries, and so require technical expertise to be able to survive in this newly technological
environment.

Writing about Marlborough College, Marcus Gray ironically puts this justification in context, "Why have a computer in a school?... Because there are a lot of computers about, and they intrude into the life and thought of just about everyone. Now there are a lot of nuclear weapons about and they affect the life and thought of all adults, but I am happy to announce that our school cadet force does not possess First Strike capability." (3) Although perhaps some teachers might appreciate some minor tactical defence weaponry.

The course designer's dilemma may be put more succinctly as two simple questions:

>   do members of the community actually need computer literacy skills to be able to operate these computerised devices?

>   do basic skills include programming skills for the writing and debugging of software?

Given that the majority of computer-controlled consumer durables are usually accompanied with comprehensible instructions, and can actually be operated with little or no technical expertise, the everyday use of such machines does not give rise to the need for a special computer literacy course. If anything is required, it is a print literacy course to ensure that the written instructions can be adequately comprehended and implemented. The concept of "user friendliness" in a machine is an intention to eliminate or reduce the need for special training and, hopefully, represents a design which makes the intended task easier to perform. In fact, the rationale for the general process of making any system "user friendly" is to hide as much of the (actual or supposed) complexity as possible from the user.

The programmable machine will usually offer a wider range of options than would be conveniently possible using purely mechanical technology, e.g. using a range of twenty four hour clocks and a similar number of interlocked, mechanical switching devices built into an electrical circuit, it would be possible to cause a video recorder to come on in a number of days equivalent to the number of clocks; a similar parallel system would ensure that the recorder was switched off again at the desired time (Heath Robinson would have approved this approach). It is, however, easier to program a circuit within the video recorder with the current date and time, and the desired dates and times of the target shows and films to be recorded over the next n days. Actually connecting and synchronising the appropriate number of clocks, and ensuring that the mechanical switching devices were all in working order, would require some manual dexterity and knowledge. Anyone with normal physical skills could be trained to do it, but might find the effort required disproportionate to the desirability of the result, i.e. complexity can be demotivating. The ease with which a wider range of television programs can be recorded once comparatively simple controls are mastered, should minimise the risk that the user will be deterred from using the machine by the

60

appearance of difficulty. The recorder is therefore considered more "friendly" when more can be achieved with less effort by the user, or when the machine does more of the work for the user.

If the user had to program any machine from scratch, without detailed circuit diagrams and a full technical specification, even the professionally qualified user would be beaten before the start. It would, of course, be possible to program and reprogram, say, an automatic washing machine so that it would start and stop at different time intervals, heat the water to different temperatures, and spin for different lengths of time. To do this given current designs, the owner would have to dismantle the control circuitry, extract the chip and cause it to accept new instructions. This is not a skill which would be transmitted in the conventional computer literacy course. If the manufacturer was to build enough memory, and a sufficiently sophisticated interface into the washing machine to make this degree of control possible, the level of decision-making required of the user becomes a deterrent. The manufacturer would simply be providing almost total redundancy of user control as against standardised pre-programmed values, and would have produced a machine which would be considered singularly unfriendly.

It should therefore be apparent that literacy is not teaching people how to program in machine code, or in BASIC, or one of the other high level languages, for "an understanding of the computer's place in society is not achieved by the study of syntactic details." (4) Literacy is teaching people enough awareness to be able to survive in the newly emerging environment, and this may include information on how to use computer-controlled machines, or systems like the standard wordprocessor packages, spreadsheets, etc., but has no pretentions towards achieving even mere competence.

Computers are nothing more than machines, but inexperienced human users often find them difficult to approach because the machines have not been given a natural language ability. Although even the most cursory of reviews will reveal that many programming languages use natural words, they are usually used in a technical sense, and these sometimes specialised usages add to the confusion in the lay person's appreciation of function. Equally, symbols which may be perceived to be of little or no significance in the real world, e.g. the intricacies of punctuation, can assume unexpected levels of importance in programming where, say, an omitted comma can cause chaos. The general mechanisms of direct communication therefore have a tendency towards specialisation, as computer specialists use keyboard skills to input encoded commands, and were it not for the development of mice, touch screens and similar devices to ease the man-machine interface, many beginners would be deterred from the outset.

3.2 Simply teaching high level languages without some positive educational justification is wrong

The main point of any computer course should be to give ordinary people a sense that they have some mastery over their environment which now just happens to include computerised devices. Thus, students should be made aware of developments such as the revolution in banking which permits the electronic transfer of funds and the imminent computerisation at point of sale where direct debiting of bank accounts may be achieved. Similarly, they should be made aware that ticket agencies can make direct bookings at theatres and with airlines, and that householders will soon be able to shop and control most of their affairs from terminals in their own homes. However, the concomitant of such computerisation is that more centralised information is potentially available about the activities of each individual. The serious public policy issues of privacy and civil liberties should therefore be addressed, alongside the more everyday and practical considerations of, say, the legal and moral position of the hacker. (5)

With the spread of computerised accounting and information systems, problems of computer crime, and both hardware and data security, become increasingly significant. Equally, computer systems like HOLMES (Home Office Large Major Enquiry System) can now make a significant contribution as an aid to detection. This is a methodology for investigating crimes backed by computer. Statements, officers' reports and house-to-house inquiry entries are stored on computer. This both provides a centralised source of all information relating to an inquiry, but also allows detectives to search rapidly for connections between seemingly unrelated incidents. Although HOLMES was specifically designed to deal with serious crimes such as the Yorkshire Ripper inquiry, a number of police forces are setting up computerised systems to deal with day-to-day matters. In August 1987, the Metropolitan Police announced the development of a £17m Crime Report Information System (CRIS) which by 1991 is to link all 75 police divisions, and to provide facilities such as fuzzy matching, to make the most of partially remembered information, while other techniques can help to verify the authorship of documents, validate disputed statements, etc. Further issues such as copyright and theft, machine intelligence, the impact of new technology on the job market, etc. can be canvassed, depending on the educational constraints for that particular course.

Some such issues will be more important than others, but regardless as to the actual course content, the essential factor is a full and proper discussion of the society which is emerging. Many of these topics will be covered without the need for the students to have access to computers, yet information on work place and leisure environments is essential, if each student is to be fully integrated into society. When all adults treat the technology as nothing unusual, children will learn by observation and imitation as they grow up. Until the generation of informed and blase parents is established, basic survival courses of this nature will serve a useful purpose.

However, it is probably not sensible to force large amounts of social comment into a general literacy course. Most students prefer to get on and use the computers, and see any introduction of politics as an irrelevance. Thus, it may be better to allow the implications to arise naturally from the use of the software, i.e. when using business software, it is appropriate to introduce ideas about restructuring employment to take account of the new technologies and, perhaps, the wider issues of the trade union response to the replacement of the traditional forms of employment, and so on. This is not to run a political campaign to fire potential revolutionaries with appropriate enthusiasm, but simply to introduce the inexperienced to the wider social realities of the information society. However, the counter argument takes two lines:

first that simply to demonstrate existing hardware and software is for the teacher to act as an unpaid sales person for the manufacturers and, although it may prepare students to deal with today's technology, it does not necessarily enable people to deal with tomorrow's advances; only with the level of understanding that comes from an ability to program can a student achieve sufficient flexibility and adaptability; and,

second that it may be better to teach some programming before allowing the students to "play" with attractive pre-programmed materials. One difficulty is that once students become interested in, say, a games program, it can be difficult to regain their attention in a class for further teaching purposes. Further, too many students may be seduced by what is already written, without gaining the enjoyment of problem solving in the creation of new programs.

It is however necessary for teachers to recognise that a substantial percentage of students will never be enthusiastic about programming. Further, such arguments ignore the quality of many of the standard packages, which will do most of the tasks which "ordinary" users will require without the need for programming skills. Thus, the present generation of wordprocessor packages are excellent. No reasonable user is going to want to learn how to program to produce his or her own wordprocessor system. Indeed, so comprehensive are many of the new computer-based devices, that it is deskilling many manual tasks, and making it less necessary to put courses on for the training of human operators. Instead of engineering apprenticeship schemes designed to equip each industry with a core workforce of skilled machine operators, new breeds of machine can turn, mill and shim with programmed efficiency under sparse human supervision. Instead of armies of clerks sorting, collating and filing a mountain of paper in overcrowded ant hills, a few key personnel input or manipulate the data in air-conditioned terminal rooms or offices.

In making these contrasts, it is not intended to create images of Utopian employment environments, for many now act as little more than machine watchers, and this is not an idyllic way of passing the time. It is intended to show that a different order of skills is now required of the many sectors of the workforce. Whereas manual competence, sometimes gained over many years of training, used to be desirable, more adaptive computer-oriented skills are now desirable, so that once sample systems have been fully understood, it will be relatively unusual that major retraining will be required to transfer staff to any new systems which will perform the same tasks.

3.3   Where does this cry for computer literacy come from?

Although there is some pressure from industry and commerce, the initiative often arises from the educational establishment which sometimes requires, or merely offers, introductory courses. The difficulty is that many of these initiatives are taken without necessarily considering whether such courses are actually needed and, if so, how best to structure the contents. It should be fundamental to the design of any curriculum, that whatever is included in one part, should not compete with other parts of the education offered. Each part should complement the whole, and arise naturally from the general work of the school or college. The real answer to the question therefore ought to be, that demand arises following a detailed discussion between all the various subject specialisms and affected interest groups, to determine what common denominator skills are required in order to undertake study at the given level. If it is decided that computer skills are desirable, but that they cannot comfortably be subsumed within the normal subject domains, the new subject of computer literacy is thereby brought into existence.

Some specific course elements will be directly vocational and will train individuals in given skills but, with respect, these are not pure literacy courses. Thus, it might be suggested that all business or commercial students ought to be computer literate. However, to give every student basic competence in word processor techniques or, more selectively, to train business studies students in the use of spreadsheet systems, is vocational and not mere literacy; although it is always useful to teach one package so that the student can generalise and extrapolate to other packages. Moreover, it is up to educators to define their students' needs in the light of both the express and the hidden curriculum. Hence, although the explicit aim of a curriculum will be obvious, education also serves other less explicit aims, viz. the development of attitudinal and social skills. However, any development of the curriculum and reallocation of study time, inevitably means that other established elements will have to be modified, or left out altogether. This may well meet opposition from the staff responsible for teaching those subjects, who may perceive their interests as threatened.

Further, independently of the internal human politics of the school or college, there must be proper advanced planning. It is not constructive to introduce disparate course elements at random through a secondary school or college career. A proper curriculum should project student development, set achievement goals for each year and show a hierachical approach. This is particularly important as computer skills migrate downwards through the education system, and all courses should be kept under review. As the social phenomenon which computers represent becomes more pervasive, what cannot today be assumed at eleven as students enter the secondary system, may soon be common knowledge among six or seven year olds.

3.4 What are the implications for teacher training courses?

In-service teachers' standards must be kept continuously under review, and appropriate updating courses should be run on a regular basis for all affected subjects areas. As potential teachers come through the general education system, the choice of course assumes new importance. Given that computer science is capable of being a distinct academic discipline, and not merely something to be contained as an element in other disciplines, undergraduate students may opt for the specialist degree, or degree-equivalent, computing qualifications. Hence, some graduates will have a detailed knowledge of computers, and others will simply have a view of their use. This creates a problem for post-graduate teacher training courses for, regardless of educational background and expertise, all individuals will require the inclusion of appropriate course elements to ensure enough competence to handle computers in the education environment.

Similarly, colleges and universities should develop undergraduate teacher education so as to include a major computing element, since more in-depth training is required for those who will teach computing skills, than from those who will merely use computers. Further, it is unfair that computer training should have to be in-service, and Local Education Authorities should have a right to expect basic competence on the part of those whom they recruit as teachers. This is particularly the case because the disciplines of computer science and education are thematically parallel. Both consider the way in which information can be represented, stored, and processed. Without the computer, society would have to be organised in a way which is less information-intensive. With the computer, education can be organised in a way which will expose the student to a far greater range of information than would be possible using conventional methodologies.

3.5 What should school computer courses teach?

At primary school level, it is important to recognise that computers are not too difficult for young children to use. A young child's world is filled with complex and exciting machines – the car, telephone, television, hi-fi stereo system, all of which are gradually assimilated into a comprehensible pattern through a mixture of observation and experimentation. A distinction might be made in that, whereas a telephone only does one thing, a computer is a more flexible tool. It is therefore helpful to know more about the computer. It also has certain practical advantages in that it is better to have exercises displayed on a computer screen rather than on card or paper which wears out quickly; non-readers can use computers by using a touch screen or a mouse to select by colour, and so on. Similarly, reading skills are often taught through the use of flash cards, where whole-word recognition is taught by showing the word on the card and speaking it. The student therefore comes to associate the sight with the sound. The problem in these more cost conscious times is that this system does not make efficient use of a teacher's time, whereas using a computer to undertake the basic work, allows the teacher to give more individual attention.

In special schools, all teaching needs to be more individually tailored to students who are outside the bounds of average ability. Such students are simply examples of mixed ability teaching. The slow learner has problems of motivation and concentration. It takes longer for such individuals to grasp a concept. Programs of a drill and practice nature can therefore fulfil a useful role. Computers also increase attention span. Glen Kleiman and his fellow Canadian researchers at the Child Development Clinic, Hospital for Sick Children in Ontario have performed a pilot study on hyperactive and other attention-deficient children. The basis of the experiment was the performance of a series of arithmetic problems. Some children undertook the solution of the problems using the traditional paper and pencil format, while others were administered the problems by computer. (6) Eighteen children participated in the study. The level of difficulty in the questions could be tailored for each child. The answer format on the computer display was designed in exactly the same way as on paper. In both paper and computer administered tests, the children were self-paced and were invited to do as many questions as they liked in a given time. Motivational features were built into the computer program, with praise statements following correct answers, and other messages relating to the child's problem of hyperactivity, e.g. advising the child if the incorrect answer had been put in too quickly.

The results of the study were clear cut. There were no differences between paper and computer work in terms of the proportion of answers correct, the average time to do problems, or the average time between problems. The differences appeared in the number of problems the child voluntarily decided to do. On average, the same child working on the same level of difficulty, did almost twice as many problems on the computer as on paper. Apparently, hyperactive children are prepared to spend significantly more time working on the computer without any significant loss of accuracy or speed. The children spent an average of twenty three minutes on the computer, which is an unusually long time for hyperactive children to stay on any one activity. In interviews, the children explained the preference variously, e.g. because it was less trouble to enter the results than to write them down, and they liked the rapid feedback.

Mike Lally and Iain Macleod (7) have developed computer-based handwriting exercises that enable handicapped students to be accurate, but active, learners. The procedure which they have evolved, emphasises the process used in handwriting as well as the appearance of the product, and requires the students to form letters on a flat-bed graphics display screen. A large cursor box may be used with children of lower abilty, and the children are challenged to follow the box and therefore draw a letter. Alternatively, a partial outline of the letter is given, and the children are encouraged to join the different elements together. With a variable cursor box, the size of the box can be reduced as the child's motor co-ordination improves. Speed and accuracy are displayed at the end of each exercise. The authors report that children see the reduction in the box size as a mark of their progress.

Slow learning often has both social and psychological reasons. If self-confidence can be improved, this can lead to better motivation and more progress. It is important to focus upon capacities, rather than their needs. Such students are usually considered dependent. If they can take the initiative, this improves self-image. The same problem can be seen in the gifted child. It may not be satisfactory to simply give the gifted young child the programs for an average older child. The younger child's perceptions, and both experiential and academic background information may be different. This difficulty can only be countered through flexibility of learning environment, hence the advantage of LOGO which has no limit to the potential of learning (see section 3.10). If a child is bright, wants to take home the manual and threatens to learn more than anyone else including the teacher, this should be encouraged. Indeed, the teacher should exploit the child as a resource to tutor other children. The reason for this is that such intellectual skills may arise from introversion, in which case, enforced communication with the peer group will help to develop social skills that might otherwise be lacking. However, there are dangers in this strategy, and the skill with the computer should not be allowed to achieve total dominance. The child should be directed towards other subject areas, and should not be allowed to hog the machine when others should be using it.

Work with the physically disabled is labour intensive, and there are few trained staff. The deaf represent the largest group to benefit from computers but there is, as yet, little software written with them specifically in mind. This does not prevent the deaf from taking advantage of the larger part of what has already been written. To help students with more severe physical disability, many adaptations of the hardware are possible to enable use. However, some of these modifications actually inhibit the implementation of the full range of software. The result is only partially satisfactory in that it may bring disabled students up to more normal standards, but it may deny them access to the more advanced materials. Only if standard software can be used, will the disabled be able to build up suitable opportunities for gainful employment whether at home, or in other computerised environments.

All schools could be directly vocational, and run courses to teach what employers will require in prospective employees. If local employers would liase with schools, and could agree on a useful range of abilities for school leavers, students could be equipped with skills of positive utility in the local employment environment. By comparison, Jack Sanger describes a class of students studying a Higher National Diploma course at a Further Education College. "There is that air of serious purpose one often encounters in further education which stems from the explicit relationship between classroom activity and future employment. This is a learning activity with real pay-offs. The processes and products of such sessions are seen by the students as having relevance and significance to their own lives beyond the institution." (8) However, if schools follow in this tradition, there is no guarantee that locally-specified skills will be nationally portable. The local requirements may be so particular, that every employee ends up geographically trapped without undertaking significant retraining during which, of course, there will be some loss of earnings.

It may also lead to individuals being typed at too young an age. Thus, at twelve or thirteen it may be decided that Student A is only fit for local employment, and is switched to the vocationally oriented course. On the other hand, Student B may be considered of greater potential, and given a more general course with a view to tertiary education and professional achievement. Such treatment directly penalises both the late developer, and

the shooting star who burns out too prematurely, for neither will
have the educational skills relevant to maximise post-school
opportunities.

3.5.1 Wordprocessor skills are becoming essential in the workplace, but should these skills be taught as an abstract exercise,
or as part of an English course on composition?

In the medium term, until a natural language voice recognition
capacity is built into computers, keyboard and mouse skills are
going to become essential and, therefore, the earlier these
skills are mastered the better. The act of writing is committing
ideas to a form suitable for communication to others. This involves reducing abstract musings to recognisable individual
words, which should be in a grammatical form to be comprehensible. This is a process of symbol manipulation but, with pen and
paper, there is a serious penalty for noticing a way in which a
page can be improved, because any alteration involves defacing
the page and rewriting it. Yet not making the improvement means
that the writer has to settle for second best.

For children, the physical act of writing is often laboriously
slow, and many never progress to develop, practice and improve
their content and style. By removing the chore of writing, experimentation with the language is encouraged, and the content
becomes the primary focus. However, without proper training in
keyboard skills, the "hunt and peck" approach of those unfamiliar
with layout is little quicker than manual writing. There is much
to be said for full training, so that the eyes can be kept on the
text during the writing process, but few are frustrated by the
slowness of keyboard use, either because they learn two or three
finger typing quickly, or because the neatness of the end product
compensates. Small children also have small hands, and this
inhibits training on a full size key board. It is therefore
necessary to balance the fact that individuals may develop what
are technically bad habits, against the fact that they actually
become comfortable in their use of the technology.

The wordprocessor allows the alteration of text simply by over-
typing the relevant word(s), and unaltered text need not be
retyped. .lthough the professional writer would have the motivation necessary to go through the traditional redrafting and
retyping process, this degree of commitment cannot be guaranteed
in the average student. The clear advantage is therefore that
there is no real penalty to improving the text, but the drawback
is that the ease of rewriting often leads to overwritten and
"baggy" prose styles. Consequently, good stylistic habits and
the art of self-criticism should be encouraged from the outset,
and the computer's secretarial productivity should be exploited
to help the user to make discoveries and to be creative during
the writing process. Thus, if desired, large amounts of material

can quickly be keyed in to promote fluency in composition. Indeed, whatever is written can be as elaborate or as eliptical as the mood dictates given that, once entered, the revision process can begin, and anything carelessly entered can be improved.

Alongside the luxury of automatic left and right justification, new material can be inserted, parts of the text may be moved around and files merged. Global editing facilities permit the alteration or substitution of words and phrases. All these, and other, parts of the everyday wordprocessor package encourage serendipity. For those who are more methodical, and whose first draft is closer to the final draft, speed of entry is less important, and the ability to get good quality printing may be perceived the advantage. Even in schools, the development of an academic writing style is important, and so control of pagination and page numbering are essential features, together with footnotes, bold facing, underlining, and other similar practices.

Because text windows are often restricted in the amount of text displayed, writing an outline can be important to keep an overview of the text, or else regularly taking a print is recommended so that a realistic control over the development and direction of the text can be maintained. Without a plan, writing can have a loose improvisational quality about it. This is not to deny the sense of freedom in being able to be able to explore alternate formats, but simply to require the writer to show proper discipline. Independently of style, self-discipline is also important in the underlying file control, for if the size of the file is allowed to become too big, handling may become sluggish, and the risk of hardware and software error may increase. The routine of file security, and the need to maintain proper back-up copies, should become automatic. In this, paper copies are safe, for even a badly written copy is better than none, since it captures some of the quick insights that may not return in later efforts to recreate lost files.

Some research into the use of the wordprocessor in assisting writing development has been undertaken by Pearson and Wilkinson. Albeit that the sample was relatively small, they report that the textual revisions made to earlier versions by the students ranged, as one might expect, from the trivial to the profound and, "The word processor was not found to be an essential prerequisite to such revision, but appeared in these cases to act as a facilitating device which increased the motivation to revise by making it so simple... [F]rom this sample the implications are that for children who are as it were at a point of readiness to develop further in their writing, the word processor may be a most useful writing instrument which could catalyse that progress." (9) The problem of student motivation is therefore fundamental. As an integral part of an English course, the subject matter of the typing is a vital part of the reason for using the technology. If keyboard skills are taught as an entirely abstract exercise, the students may become bored and demotivated if no immediate relevance or utility is perceived.

When the computer is being used on an instructional basis, say for example, for drill and practice in vocabulary and grammar, the learning may be directed towards simple skills and elementary knowledge, but the use of the keyboard is consolidated alongside the intake of subject material which aids the development of comprehension and visual interpretation skills. Formal word or adventure games can be used to familiarise individuals with computers generally, and keyboard skills in particular, as can both revelatory programs which communicate ideas and concepts, e.g. in simulations, and conjectural programs which encourage thought rather than mere assimilation, and where the emphasis is on the manipulation and analysis of data.

However, there is a further issue in that if a professional level of technical expertise is required, employers frequently demand a greater level of sophistication than is usually taught in schools, and Further or Higher Education is required to add a professional gloss, or in-service training is given. The major difficulty is that individual centrally-funded schools cannot afford the range of machines and software packages that would be required to, say, train students on all the major database packages, or in even some aspects of hardware maintenance. A general computer literacy is probably of more use. Given the difficulties, perhaps the school courses ought merely to prepare students for Further or Higher Education courses by covering specific topics to a suitable level, and introducing the students to the study skills which will be required in tertiary education. Such a strategy might assist the British education system to encourage more students to stay on in the colleges and universities to achieve better educational standards.

In comparison with other developed Western countries, an embarrassingly small percentage of British students actually avail themselves of educational opportunities beyond the compulsory school leaving age. In Japan and the United States, for example, staying on approaches 90%, while in France it will soon be 70%. In Britain, even if account is taken of those in the Youth Training Scheme, it is only just over half. In France, as the French Government carries out its pledge to aim at 80% in full time education until the age of 19, twice as many young people will be qualified in engineering as in Britain, and in office technology the figure is ten times as many. Against this level of competition, the apathy of the young in Britain is encouraged though the lack of true opportunities for improvement. Britain only has schemes like the YTS. But while the new two year YTS is a vast improvement on the old because it should lead to at least some vocational qualification, the British government should adopt urgent measures to upgrade education for the 16-19 age group. The hope is that the TVEI (Technical and Vocational Educational Initiative) will increase motivation through its technological approach but without proper grounding in the schools, little work of real substance will be achieved.

In fact, in some subject areas, there is such a lack of co-ordination between the syllabus requirements of different examination boards, that further and higher courses take little for granted, and cover the basics in introductory lectures. To some extent, this situation will be mitigated by the proposed national curriculum in the core subjects. However, this presupposes that all higher level courses require the same basic information, and that all the schools will not teach down to the pass mark. It is easy to produce a coherent course which will develop knowledge and skills to be exploited in particular trades or professions. It is more difficult to agree upon general core skills which will offer the best support to study in the sometimes eccentric world of post-compulsory school age education.

3.6 What programming languages, if any, should be taught?

In a sense, all programming languages are the same because most languages can be used to solve the same problems. In fact, the variety of languages goes to underline the point that hardware is absolutely dependent upon the software created by humans, but that there are many different ways in which to solve similar problems. The differences between languages lie in the fact that some problems are easier to solve in one language than another, because the language designer had particular tasks in mind when making design decisions. However, the most important criteria for language selection are that the one or more languages chosen should be easy to learn and, from the teacher's point of view, they should be easy to teach. Similarly, they should provide a good learning environment where data manipulation and problem-solving skills can be learned, and they should be of some value to the student after leaving school – this might suggest teaching the commercial languages like COBOL rather than BASIC.

Whatever decisions are ultimately taken, it is more than a simple truism that any language, package or system must be learned by the user before it can be mastered, but the greater the degree of learner control which is included in the system, and the more autonomy which results, the greater the learning cost to the user. Achieving a workable balance between the learning cost and user control is a key issue when deciding which languages and packages to give to students, particularly given the amount of time available to the students. The common high level languages give significant long-term control to the user, but the necessary investment of time can only really be justified if a substantial later amount of programming work is envisaged.

3.7 Are there advantages to teaching BASIC?
- (Beginners' All-purpose Symbolic Instruction Code)?

BASIC was aimed at liberal arts students in America who disliked the detail of programming in FORTRAN or ALGOL, but who wanted to be able to write programs. The most important aspect of BASIC was that it worked in an interactive environment. In the early days of programming, the only computers were very large, and many computer professionals objected to the idea of timesharing because it appeared to use an expensive and valuable resource inefficiently. In a historical context, the development of BASIC may therefore be seen as quite a brave step.

It is now a common language, having many variations, some of which represent a more advanced form. However, regardless as to the level, all the dialects are aimed at fulfilling the original design expectation that the commands should be easily learned. This latter is achieved because the system depends upon the use of everyday words, e.g. save, run and print, as commands, and it simplifies the handling of strings and formatting. From the teaching point of view, it may be considered highly suitable not only because it is apparently easy to learn, but also because there are many programs already written in BASIC, and a library of books is now available at a wide range of ability levels. Moreover, because it happened to be an easy language to provide on micros, the myth has grown up that programming is BASIC, and many students are predisposed to believe that the acquisition of the language is desirable and necessary. But the opportunities to enhance knowledge are often lost because BASIC is frequently taught with an emphasis on syntax rather than on computer-based problem-solving as an independent skill.

Albeit in a flowery way, Christensen states the problem, "God created the computer to make life easier and more diverting to man. Shortly after, the Devil invented BASIC to confuse man's mind and make it harder for him to use computers." (10) The language appears to have the advantages of convenience and simplicity, but because it is easy to change the program, it encourages bad programming habits. Instead of good design from the outset, many attempt to create programs on a trial and error basis. This can easily lead to programs which contain hidden bugs. These do not show up under normal circumstances, but can suddenly appear and paralyse the system. Further, it was intended as a beginners' language and so, while it is effective for easy problems, it can be excessively complicated to produce solutions to more demanding problems, with programs being a mass of GOTO statements and subroutines. The original intention was that these more difficult problems would be solved using FORTRAN, but BASIC has been forced into the role by the computer manufacturers' discovery that BASIC is easy for the machines to execute.

If BASIC must be taught, the best strategy is probably to teach it in tandem with one of the list programming languages to demonstrate the weaknesses and strengths of both. Hence in BASIC, the programmer must rely upon the array, whereas a list is not necessarily fixed in size, and it does not have to contain information of only one kind. Conversely, hierarchies of lists can be used to set up complex data structures, but it is not possible to directly access specified elements in the list, so list manipulation can be slower than the use of an array. This form of comparative teaching should lead to a more rounded appreciation of programming and machine capacity.

If only BASIC is to be taught, one approach is to have a file of BASIC programs for students to debug. This strategy may be described as the concept of deliberate imperfection. The student is given material known to be incomplete or non-functional, and is invited to repair or remedy the defects. Research among experienced programmers tends to suggest that this process of error identification (debugging), depends upon the adoption of various tactics, based upon existing knowledge and experience in debugging generally, to find clues to explain the non-performance. The detection of a clue, "leads to the generation of a hypothesis about the bug, which in turn leads to the adoption of a (probably) new debugging tactic... If nothing suspicious is found as a result of using a particular tactic, this lack of a particular clue may provide a subject with some useful information that may lead to the generation of a new hypothesis." (11)

For these purposes, a hypothesis is a concatenation of those more general thoughts which have been gradually formulated into testable terms. Some errors can be detected at a grammatical or syntactical level without any need to understand in detail what the program does. Others require an understanding of the substance of the program, because the basis of the correction is to enter what the correct program should be. This approach will also prove to both teachers and students that BASIC programs are difficult to read. It will assist the appreciation that other languages which, for example, name subroutines and processes, are more effective because, assuming that relevant names have been given, it will be clear what the program is doing at each point, rather than having to chase line numbers. (12) As a matter of programming style, it must be admitted that consistently using REM statements does help potential debuggers to understand the function of each group of lines. But even this act of professional thoughtfulness lacks the clarity of structured programming, where the conceptual gap between the written, and therefore static, program and the dynamic process is only nominal.

However BASIC is taught, there remains a fundamental problem with structural languages like BASIC and FORTRAN in that they require the programmer to think in closed loops, and the facilities to alternate and iterate are minimal. Further, the ability to create subroutines is limited, and this inhibits modular design. Conversely, list programming languages require the programmer to think in the repeated application of the same procedure, and have a more natural and logical feel to programming. The ease with which any language can be learned is a function of the ease with which the learner can see how the language works. The learner needs elegance and simplicity. BASIC hides behind comparative complexity. It also generates frustration through the unforgiving rejection of typing or syntactical errors, and users can become quickly frustrated and discouraged.

3.7.1 What other languages should be considered, and what should they be used to teach?

Of the many languages, mention is made of two. PASCAL was derived from ALGOL, and was designed to be easy to use. It requires data to be explicitly declared – a useful discipline which makes debugging easier because it forces the programmer to clarify intent from the outset. The system depends upon alternation and iteration, i.e. if – then – else for a simple fork, or case – of – otherwise for multibranch, while repeat – until, while – do, and for – do provide variations on the theme of repetition.

PROLOG (PROgramming in LOGic) is a descriptive and not an imperative language, i.e. rather than using commands, the programmer describes what is required. This removes any distinction between database and program. It has a powerful list processing capacity, but minimal alternation and iteration, the latter being implemented as recursion. All academic subjects can exploit the data structuring capacity of the language, with programming being learned incidentally. However, the logic which the language provides is not all–embracing. It may be good for many uses, but is not best for everything.

To the computer, everything is in binary code. The term 'data' refers to the symbols which an individual uses to represent ideas or facts. Similarly, 'information' is simply the meaning which the reader attaches to data; it is a pattern that has meaning and, as such, it is distinct from the medium within which it is stored. It is therefore irrelevant whether the code represents numbers or letters. Although their design depends upon logic gates and the trappings of scientific rationalism, the computer need not simply be a number cruncher. All data can be processed and transformed into new configurations. There is no reason why it cannot analyse literature in an attempt to measure or define style, help to make guesses about the shades of meaning in ancient languages or assist in the evaluation of historical or archaeological evidence. "[The computer] inevitably works in partnership with the curriculum that it has been designed to explore and serve." (13) There is little difficulty is placing specific subject domain software within its appropriate curricul-

um. The real problem is to identify a role for the generic software. Data collection and interrogation packages, or general
framework software are not of great utility unless a sensible
educational use is found for them.

Hence, in Micro-PROLOG and classroom historical research, Richard
Ennals describes list manipulation and retrieval skills being
developed by a group of twelve year olds in their study of history. (14) This form of use stands alongside the subject-specific
packages like Choice, Campaign and Shallow Hill (Archeo), where
subject materials are directly addressed by the software. Other
subjects which have gone through the process of quantification,
have been geography and economics which, by virtue of adding
statistical and numerical techniques, have emerged into the computer purview. Thus, programs like DEMOG2 allow the user to make
population projections using data provided or new data, and Agcom
deals with Agricultural Commodity Price Stabilisation, leaving
the teacher free to develop in-house uses for generic packages,
e.g. local history studies based on data gathered from grave
stones can be manipulated in programs like Cardbox, or biological
studies of the local ponds analysed in programs like DBase or
Lotus.

Until recently, the use of computers for the teaching of art and
design has largely been limited to inexpensive software which
could illustrate the possibilities for graphics. Now computer-
based painting and design software which is built around the use
of the mouse and icons, has been dramatically enhanced, and made
available on the cheaper micros. This overcomes many of the
disadvantages of keyboard entry, and creates a physical activity
which is similar to that of drawing or painting. Because the
technology is easy to use, creativity is encouraged. The computer
is capable of great representational accuracy through a zoom
facility which allows adjustments of colour and design at a pixel
level. The residual problems are that suitable printers and
plotters remain expensive, and the software control of the peripherals remains poor. Whether schools and colleges develop in
this field depends upon the perception of relevance of the techniques to art and design education. (15)

3.8 What is LOGO?

LOGO is a derivative of LISP (a LISt Processing language developed to promote research into Artificial Intelligence) which emphasises the graphics capacity of most modern micros and PCs. It
was created by Seymour Papert and others at the AI labs at MIT
specifically for children, in some projects the children being as
young as 3 years old (e.g. at the Lamplighter School in Dallas,

Texas). LOGO may claim a degree of uniqueness in that it is the only computer approach which has been deliberately developed from a specific theory of learning, viz. Piaget's model of children as builders of their own intellectual structures, and it is "design-ed to enable children to use computers in a masterful way, as tools for actively exploring, planning and programming projects that interest them." (16) Unlike BASIC, Pascal and APL which were developed as introductory mechanisms either to programming or mathematics, LOGO is not intended as an easy introduction to anything else. "Instead, it's a door into the territory of the computer as an object for intellectual exploration." (17) To that extent, it is suitable for introducing concepts and ideas to people of all ages, including the general theory of relativity to undergraduates. (18)

Piaget asserts that the mind naturally acquires knowledge, and argues that children learn best in an activity-oriented environ-ment. The child must be challenged with problems, have the oppor-tunity to question, to test and experiment. The child is there-fore encouraged to develop strategies, and to test out their effectiveness. If such an approach is applied through the quick-ness of the computer's responses, the child should more rapidly become aware of his or her own thinking processes and begin to evaluate ideas. As the child draws on reserves of skills and knowledge to solve the problems posed, not only are feelings of self-confidence and autonomy encouraged, but intelligence is developed. In turn, this provides motivation to develop further skills because education is perceived as being more relevant and useful. In such an environment, a mistake is not, and should not be perceived as, a catastrophic blow to self-esteem, it is a natural part of the learning process. Because better continuity of activity is maintained, learning skills are refined over a period of time and are improved with experience, subject to the availability of both the software and teachers who understand, and can support, the educational task engaged in.

The most famous application is turtle geometry. The main problem in subject areas like solid geometry, is that students find it hard to visualise shapes, planes and surfaces. Some children who are exposed to Meccano and other three dimensional construction toys, develop an ability to mentally manipulate space. Without the experience and stimulation of manipulating solids in three dimensions, many people never develop any real spatial awareness. However, a substitute for practical experiment is offered through the graphics' capacity of the computer which allows the user to manipulate a representation of reality.

LOGO graphics are not described in absolute positions in a (Cart-esian) co-ordinate system, but relative to the position and direction of the turtle, a conceptual animal that moves around the screen. An environment is therefore created in which space and geometry can be intuitively explored. Just moving the turtle at random (called turtle humming) might create a recognisable shape or a meaningless doodle, but it leads to an understanding of the effect of the commands, and the ability to plan and direct movement. This may be seen in the three line procedure POLYSPI (polyspiral) which creates designs based upon the three variables, distance, angle and change in distance, allowing the user to create beautiful pictures. This might be purely an artistic endeavour, or it might be used to introduce the user to the idea of variable separation, the difference in relative potency of the variables, and the stepping of variables. Thus, by holding two variables constant and adjusting the third variable incrementally, the user observes a model of how things are generated through their intersecting dimensions of variation.

The ultimate aim is to produce a learning environment where thinking is fun. The problem in seeking to promote learning through the use of other languages is that the sort of problems which are usually given to beginners are not inherently very interesting to solve, or if they are interesting, they are not very easy. Thus traditional arithmetical or algebraic problems are offered and deter the non-mathematically oriented. LOGO avoids this difficulty, and enhances the fun aspect of learning through, say, the ability to abandon the turtle and to create multiple conceptual animals called sprites, which can be given shapes and moved around the screen either synchronously or asynchronously with commands similar to those used to control the turtle. The result is the opportunity to create scenarios that have many moving objects with different shapes and colours, and a static, but vivid, background. LOGO is therefore like Meccano (19), i.e. it comes in a form of kit and the user starts by making simple assemblies out of a few simple procedures, and gradually builds up to complex assemblies for the solution of problems.

These environments are termed microworlds and may be considered a subset of reality where powerful abstract ideas may be encountered and explored. "A well-designed computer microworld embodies the simplest model that an expert can imagine as an acceptable entry point to richer knowledge." (20) A microworld can be an environment where users become familiar with concepts and ideas, and where phenomena can be observed and interactions may take place. If the phenomena are sufficiently interesting, and the interactive capabilities sufficiently stimulating, the users will be motivated to experiment and therefore to learn in a natural fashion as approved by Piaget.

Papert advocates that microworlds should always be constructed around powerful ideas, i.e. ones which it is worth the teacher spending time on creating, and worth the students' time to explore. The criteria for determining whether the idea is sufficiently powerful are that it should be: simple, general, useful and syntonic. The feature of simplicity aids understanding and the generality of its application guarantees utility. Papert uses syntonic to mean any idea which relates and unifies already acquired knowledge gained in diverse experiences. This linking of information and concepts creates more powerful understanding, and the ability to reduce ideas to a concrete model that can be used as a metaphor for problem-solving, gives a greater generality to analytic skills.

The language itself does not instruct. It is attractive because each of the commands produces an immediate visual response and, it does what the users tell it to do and does not comment. Thus, the procedure to create a yellow ball on the screen can be called SUN. The procedures which are to change the y coordinate of the sun can be descriptively accurate as UP and DOWN. This freedom to create new keywords means that the vocabulary of the resultant system will only contain words with which the student is familiar. Moreover, because writing is an essential part of controlling the computer microworlds, small children may be strongly motivated to learn a considerable vocabulary if each sprite and procedure is given a natural language name. The system can also be more strongly tailored to the student's own interests, and the level of complexity will be more under the user's control. LOGO has also been linked to the use of robotic turtles. Getting the movements right in the physical world not only helps a student bridge the gap between the theory of a program and the actual spatial movement of the robot, but also helps to lead a student into solving problems symbolically.

It is therefore for the user to attach values to what has actually been achieved, and the user is more able to enjoy and learn from mistakes. The user is simply allowed to see the results of each experiment and, since the results of experiments can be stored, the user can build up a library of successful experiments, and also gain prestige by swopping program elements among the peer group. Further, by watching how a program tackles a problem, the learner can often gain insights into the thinking processes involved in the actual writing of that program. The student also learns to investigate a phenomenon by making a model of it. In general, LOGO is perceived as less threatening than other languages because it does not depend on an overtly mathematical approach, but nevertheless has the flexibility to be used to allow children to explore concepts in maths and physics, to write, to create art and to play music. In this latter function, LOGO music uses a synthesizer board for sound generation, but otherwise relies upon the same intuitive system's approach for creating music as, say, learning physics. Thus, the users must generate the notion of meter. The structure of the scales is not simply taken for granted, but rather can be constructed as a procedure that chooses from the complete pitch collection as a special case. Procedural design is therefore a model for musical thinking, allowing the students to learn about sequence, intervalic relations, texture, harmony and so on, through a process of constructive experimentation. (21)

3.8.1 How does LOGO compare with the other languages?

LOGO structuring is more flexible than in BASIC. It consists in separate procedures which are written for each part of the problem on an interactive basis. Although a similar effect can be created in BASIC by using GOSUB, the resultant subroutine is not an independent program. This distinction is further reflected in the fact that a LOGO interpreter does not create a permanent machine language version of the program. Each statement is compiled each time it is to run. The programming style permits recursion, i.e. modern procedural languages allow one procedure to use another procedure as a subprocedure to do a part of its work – recursion is where one procedure can be a subprocedure of itself, and differs from mere iteration which simply calls for a repetition of the same procedure.

LOGO also permits list processing. The mechanism to deal with groups of variables in BASIC and FORTRAN is the array. An array has a fixed size, while lists can grow or contract as the program requires, and it can only handle variables of the same size and type. This is efficient because if the computer knows the address of the start of the array, it is easy to calculate the position of the nth item. A list in LOGO can be a number, a word or another list. Because the size of each element is variable, lists are stored in a more complex system and are slower to process. Generally, it is not necessary to type variables as either numeric or non-numeric, for variables are treated as particular to given procedures. In BASIC extra statements would be necessary to assign values to the variables, whereas LOGO simply specifies inputs to procedures. Compilers are more easily designed to run with typed languages, but interpreters work as easily with typed and untyped variables.

Finally, LOGO is an extensible language in that the user can define new procedures and, thus, expand the capabilities of the original system in a permanent and personalised way. This can lead to the creation of a toolkit. Given the modular nature of the language, programs can then be constructed systematically using a hierarchy of the procedures. Because each of the procedures has a relevant name, the program is self-documenting and easier to understand than a conventional high level language program.

For these purposes, a procedure may be defined as a set of behaviours or activities which direct the search for the solution. The product is the actual solution. Both are essential parts of the problem-solving experience. If one has a goal but is not immediate familar with the means, thinking is necessary. The quality of persistence is also necessary. Not only is planning and experimentation a part of the process, but also a retrospective evaluation of what has been done to consolidate the learning experience. The programmer makes a plan – which may be a flowchart – and seeks to understand the problem. A partial or incorrect solution is a program that does not run at all, or only runs in part. Debugging is useful because the programmer must find and interpret clues to the cause of the malfunction – all part of the problem–solving process. Many of the procedures contained in a problem–solving toolkit may be treated as "black boxes" by the users and not amended (i.e. many modern pieces of equipment come in black boxes, but it is not necessary to know or understand what goes on inside each box to be able to get the desired results). Others may be treated as grey boxes, and can be modified as the users require.

Peter Goodyear suggests that this flexibility is of great educational significance because it allows students to tune the system to their own investigative learning strategies. That a group will have a diversity of cognitive style and of computing skills can be a difficulty in a rigid curriculum. "In the more flexible LOGO modelling environment, however, our initial observations suggest that this diversity is less a problem than a positive advantage – allowing us to capitalise on the variety of learner confidence and expertise through a considerable degree of peer–teaching." (22)

Unlike Pascal and FORTRAN, LOGO is interactive in that any command which is communicated to the computer will be executed immediately. It is therefore quick and easy to create and test a program, making any changes that are necessary on a trial and error basis. In commercial terms, program development is often more efficient using an interactive language, but programs run more efficiently when written in a non–interactive language because the machine–readable version is permanently stored. LOGO is therefore a slower language because the program must be interpretted for each run. However, most students have no real interest in the speed of the end–product program. If a class exercise has been set to solve a particular programming problem, the interest lies in the solution of that problem, and not in the degree of efficiency achieved in running the program when it is completed. For this purpose, interactive languages can be preferable. But, if the students are being trained for real–world tasks where the speed of operation in the completed program might be significant, then programming in the non–interactive languages would be essential.

3.9   Conclusions

That programming is not a simple art can be evidenced by the number of home computers, bought in a flush of enthusiasm, which now lie unused because the reality of programming from scratch is too difficult for the average person without proper support and encouragement. It is therefore better for the teacher to plan courses on the basis of flexibility, and to try to select elements that could be incorporated into the computer environment, rather than trying to decide which programming language, with all the limitations that might bring, the students should be taught. If it is decided, on the best educational grounds, that actual programming languages and skills should be taught, whatever language(s) or system(s) are selected, there should always be a good editor and the relevant syntax should be flexible. Students will also need good memory provision, and comprehensive search and retrieve commands are useful.

However, independently of the issue of specific high level language tuition, an introduction to the techniques of list manipulation is probably desirable, and experience of using the more advanced routines such as the pattern-matching utilities, ought to be considered. Given the need for a literacy course to have a broad base, it will also be advisable to mention the concept of expert systems, and so a suitably simple example should probably be available for student experimentation. The provision of computer resources with good graphics is vital if LOGO is to be used, but it should also be remembered that the best use of LOGO depends upon the system being used to teach powerful ideas. Thus, either the teachers must have powerful ideas to communicate to their students, or the teachers must understand and care about the pre-programmed powerful ideas. Any failure in this area is likely to result in unsatisfactory learning. Finally, to help beginners, a library of general procedures should be compiled, which the students can play with and, for those who want to learn a language, intelligent programming aids like APES should be made available, remembering that beginners need sophisticated not simple systems.

In the last analysis, it should be recognised that if students are taught only one language like BASIC, this can cause them to become used to a language which is unsuited to the demands of advanced modern computing. The exclusive use of BASIC also teaches good students bad programming habits, and can turn the weak or average students against computing. Moreover, no matter what its advantages, LOGO on its own will not be enough. LOGO will not replace the commercial programming languages because it does not attempt to solve the problems of industry and commerce. Properly used, however, it is an excellent language for stimulating thought and, in the classrooms of tomorrow, that is a most desirable result.

References

(1) Computer Assisted Learning in Geography. I.D.H.Shepherd, Z.A.Cooper, D.R.F.Walker. CET, London. 1980. p.116.

(2) Adult Computer Literacy: Analysis and Content. Stephen Bostock and Roger Seifert. collected in Microcompueters in Adult Education. pp.1/17 at pp.4/5.

(3) UNIX and the naive user: children meet a grown-up operating system. Marcus Gray. collected in New Horizons in Educational Computing. pp.272/81 at p.273.

(4) Computers: Promise and Challenge in Education. p.160.

(5) R v Schifreen and Gold, discussed (1986-87) 1 CLSR 146.

(6) Microcomputers and Hyperactive Children. Glen Kleiman, Mary Humphrey & Peter H.Lindsay. (1981) March. Creative Computing 93/94.

(7) Development of skills through computers: achieving an effective, enjoyable learning environment. Mike Lally and Iain Macloed. (1982) 32 Impact of Science on Society 449/60.

(8) Programming Learners or 'Algorithm, who could ask for anything more?' Jack Sanger. (1986) Vol 28 No 1 Educational Research 56/65 at p.56.

(9) The Use of the Word Processor in Assisting Children's Writing Development. Howard Pearson & Andrew Wilkinson. (1986) Vol 38, No 2 Educational Review 169/87 at p.187.

(10) COMAL - an educational alternative. Borge Christensen. collected in Microcomputers in Education. pp.75/81 at p.75.

(11) How People Debug Computer Programs. John D. Gould. (1975) 7(2) International Journal of Man-Machine Studies 151/82 at p.165.

(12) Each line of a BASIC program must be given a number, and in moving from one part of a program to another, the GOTO command relies upon giving the appropriate line number rather than giving the name of the particular process to be performed. At the discretion of the programmer, descriptions of the function of each batch of lines can be included as REM statements.

(13) Developing CAL: Computers in the Curriculum. p.34.

(14) Micro-PROLOG and Classroom Historical Research. Richard Ennals. collected in Teachers, Computers and the Classroom. pp.130/7.

(15) For more detail see Microcomputer Graphics in Art and Design Education. John Gardner and Robert Paisley. collected in Trends in Computer Assisted Education. pp.77/87.

(16) Computers: Promise and Challenge in Education. p.64.

(17) Why LOGO? Brian Harvey. (1982) 7(8) Byte 163/93 at p.188.

(18) Turtle Geometry: The Computer as a Medium for Exploring Mathematics. Harold Abelson and Andrea diSessa. MIT Press, Cambridge, MA. 1981.

(19) Model Building, Mathematics and LOGO. J.A.M.Howe, P.M.Rose, K.R.Johnson, R.Inglis. collected in New Horizons in Educational Computing. pp.54/71 at pp.55/6.

(20) Designing Computer-Based Microworlds. R.Lawler (1982) 7(8) Byte 138/60 at p.140.

(21) LOGO Music. Jeanne Bamberger. (1982) 7(8) Byte 325/8.

(22) A Toolkit Approach to Computer-Aided Systems Modelling. Peter Goodyear. collected in Trends in Computer Assisted Education. pp.88/96 at p.94.

CHAPTER 4

THE ADVANTAGES AND DISADVANTAGES OF CAL

This chapter examines the second theme of the book in looking at the possible uses of a computer as an aid to learning. It is inevitable that different schools of thought have emerged as to the effectiveness or otherwise of the computer in this role, and this chapter lists and comments upon the main arguments for and against the use of CAL

4.1   Introduction

Whatever formal education theories one chooses to formulate or espouse, certain basic skills need to be imparted to the student. Firstly, the student must have "knowledge", i.e. be able to name things, recognise a phenomenon, and so on. Secondly, the student must have comprehension, i.e. be able to demonstrate understanding by selecting an example of a known thing or by classifying phenomena, etc. Thirdly, the student must be able to apply abstract rules to real situations. Fourthly, the student should develop powers of analysis, i.e. be able to compare and contrast alternatives, justify the adoption of one such alternative as opposed to the other, break a problem down into its component elements, etc. Finally, the student should be capable of evaluation, i.e. should have the competence and the confidence to judge the value of knowledge, argue for and against a proposal, defend a proposition, and demonstrate the normal characteristics of rationality in decision-making.

The problem for those who are responsible for managing the education system, is to determine how these skills are to be transmitted to students at a time when they are faced by significantly reduced budgets at the primary and secondary level, and by, "diminishing resources available for higher education, and the need to use those resources with maximum effectiveness across the whole of the higher education system". (1) A standard response to these pressures and performance criteria, which are based upon arithmetical and not academic grounds, is to teach larger groups. But although it is true that the large class is an inexpensive form of teaching in economic terms, overt student behaviour is generally limited to the taking of notes and, since there is very little feedback as to the quality of those notes, incomplete learning may result. Thus, for example, the note-taker may ignore or misconstrue points which the teacher intended as main points, or may mistake minor for main points. Such gaps or errors simply multiply the chances of misunderstanding later lectures. (2) If these problems are recognised and the system permits it, a form of salvage operation can be mounted in the parallel tutorial or seminar program, or the difficulties reduced by dictating notes or, if resources permit, distributing handouts, but these are often only stop-gap measures and may not provide effective remediation to those in error.

Hence, the wholesale dictation of notes is educationally stultifying, although it does guarantee a consistency of notes in the hands of the student. Indeed, research has shown that students prefer a "good product" in the form of notes for aiding recall and in revision for examinations (3). Handouts should be considered more useful because time is thereby released for the discussion of the material and its implications, but remain educationally controversial. In as much as it is relevant for these purposes, the view expressed by the National Union of Students is preferred, namely that, "The opportunity to grasp basic ideas is hindered by the necessity to take notes." (4) and therefore educationalists should look for delivery systems which will provide a good product, yet leave time as free as possible for constructive learning.

In a tutorial or seminar, the ideal would be individual tuition. The student/tutor relationship is Socratic and one of direct interaction. Hence, the student's performance depends upon what the tutor communicates, but what the tutor communicates depends upon what the student does. In a one-to-one teaching situation, fine adjustments can be made. However, more usually, the tutor will be confronted by a group of students. Here much of each student's time is spent in observing others in action, but such vicarious experience has serious limitations. It is not as positive and memorable as an interactive experience. The student may simply spend time dreaming of better days or, having heard another answer a question, mistakenly believe that he or she could have produced the same answer, or that such information is now memorised, to be recalled upon demand. In fact, depending upon group size, very little personal attention can actually be given to the individual learner and, the larger the group, the more depersonalised the teaching becomes. CAL may be one of the ways in which this tendency can be counteracted, and it is now necessary to consider whether its use could make teaching more personalised and therefore more effective.

4.2　A definition of CAL

By way of introduction, three interconnected propositions should be made about CAL.

4.2.1　Computer-aided learning techniques are an inherently flexible way in which to present any material for student consumption

Many different types of CAL packages and suites have been designed as delivery systems for the presentation of information. Thus, one can exploit the data storage facility of computers as repositories of information in the same way as a book, a series of handouts, or a conventional lecture course. The extent of the information stored will vary with the size of machine, but full-text and abstract retrieval systems can give direct access to textual materials not necessarily available in the school or college library, or maximise the effective use of existing library resources. Further, with the ability to link into other delivery vehicles such as interactive video systems, models and examples totally outside the possible range of the ordinary classroom or laboratory can be cheaply and conveniently given to the student. Thus, some demonstrations might be too expensive or dangerous to perform live, but on video, backed up with computer-generated graphics, cut-away diagrams, and explanatory materials with comprehension exercises, a complete topic can be packaged for student consumption.

and

4.2.2　Computer-aided learning techniques are an important way of testing a student's understanding of any given topic

Equally, computers can be exploited as test mechanisms. This may be done in one of two ways. Firstly, the teacher can devise batches of objective questions or other similar educationally

87

acceptable tests, and leave the student to work through them. Alternatively, the teacher can require the students to program a topic or to enter data into an expert system shell. If a properly functioning branching program is to be created, or a compiled version of a knowledge database is to come into being, the student must be able to analyse the given subject-matter into a logically sequenced series of propositions or rules. There are few better tests as to the accuracy of any individual's understanding of any topic. More importantly, this type of use corresponds closely to the student's later possible professional use of the computer, where either support or expert systems will be exploited. For these purposes, the student does not key in the material in order to learn how to program. Indeed, given a user friendly front-end, there is no necessity for the user to know anything of the internal workings of the software. The computer is simply being used as an intellectual tool which can augment the student's capacity to understand.

but

4.2.3 To optimise results, the CAL systems should be as "expert" as possible

In teaching terms, the strength of any computer-based teaching system is that the program can be given criteria against which it can evaluate the learner's responses: it can judge whether remedial action is necessary, and it can keep the overall performance of the students, and of its own materials, under review. Thus, if it is decided that a student's performance is poor, a detailed reading list can be given, or alternative question and answer sequences can be tried in order to lead the user through the concept by a different route. If this latter sequence proves equally incomprehensible to the user, the remedial reading can then be given, or a human tutor called.

Intelligent CAL packages on an interactive mainframe or networked system can also supply detailed statistical information to teachers. It is possible to acquire this information from stand-alone systems, but it is administratively less convenient and relies upon the teacher either visiting each separate machine, or working through the floppy discs used by the students, to extract each individual's progress report. At a macro level, it is always useful to know which sections of any given learning package are being used at any given time during the course of studies. It is also possible to identify which students are procrastinating and need encouragement, and which students are finding the course difficult and require extra help. At a nuts-and-bolt level, the answers to each question or group of questions can be monitored, and can show that students are having difficulty with particular concepts. Such concepts can be made the subject of more intensive study in the face-to-face tutorials. Equally, topics obviously understood in computer-based study can be glossed over, thus making the use of "expensive" live tutorial time educationally precise and more cost-effective.

If sections of the CAL suite are shown to be causing the students difficulty, the offending passages of text or sequences of questions can be rewritten. The monitoring capacity of the computer will then continue the evaluation of the teaching materials, now including the new passages, as the students use the system. It is therefore possible for the programmer/teacher to develop and improve the package using "real" criteria rather than the combination of instinct and experience which is all that teachers normally have to guide them in the preparation of teaching materials. Moreover, revision classes can pinpoint areas known to be found most troublesome, and new material can be incorporated into subsequent year's teaching schedules in an attempt to pre-empt the future generation of students' difficulties. In short, the computer's responsiveness and analytical abilities can substantially assist the teacher to become a more professional and effective communicator.

4.3 What are the different types of CAL program?

At the most general level, CAL programs may adopt one of two basic forms. First, CAL can be linear where the student is taken along a single path from one topic or skill to the next. The path is the most economical conceptual route which can be devised to take the learner through the material. It may wander about like a small stream through the landscape, but it offers no branching, i.e. no element of choice is allowed to the learner as to the route to be followed. Hopefully, it will always contain illuminating examples and analogies, but it is always orderly. That a topic is complex is considered no deterrent to breaking it down into a linear sequence which, it is hoped, will succeed by demonstrating the difficulites and showing solutions in the best order. This is academic linear programming, and is based upon the Skinner proposition of conditioning through reinforcement, the material being so arranged as to maximise the chance of the correct response, or to approve close approximations to the ideal response. There is no real individualisation, save that each student can work through the material at his or her own speed, and the underlying educational assumption for this form of program is that students learn by being told.

Before the advent of the computer, programmed learning texts were limited by size, the constant page turning was inconvenient, the student could cheat by looking up the right answer, and such books were not very enjoyable to read. The computerisation of linear texts can overcome all but the last difficulty, and even

89

that can be mitigated by good layout and design. But the only real design considerations are mechanical, i.e. what should the screen display look like, and should the students be allowed one try or two before giving the reinforcement? Morever, given that the normal expectation is that the right answer will be given, most programs are designed on the basis that reinforcement will only be given when the right answer is produced.

Alternatively, CAL programs may be branching, i.e. allow for a variety of possible user inputs at each point. This does not accord with Skinner theory because the optimum path through the material has not been devised, nor need it be followed. However, the point is that the computer can be made sensitive to the answers given by the learner, and will then seek to set the level of explanation to suit need. This is real individualisation. It is true that the good student can feel cheated because there are so many pathways which cannot be explored unless answers known to be wrong are inserted, but this is a small price to pay for the variety of educational opportunity which the system can offer. Perhaps an economic argument would have more substance. If a good student purchased a CAL software package, and found that a signi-ficant part of the cost of that large program was a long sequence of remedial sections, the program would not represent good value for money to that student.

In design terms, there are also problems because, although good students can make bigger conceptual leaps through the material, it is difficult to provide for students of different "leaping" abilities. The programs must therefore offer feedback which can quickly correct any misunderstandings which are detected. The branching options allowed by the programs may be forwards, back-wards or sideways. Thus, the student may go to a more advanced example or a new topic, may be referred back for revision pur-poses, or the student is exposed to information which most stud-ents skip. The decision as to where to go next may be by student choice, e.g. menu-driven, or by criteria built into the teaching package which refer to the immediate answer or to a pattern of past answers.

Both linear and branching programs, whether created from scratch or, say, through the use of authoring languages, share the same philosophy. They both rely upon the systematic presentation of information and, in many systems, there is an implicit assumption that this takes precedence over any other learner activity. Further, both types of system are likely to have as one of their basic concerns the efficiency of presentation rather than the quality of learning, seeing learning as the acquisition of know-ledge rather than experience, i.e. they are both aspects of pro-grammed learning. This is understandable given the present state of the technology, for the machines cannot really make decisions about the students. Thus, until the development of a natural language interface, the content of each section of information is preset, giving only marginal control to the level of difficulty in the presentation of that information, and the switching capacity at each decision point or node in the standard authoring systems, tends to be limited without major programming surgery.

4.4　What are the main features of CAL systems?

4.4.1　Information is presented to the individual student user in a structured form

This most conventionally quoted of the CAL features is simply making a virtue of a necessity. It arises from the simple fact that scrolling text (i.e. text which is serially displayed) on a visual display unit (VDU) is educationally unsound for a variety of reasons (see later), and so information is presented to users in screen-sized windows or frames. Alternatively, if the system is print-based, it may be wasteful in terms of time and materials to print out the same long batches of material for every cohort of students, when a small number of books on short loan in a library could serve the same purpose. However, some proponents of CAL gloss over this limitation by implying that the computer is therefore effective in the communication of a technique, since most techniques are capable of being broken down into small intermediate steps.

It is also said to be useful in the study of a subject where there is a hierarchy of facts and/or rules, adopting Gagne's hypothesis that even complex learning is capable of being achieved through the assimilation of groups of interdependent rules and strategies. In such subjects, mastery of each step is a precondition to being allowed to proceed to the next step, and fits into the standard CAL pattern of presenting information in discrete lumps. Other subjects which are supposedly suitable for computerisation are those described as authoritative, i.e. they deal with absolutes where the learner is either right or wrong. An example of this would be a simple arithmetic exercise but, in making design decisions about the CAL style for the presentation of such a subject, the fact that the subject is authoritative does not mean that it has to be taught authoritatively. ⌜One of the advantages of the computer is its inherent flexibility of presentation style, and to neglect to exploit the many possible variations of both visual and aural stimuli is to waste the resource. Finally, there is the ⓥrevision function, where information is often presented in a schematic form to assist recall, and to provide a framework about which to assemble the complete understanding. This use is claimed to be particularly suited to exploit this feature.

Of course, there is no obligation to adopt the conceit of feeding information to students in small bites, given the power of the new full-text retrieval systems to efficiently locate relevant sequences of textual material held in a continuous and coherent form. The user can then call for as much or as little of the material as is considered appropriate, with each page of information presented to the user for consumption. However, to simply rely upon the user to select appropriate key words in the most useful combinations or permutations, is to do no more than to give the user a book with a superior index. Although it does overcome possible difficulties in gaining access to materials in libraries, it does not exploit the teaching strengths of computer systems, nor does it necessarily challenge the passivity of the students. Thus, while work might be invested in the creation of specialist subject-oriented thesauri which could offer more effective learner-support, and make topic access more coherently feasible, in the final analysis, all this effort is really doing no more than to provide a computer-based sources and materials book.

One of the major design considerations is therefore to identify the purpose for exposing the learner to the given material, and consequently to fix the size of each unit of information. Sometimes it may be considered appropriate to provide moderately long units of more narrative information, followed by detailed comprehension questions. On other occasions, small units of information may be considered better suited to the subject matter, and more likely to meet the learning objectives. The problem with small units is, however, that unless care is taken in the drafting, they can become repetitious with a risk of loss of interest and boredom on the part of the student. It is alleged that this "pall effect" weakens the powers of assimilation. To some extent, the answer to this question is a matter of design style. If only one path through the technique is provided, and it is unimaginatively presented, boredom may quickly set in. However, several versions may be provided to meet different purposes or standards of student, viz. a more pedantic and intentionally detailed introduction for the weaker student, or a fast encapsulation for revision purposes. This type of material most usually appears as a tutorial, or as a dialogue question-and-answer sequence, and it is this general CAL approach which competes most directly with a lecture or a book.

However, there are significant educational problems to be overcome in the design of these tutorial-style systems. Any badly thought-out programs which simply call for rote learning, or which reinforce the strong student tendency towards formalistic thought patterns, are of little long-term benefit. Thus, the 'obvious' educational use of the computer to more effectively provide information by automating the tried and tested linear programming techniques, or as a mere repository for banks of objective test questions, has real dangers. Simply dividing up teaching material into small segments, with one or two cursory comprehension questions, is not a constructive use of a computer's capabilities. However, it is equally easy to go too far in the opposite direction. If the student is bombarded with alternative explanations, none of which are truly understood, the student may become confused and demoralised. Thus, the computer should quickly point students in the direction of different forms of learning activity, which not only provides a variety of learning experience which helps to maintain interest, but may also provide fuller or more helpful explanations than can conveniently be stored on system.

Although CAL systems can be made very sophisticated, duplicated explanations are costly both in terms of staff time for preparation, and in computer storage terms where memory space may be restricted (save that, in the more modern hardware, this is increasingly less of a problem). There is also a risk of textual redundancy. The in-built statistical report package will show what percentage of students fails to understand the preliminary sequence, and therefore requires the alternative explanations. If a high proportion of users fails to understand the introductory elements, this may be a criticism of the way in which that early information is being presented, and the beneficial redrafting of that early material may make reference to alternative explanations less necessary.

Through this process of redrafting and refinement, success might therefore be claimed when, in simple statistical terms, the stage is reached where only a small proportion of users fails at the first hurdle. One facet of this result is that a great deal of development time and effort may have been invested in the alternative sequences for little continuing return. However, education aids should not simply be judged in such hard utilitarian terms. The programmer can provide a whole range of different examples and explanations to lead the learner towards understanding. This need only be done once. For a topic which is static or only marginally dynamic, the fact that only a few students in each year might make use of it, does not detract from its longer-term utility. Further, the computer can devote more time and patience to the presentation of this material immediately the difficulty is diagnosed. Whereas even if the relevant member of staff can be located before the ephemeral initiative to question has been lost, there is no guarantee that the member of staff will have the time to devote to the solution of the problem on a face-to-face basis.

Alternatively, the designer may deliberately have made the opening remarks difficult to indicate the need to maintain proper intellectual standards, and to avoid the simplistic explanation. If, say, Taba's theories are adopted, (see section 2.4) the student must be challenged and, if necessary, baffled by being confronted with problems not immediately understood. Similarly, Gestaltists and cognitive psychologists would argue against simplified explanations. If "insights" are to be encouraged, the students must be encouraged to think and reflect upon the material supplied. The less challenging the presentation of the material, the less effort the student is required to make, and so the more passive the exercise may become. If teachers wish to avoid the simplistic stimulus–response model and to lead the students to a more complete understanding of complex issues, the computer must represent a mechanism for the exploration of ideas, and not be a mere Skinner box in sheep's clothing.

Another aspect of this feature is that students will often experiment at their own initiative with the responsiveness of CAL suites by inserting random or perverse answers. Equally, in a human–supervised CAL tutorial environment, it is a useful teaching device to challenge the student to predict what the response of the system will be if the 'wrong' answer is offered. (5) Either way, the completeness in the range of a system's explanations or in the variety of assistance offered, may give the students more confidence in the overall system's ability to help them, and thus enhance its use. Ignoring all the intangible benefits of student confidence and a reinforcement through reading derived from an exploration of the system's capacity, even if only one or two students directly benefit from the alternative explanations, this is still a gain because these are students who might not have brought their difficulties to the attention of the teaching staff, and who might have gone through the course without ever having grasped the particular concept. On the other hand, the danger of the comprehensive system is that it can tend to make the user too dependent upon the computer without coming to recognise the value of other forms of information such as books, micro fiche, and so on. This is a problem of presentation, and the teacher must ensure that the computer is seen in its proper educational context.

To introduce a note of realism, it should also be acknowledged that in many subject areas, teachers believe that students require detailed practice and, in this, the computer can offer considerable variety. Students can be supplied with a series of short drill exercises, and they are invited to solve them and to enter the answers. Thus, in a modern languages course, exercises might be given in grammar or vocabulary. Similarly, in a course based in whole or in part upon mathematical techniques, the ability of the computer to generate random numbers may be exploited to create an infinite number of test questions on set formuli. When difficulty arises in the solution of any such exercise, the computer may give aid. This assistance might simply be to give the correct answer. Alternatively, the computer may diagnose the particular problems which the student has shown through the answers given, and give assistance in the form of learning sequences tailored to the individual student's difficulties. Whether or not such drill and practice is educationally sound is not within the scope of this book. It is simply recognised that substantial amounts of time are devoted to the activity in many subject areas, and that the computer may save a significant amount of time and effort on the part of staff who would otherwise have to set and mark the work.

This feature as defined need not be confined to the literal presentation of information in a programatic form. It may equally apply to information supplied in a controlled situation. Thus, for example, another relevant type of computer software is the game or gaming simulation as a learning device. Games and simulations, computer-based or otherwise, have a high motivational value, and may have useful educational components in introducing students to a concept or idea. This is achieved by confronting them with a situation where the idea would produce a good solution, or in allowing students to apply learned principles in a non-threatening environment. In a classroom, a student only has self-esteem at risk in a simplified version of reality. In the real world of employment, mistakes may produce unemployment.

The advantage of the computer-based game is the speed with which relevant calculations may be made and displayed, often permitting the game to flow more smoothly than the manual equivalent. This minimises boredom and enhances the dynamic of enjoyable competition which the gaming simulation relies upon as its primary motivating force. There is a further possibility which is playing with the computer as opposed to playing games on the computer. Independently of the use of computers to permit the playing of games, there is the use of the computer for play. One example of the recreational use of computing power has been the endless repetition of a very simple calculation. This has led to results such as the Henon attractor (6), the game of life (7), and cellular automata. (8) In most of the cases, although the calculations are inherently simple, they generate irrational numbers, and are unsuitable for mental arithmetic. They are also impossible by a single human, because the obtaining of an interesting result can easily involve a million repetitive calculations.

4.4.2 The student is required to make an active response to each unit which contrasts sharply with the more passive role in reading a book or, to some extent, attending a lecture or tutorial

In educational theory terms, the second feature is that responses are elicited from the students, and this provides a measuring mechanism of student performance. This may be directly exploited in an expert system. Thus, for example, the system can keep a record of responses and determine whether the student is using the system "intelligently". Some students seek to exploit the reinforcement mechanisms which will tell the user whether the answers actually given are correct and, if not, indicate the preferred answers. If it is decided that the student is entering random answers in the hope that the system will provide the correct answers 'for free', i.e. not require genuine work on the part of the student, the student may be reprimanded and/or excluded from the system until evidence of effort is provided. It also represents the basis of the statistical package which will assist the teacher to judge the performance of students both individually and collectively, and to evaluate the quality of the stored materials.

4.4.3 The student can be given immediate feedback on performance

The value of this proposition in education theory terms is that, as Skinner requires, the student can immediately be told whether the response given was correct. This feature does give rise to debate. Some argue that the feedback should be immediate to prevent the student from being passively confirmed in error; others prefer deferred feedback, so that more questions can be asked of the student to diagnose the reason for the error. This latter strategy therefore allows the cause of the error to be corrected, which is more useful than simply treating a symptom. Even when the correct response has been given, it is often useful to have a back-up question, or a series of questions, which probes to ensure that the initial answer was given for the right reasons, and was not a guess (see 2 above).

4.4.4 Each student is free to work at his or her own speed, making mixed ability group teaching more approachable

Many criticise CAL on the ground that the student often does work on his or her own, and so does not get the stimulation of the peer group in discussion. The line of argument starts with the correct proposition that the Socratic dialogue is the ideal learning environment, but that the social advantages of joint exercises in a group may have equal or greater values. The problem with this critique is that it implicitly assumes that a CAL system will totally substitute for the teacher. It also assumes that students will always work through CAL suites on their own and not as groups. Neither assumption is necessarily justifiable. Although the computer is recognised as a valuable tool, schools and colleges have not had the resources available to buy in the level of hardware which would be required to provide terminal access or work stations for every student. Even in those schools and colleges where substantial facilities exist, the amount of software available does not permit the removal of teaching staff from the teaching environment. Finally, the existing structure of courses, and the institutional and educational philosophy under-pinning them, is incompatible with the idea of complete computer-isation. The computer should therefore be considered merely as one more option available for exploitation by an individual teacher or group of staff.

4.5 What are the advantages of CAL-based teaching?

4.5.1 Controlled experiments have demonstrated that a good CAL program can achieve the same results as a good teacher, often in less time

Anything which a teacher might want to say to a group of students can be written down. If the objection to CAL is that it can mentally strait-jacket a student user by providing material in a predigested form, how does it compare to a text book, a handout or dictated lecture notes? Such written forms can only sequence the ideas in the order in which the author has presented them. A properly constructed, branching CAL program can present the required information in a variety of different ways, such ways being determined in direct response to the student's understanding, comprehension and general progress. Although books can be written in a scrambled form, the written product is frequently the victim of student passivity (9). It has also been shown that properly constructed CAL packages have the capacity to diversify the learning experience and to enhance the effectiveness of other educational resources, e.g. they can significantly increase the use of library resources through targeting precise sources in remedial help sections (see later this chapter).

4.5.2 Training can be at any time the hardware is available, and at any place where the software can be accessed

A teacher can only be contacted at certain limited times of the day or evening. Self-evidently, a student could work through CAL sequences at any time during the opening hours of the school or college, whether the material is available for use on a micro, mini or mainframe. The only limitations will be either the number of floppy discs prepared for each topic, or the number of terminals. If the software is designed for a micro or PC, and the user has access to an appropriate machine outside the institution, there is no reason why the student should not take out a copy of one or more discs in the same way as library books - something which is particularly useful for part-time students (cf. Bristol Polytechnic and their existing microfiche scheme, and the proposed Open University scheme). Finally, if telephone access to a mainframe facility is possible, schools and colleges might rent out a suitable modem for access outside opening hours.

Once software holdings build up, a software librarian is necessary who can catalogue all the features of the available packages. Thus, software is written in different languages and in different dialects, and many packages take advantage of specialised peripherals which make them inoperable without these devices. All the idiosyncracies of the package must be carefully noted. Busy staff and students do not have the time to work through the software itself, looking for the desired educational features. A short summary of the intended aims of the software package should therefore be included in each catalogue entry. Further, because software in machine readable form is not easy to read, good documentation is essential if software is to be evaluated with a view to use, and it must be stored with the software.

4.5.3 All the students get the same basic instruction, and there can be no doubt about what is being taught

Current practice to reduce the level of uncertainty inherent in the conventional lecture/tutorial system requires that the students are supplied with a "good initiating product", i.e. dictated lecture notes or handouts, and standardised access to information, i.e. the recommended text book(s) or reading list. However, inequalities are almost inevitable. It is impossible to guarantee that all the students will have the funds or the inclination to acquire the recommended book(s) and/or gain access to the materials on the reading list; or that, even should they all do so, that all will read, or read with equal understanding and learning effect. Further, many students simply file handouts away in a convenient file to be carried around, apparently expecting that the information will be absorbed through the pores by some, as yet barely understood, human osmotic process.

If CAL is utilised, and it is assumed that suitable printers are available in conjunction with the CAL suites, users can always be given a copy of the work which they have undertaken. It is, of course, true that this material may suffer the same fate as the handout. Print-outs may lie unread for the rest of the course but, unlike the ordinary handout, at least the users have had to pay a price in the form of work in order to obtain it (see Richard deCharms and the concept of personal causation (10)). Further, as well as a source of 'good product', it is also a clear record of that which the individual user failed to understand together with individualised suggested remedial action. The student may therefore have a much greater incentive to make further reference to this form of product, either because effort has been invested and the student consequently places more value upon it, or because it may be more directly helpful than the conventional handout. It also has the advantage that, in the event of loss, the student can always return to the system for a new copy and thereby recreate the learning experience.

4.5.4 It enhances the role of the teacher or tutor, freeing such persons from the chore of routine instruction, exercise setting and marking, and allows the opportunity to give more individual guidance and special help

The repetitive task of communicating basic information by formal classes or lectures is an inefficient way of using the valuable information and teaching resource which is the school teacher or college lecturer. If students are to be given skills, they must be allowed the maximum opportunity to grasp and practice those skills. This cannot be achieved in the conventional classroom-based lecture format. If all routine or narrative material is included in suitable CAL suites, the teacher is then free to spend time on the explanation of more difficult material, and to devote more attention to students on an individual or small group basis. Both tasks exploit the real ability of the teacher, and make a positive effort to humanise the teaching situation. Further, if the student takes tests or examinations at his or her own work station, the results can be given immediately, without having to wait for the chore of marking. Moreover, through the use of the computer, the form of the tests or examinations can be more inventive than the standard written forms of multiple choice questioning adopted by some examining bodies and institutions; and, perhaps more importantly in pre-examination tests, the students can be told what they must study further at a time when they are more predisposed to use the information wisely.

4.5.5 It can relieve the teacher and the student from the boredom of 'unauthentic labour'

An example of this would be the long arithmetical calculations which would normally be machine-based in the real world, and by allowing the computer to perform such tasks, both teacher and student are free to concentrate on the more genuine educational issues. To perform all the calculations which may be necessary using pen and paper, is sometimes to give the opportunity to the student to loose sight of the overall process involved. The speed with which computers can perform these calculations allows students the opportunity to experiment with the process, something which would be more difficult by manual means. However, this begs the question as to the precise nature of the 'genuine educational issues'. The criticism may equally be made that the general use of computer-based systems has the effect of deskilling the particular task undertaken. If, say, a pocket calculator can perform routine arithmetical tasks, is it educationally necessary to teach students the methodology of arithmetic? Is it necessary for the student to understand how the machine arrives at any particular result, or is it more constructive to shamelessly exploit the machine and to teach machine applications? This issue becomes progressively more important as the technology of the programmable pocket calculator develops, for it is now possible to include topics in the elementary curriculum that were computationally too difficult without the use of a machine.

In this, a distinction needs to be made between the concept and the process. By using the power of the machine, the educational outcome is not simply that more problems can be solved in the same time, it is that more aspects of the procedure can be examined in the same time. It is not sufficient to naively treat the computer as a variation on the labour-saving device. It is true that it can do more calculations more quickly, but that enables one to see the underlying pattern more easily. Hence, relationships between concepts should become more apparent, and the students should become more proficient in the manipulation of ideas. Consequently, the constructive use of a wordprocessor package can lead the writer to view every manifestation of the document as a mere draft because of the ease of amendment. This can have a real and beneficial impact on the the writer's creativity. Similarly, any mathematical problem can be investigated through the agency of a computer. Thus, instead of merely illustrating a phenomenon, the student can be encouraged to build a model, and to predict real world results.

However, many of these good educational outcomes can really only be achieved if properly designed software support is made available to the students, or the students develop some programming expertise. There are two problems in the latter solution, viz. programming can be time-consuming, and the detail of programming may also contain unauthentic elements, e.g. it would be inappropriate to force students to write graph generating software from scratch. However, by a constructive use of the computer and a tool box of software packages, students can be encouraged to more thoroughly investigate numerical and analytical techniques than would be possible using manual means.

At this stage, social policy considerations become relevant. As computer systems become more prevalent and more competent in the performance of 'human-like tasks', the overall need for human personnel who are trained in the performance of routine tasks is diminished. The requirement is therefore for a new para-professional class of information technician which will manage the machines, and represent an interface or buffer between the remaining professional planners and decision-makers, and their support machines. This has significant educational implications which are outside the scope of this immediate chapter, but which should implicitly be born in mind.

4.5.6 Small group teaching is uneconomic but better academically

A computer-based system can give individualised tutorial guidance of a high standard, and therefore potentially produce results which a labour-intensive teaching system can no longer afford to offer. The existence of such systems also enables academic staff to devote more time either to remedial teaching, or to the generation of much greater sophistication than might otherwise have been possible in the time available. Moreover, since the better CAL suites will identify both the weaker and the stronger student users, the tutor may target teaching very precisely, helping the students known to be in difficulties, and extending the frontiers of knowledge in those students seen to be in command of the more obvious material.

4.6 What are the disadvantages of CAL-based teaching?

4.6.1 There are real costs associated with the development of CAL systems

Even given the technical expertise, it is very expensive in terms of staff time to devise and program effective CAL suites. A single tutorial on a moderately straightforward topic must be designed, keyed in, debugged, tested educationally, copied and distributed. It may be self-contained, or it may require the production of accompanying support documentation. Existing teaching materials will then have to be reconsidered, and face-to-face tutorials redesigned, to take account of the software support. If the production of the software was not team-based, colleagues may have to be shown the new software, and persuaded to adopt it and/or amend their approach in classes and tutorials so that what they say and do is at least compatible with the CAL materials.

Without the expertise, schools and colleges must either train their staff to adopt the same educational and software standards, or run the risk of their staff continually reinventing the square wheel. If schools and colleges decide that in-house production is not feasible, it must be recognised that there are also significant costs involved in the purchase of CAL suites. Apart from the capital and revenue outlay represented by the host machines, printers and disposables, the licence fees (if any) and the purchase price of the software, the receiving staff must evaluate the packages, and determine how best to incorporate the material into the structure of existing courses.

During this evaluation process, amendment to the software may be found desirable and/or necessary. This is not to suggest that CAL suites will be supplied with substantive errors contained within them. There are always differences in the approach to, or in the interpretation of, academic topics quite apart from the level of emphasis demanded by individual syllabi. Some ability to tailor software to particular course requirements, or to add an explanatory commentary, is therefore always desirable. There may also be problems of portability, particularly in mainframe systems, and there may be software bugs. All of these factors add time and therefore money to the cost of acquisition, even assuming that there is in-house expertise available to remedy any defects. If outside help has to be sought, the cost inevitably goes up. When running, the better designed systems are also going to supply staff with student profiles and statistical data, all of which should be considered if the best use of the teaching aid is to be made. Ironically, although this information will permit staff to perform their job more professionally, it does require more time to take proper advantage of it.

4.6.2 Most schools and many colleges already operate a high class contact timetable with little time allocated to the use of library facilities

The adoption of a high CAL input may further lure students away from books and the written medium, and might lead to an unhealthy dependence upon the programs. Unless the software is well-designed, this may lead the students into an undesirable intellectual formalism. Further, students may become more interested in the mechanics of instruction rather than in the subject matter to be communicated. On the other hand, if the software is well-written, it may direct the students to make much greater use of the library resources. In some educational establishments, this may run contrary to the policy represented by many existing timetables. It may also highlight the inadequacy of many school's and college's library stocks. The irony is that the better the CAL suite, the more likely is it that greater library expenditure and use must be planned for. After all, the library is an information resource of considerable power and, in any event, all students should be taught information retrieval both manual and electronic as a part of every curriculum. This becomes even more relevant as more libraries install automated circulation, cataloguing, and enquiries systems, and provide access to on-line database services. Students therefore need a good grounding in the use of boolean descriptors, and in the development of search strategies, if the best use of the databases is to be achieved. In-house, libraries also regulate the ordering of, and payment for, both books and periodicals through computer systems, and the training of library staff as well as teaching staff is necessary as more information only becomes available in machine readable form.

A remedial CAL section can tell a user to read just the right pages in identified books or periodicals. Library shelf-counts in institutions where detailed CAL research has been performed, have shown a significant increase in book use where exact page guide information is given by the CAL suites. Students seem signific-

antly more willing to use the library when the required information is precisely identified and delimited. There is only a
marginal increase demonstrated where students are referred simply
to books or articles in an apparently open-ended way. The
suggested reason is that a student is more prepared to use the
library resource if, in advance, it is known that only, say, four
pages need to be consulted. A special journey may therefore be
seen as feasible within time available, or worth the effort given
the weight attached to the topic within the overall context of
the course. If this information is not known, students are less
willing to invest the effort in going to the library, finding the
book and checking the index to see how much work is going to be
involved.

One of the key variables seems to be the distance between the
computer resource and the library. If the resource is situated,
say, in the students' department or in some centralised facility,
students are shown to be significantly less willing to move
within the institution if the work is not quantified in advance.
Other factors intrude and affect the decision whether to leave
the computer resource, the most important of which are: if the
student recognises that, having given up his or her seat, such is
the pressure on the resource that he or she may have to queue to
return to the computer, there is every incentive to defer the
visit to the library – the time available for the visit may then
expire, or the inclination may be lost through tiredness, a
general loss of interest or other comparable reasons; if the
journey involves moving from one building to another, it may be
seen to be raining or otherwise unsuitable for travel; once
undertaken, fellow students or staff may interrupt the journey
and cause a loss of motivation, and so on. However, if the computer resource is next to the books and little effort is required
to check the book(s) referred to, there is a greater likelihood
that the remedial reading will be done, even if fully detailed
page information is not given.

The practice of referring the student to the library is the
correct way of framing the help because:

(a) copyright will forbid the unauthorised storage of the
text of the relevant books; and

(b) given (a), it is usually cheaper to buy the books than
to pay the licence fees demanded by the publisher(s); and

(c) even if the licence fees are not prohibitive, unless the
text is available in machine readable form, the cost of
keying in the material will be substantial; and

(d) the student should be encouraged to experience a variety
of educational stimuli, both to assist in maintaining interest, and to give the greatest opportunity to discover a
satisfactory resolution to the difficulty.

4.6.3 There are also administrative problems associated with computer installations

The problems particularly relate to the physical location of the computer resources, the cost of hardware maintenance and insurance (if the school or college is allowed to insure against loss and/or damage), and timetabling difficulties which may draw heavily on staff time. If it is assumed that, in the first instance, schools and colleges will not be able to afford the installation of major computer resources, the problems are two-fold. In the first instance, the staff must be allowed significant access to the resource, to both familiarise themselves with the hardware, and to begin the process of developing new software or modifying existing software. Without this staff development exercise, little use would actually be made of any resources actually installed.

Once this initial phase is complete, and the staff at all levels have accepted the course implications of adopting substantial CAL input, specialist terminal and/or micro rooms must be created at strategically sensible locations within the available buildings (in particular, seeking to balance the need to have computer resources close to teaching rooms, as against the need to have the computer resources close to the library facilities). Additional power points or ports will be required in most major teaching rooms for demonstration or tutorial purposes, with academic support staff responsible for moving equipment from one room to another as and when required. Technicians will have to be trained in the maintenance and repair of the different types of hardware, bearing in mind that while resources remain limited, only the most robust of equipment will survive the level of use envisaged without regular maintenance. This retraining and redeployment of staff, refitting of class rooms, and the consequent timetabling implications, have significant costs attached to them. The alternative to this high-profile and costly exercise is piecemeal development by one or two enthusiasts which is frequently counter-productive.

4.6.3.1 Where should the computers be located?

The immediate answer is that proximity of the equipment to the classes, and to the staff facilities, enhances the dynamic impact on the staff. However, it should be noted that the primary purpose of the computers is to assist the students' learning and, thus, no matter how worthy, once the computers have been introduced to the students, they should not be taken off by staff to their own rooms for development work. The more remote the equipment, the less the incentive to make special trips to use it. Modern school and college architecture may have to be completely rethought. Current school and much college architecture is based upon the circulation of students from one classroom to the next, to a laboratory, to a library and back to a classroom. All must be within a reasonable walking distance if reasonable continuity of activity is to be maintained.

If CAL becomes more prevalent, the circulation of students is not so important. Instead, information comes to the terminal. Design of the terminal and its environment therefore becomes the predominantly important focus. The layout of the room should strike a balance between allowing user interaction, and allowing each user a degree of privacy. Again a balance must be struck for the sharing of information is a vital part of the learning experience, but interaction can be distracting to other users. A compromise layout would therefore be to arrange the terminals or micros in U or L shapes, or as an island. Students could then select a keyboard where other users are communally grouped, or where other users are not in immediate line of sight. In designing the layout, space should be made available to both sides of the machine for books or other materials, remembering that some students are left handed so enough room for writing must be allowed on both flanks. Moreover, noise insulation on printers is essential if work is to proceed in a reasonably pleasant and relaxed atmosphere.

All logging on and off procedures should be simplfied on mainframe systems, particularly where there is a network protocol involved, and standalone systems should just be switched on with operating systems which are easy to boot up. Just as all barriers to access should be as minimal as possible, getting a print of teaching materials should also be simplfied so that students see no real disincentive to obtaining the good initiating product in the form of notes, etc. The question of ergonomics should also be considered. There may be problems of eye strain if users make significant use of VDUs. The best solution is probably indirect lighting, with blinds at the windows which minimises reflected glare. However, even with good lighting when using keyboards and screen, the continual refocussing from documentary source to screen can promote muscle tiredness. The problem is particularly acute in those who already wear glasses. Most opticians set the focal length of the lenses for what is thought to be the most comfortable reading position, viz. about 15 inches. The problem cannot simply be overcome by changing the position of the screen. The answer lies in tinted variable focal length lenses and better screen character definition. (11) If long teaching sessions are to be encouraged, comfortable chairs with suitable adjustable back support are also essential.

Electrical safety is also a primary concern, and cables should be safely installed, and not left to festoon the room or work tables like the rigging of a dismasted schooner. Any failure could lead to the problem of accidentally switching off or otherwise disconnecting equipment, e.g. by catching and pulling wires or plugs. Similarly, continuity of power should be ensured and power surges must be protected against. Although data may not be lost, it is also wise to avoid thick pile or nylon carpeting which will minimise the sometimes painful consequences of static. Without air conditioning, excessive dryness will enhance the risk of static, while excessive humidity will damage the paper and disks. All round safety requires the presence of fire extinguishers close to hand, and to help preserve the machines, no eating or drinking to be allowed. In general, electrical contacts do not react well to a mixture of, say, a fizzy drink and biscuit crumbs.

One of the by-products of the increasing portability of the new hardware is the increased risk of theft. When being created, the computer facilities may not be able to command a room of their own which meets security constraints, particularly since education authorities tend not to insure their property, premiums exceeding the cost of replacement. So for example, CAL language laboratories, both mainframe and stand-alone are becoming more common. Dale V.Gear even reports on a CAL system to teach classical Greek, "The laboratory was staffed whenever it was open, both for the students' aid and for the protection of the easily transportable microcomputers." (12) For such a use, reinforced doors and special locks, bars on windows and burglar alarms should all be considered. But although anchoring the equipment to tables or work benches, may be more secure, it has the disadvantage of making what may be a scarce computing resource available in only one location.

A secure way of keeping floppy disks must also be found. Data may be lost if disks are bent or exposed to dust and dirt. This is problematical in an environment where there may be large concentrations of chalk dust. There is also a problem with regard to disk security. They are relatively easy to steal. A supervised library system of borrowing disks is therefore desirable, and it should be accompanied by a shop or dispensory of blank disks for student use. If inter-site networking is to be encouraged, telephone lines must be connected to the labs. This involves much official red tape and can be expensive for the school or college, particularly because it offers horrible temptation to any student who happens to have an aunt in Australia.

The short-term answer to the hardware problem may lie both in non-specialist applications, and in fixing the equipment to trollies which can be moved from one site to another as required and minimise any disruption to existing room designs. This does not solve the problems of doors that are too narrow nor of stairs which are impassable, but this mobility may enhance general access to the equipment, and offer greater opportunities for the demonstration of software. The decision whether to have fixed or movable resources is also tied up with the problem of scheduling access. Although formal classes must be allowed to book access to the facilities, free student and staff access is equally important if consistent self-development is to be maintained. If individual schools and colleges are short of hardware, the equipment must come to the site. Thus, the initiatives of the British Schools Technology programme in equipping buses which can tour schools is matched in America where, for example, one school authority in San Fransisco has created a computer bus to provide more immediate access to schools which could not individually afford the hardware. (13)

4.6.3.2 Should a formal Computer Services Unit be created?

It is unlikely that one person can adequately support anything more than a very small installation at a small institution. Thus, when planning the acquisition of hardware, the support and services personnel should be considered first. In this, it can be useful to have a computer co-ordinator who stands independently from either the maths and science departments that might otherwise monopolise the resource, or from a support unit. Such a person should be sensitive to the legitimacy of claims from non-science departments to access and referee in any disputes. To simply give the school or college computer to one person or department is not productive. A properly set up Computer Services Unit should offer the following support for the system:-

(a) The use of the system should be strongly promoted. It is not sensible to invest capital in hardware and then not gain the maximum benefit from it. Consequently, there is a need to stimulate initial enthusiasm and then maintain it, e.g. by creating user groups where people can exchange information and jolly each other along; and by offering both software support, and programming and development consultancy to help to maintain enthusiasm in the new users.

(b) Once the principle of computerisation has been accepted, it is necessary to provide advice on what hardware and software to acquire in order to meet future need. This involves keeping pace with pricing generally, and educational discounts in particular, and dealing with suppliers on a regular basis to get the best terms. For larger institutions, this purchasing function can be a full time job, and it is helpful to belong to an association such as ACUCHE (Association of Computer Units in Colleges of Higher Education), which surveys prices for the membership and seeks to standardise the terms of purchasing and licensing agreements. Without this form of back-up, it is useful to build up the expertise in two members of staff who can co-ordinate the function, and reduce the risk of skill loss if the key person leaves that employment.

(c) Having ordered suitable kit, someone must accept the responsibility of physically setting up the hardware when it arrives, and of maintaining proper records. Software acquisition and licensing also needs careful attention, and policing the use of licensed software can be demanding.

(d) Introductory and continuing support should be given to both users and owners (more students and staff now own computers). This should be followed by newsletters and documentation to keep people abreast of technical developments, while workshops should provide experience in new acquisitions or developments. It is also useful to maintain a library of the manufacturers' manuals or abstracts of the most useful parts.

(e) The hardware must be properly maintained. This can be done in-house but may not be contractually possible, or may become too great a problem when a variety of hardware has been purchased. If guarantees are invalidated should the user undertake the maintenance, the normal spectrum of maintenance contracts must be administered.

(f) Staff must be provided to assist in moving the equipment around, or in supervising the labs.

4.6.4 CAL is perceived as a threat to jobs

In an economic environment where Government policy is seen to threaten contraction rather than expansion in all levels of education, combined with a decline in the birth rate which is working its way through the system, there is also teacher hostility to the concept of the computer which is seen as a direct threat to jobs. This adds to the problem of innate conservatism in the teaching profession which has always represented a potential barrier to the trial of any new ideas. Without the active support of staff and their administration, the promotion of CAL cannot really make progress. This point is fully examined in Chapter 6.

4.6.5 There may be health problems associated with long-term exposure to VDUs

It has been suggested that there may be health problems associated with long-term exposure to the electromagnetic radiation which is emitted by VDUs. Electromagnetic radiation is a form of energy capable of travelling as waves through a vacuum. The radiation may either be ionising or non-ionising. In both the educational and the commercial world, there has been some controversy, both informed and uninformed, as to the possible risks, while lay opinion has run the whole gamut of possible medical dangers. Thus, there may be risks to eye sight, e.g. through the development of cataracts, that facial dermatitis may arise, that for those who suffer from the condition, photosensitive epileptic attacks may be induced, that bodily fatigue may be caused or, more extremely, that there may be risks that pregnant women may have a miscarriage or give birth to children with defects, or more generally, that cancer may be induced. By any criteria, this amounts to a frightening catalogue of possible medical consequences. However, that which is possible is, by definition, not necessarily probable.

In fact, at a purely technical level, British VDU manufacturers have adopted lower emission standards than the formal international guidelines. Most British regulating bodies now subscribe to the ALARA principle (As Low As Reasonably Achievable) for ionising radiation. If this were not the case, (and it must be emphasised that no VDU would have the required power levels), at the extreme end of physical possibility, acute exposure to ionising radiation invariably results in death, while cancer or other genetic damage is the usual result of low level chronic or intermittent exposures. The effects of low level ionising radiation on sensitive organs, e.g. the reproductive, tend to be cumulative and irreversible, so the 'total absorbed dose' is the relevant criterion.

The standards for non-ionising radiation tend to relate to the possible thermal effects of the radiation. At sufficient power, the thermal effects can be severe, particularly in tissue which is sensitive to heat (e.g. the eye where exposure to microwave radiation can lead to cataract formation. Very little is known about the biological effects of low frequency radiations but the Institution of Electronic and Electrical Engineers (USA) has said "Cumulative irreversible damage can occur in tissues that are continuously or repeatedly exposed to ionising radiations at low levels, but there is no scientific consensus to support to proposition that continuous exposure to low level (less than 1mW/cm) RFEM fields result in damage irreversible or otherwise to biological molecules." (14) However, a European survey carried out by ERA Technology Ltd on behalf of the National Radiological Board for the UK Health and Safety Executive found that,

> The measured radiation emissions from corectly operating VDUs are much less than the limits for continuous occupational exposure in the various regions of the electromagnetic spectrum given in many national and international standards...
>
> the conclusion must be that the radiation normally emitted from a VDU does not pose a hazard to operators either in the long or short terms. (15)

Further, there is no medical evidence to support the fears of cataract formation from the use of VDUs, and the introduction of better lighting and controls to reduce screen glare have reduced the incidence of the more common simple eye strain. The cause and effect of VDUs and facial dermatitis is not clear. It is true that some operators have reported the condition, but this may be caused by working in centrally heated and dry atmospheres near a source of static electricity. If offices were to introduce humidifiers and to take anti-static precautions, it is probable that the incidence of this condition would decline. It must be accepted, however, that bodily fatigue is a more real danger. The remedy is to promote good posture, and to allow the opportunity for staff to move around and, thus, avoid a build up of fatigue. Even where the environment is ergonomically designed to minimise discomfort, repetitious muscle strain injuries are becoming more common as keyboard operators spend more time making rapid finger movements. Ironically, mechanical typewriters, and the early electronic keyboards slowed typists down and prevented this form of injury. Now that the keyboards can keep up with the pace of the faster typists, more injuries are being sustained.

Unions and employers in some countries have responded to these verified hazards by limiting the length of time spent in the use of a VDU at a single sitting, and rotate their staff to different activities. Although it might be reasonable to argue that until all of these risks are quantified, or the fears shown to be groundless, it may not be responsible to encourage the wholesale adoption of VDUs, and therefore of CAL, it seems equally clear that such risks as do exist are minimal and cannot cause serious injury even when the technology is used to excess.

4.6.6 Even when software is made available, there may only be one terminal or standalone for an entire class to use

The only answer is to demonstrate the software to the class, or to use the software on behalf of the class. For such demonstrations of software to a class, the teacher must get the students and the computer in the same place at the same time, must get the hardware working (not necessarily easy for a harassed teacher with a large class of school children), and must try to take educational decisions about how quickly the students can absorb information from the screen when it has not necessarily been designed with this in mind, e.g. with large format print. Further, this function reinforces the role of the teacher as the controller of access to information, and formally places a barrier between the student and the machine. Although this may be for the entirely practical reason that there is only the one machine for this school or college, the situation is sometimes stage-managed, because the teacher does not believe that un-restricted access to the computer is desirable.

4.6.7 Various polls and questionnaires have determined that the response of students to CAL is rarely neutral

Views and attitudes tend to polarise. While there is no difficulty associated with those students who are enthusiastic, it can be difficult to motivate those who are hostile to the use of computers. In many instances, the hostility is rooted in simple unthinking prejudice, but students also identify other factors such as a lack of keyboard skills as a rationale. Some dislike their new-found inability to hide. The monitoring and reporting advantages which teachers may identify, undoubtedly alarm both those students lacking in confidence, and those students whose laziness will be exposed. While the latter's performance may be improved through shame or exhortation, the former need careful counselling and advice to put the responses of the system into a proper context.

From a software design point of view, there is always a need to provide a genuinely friendly front-end to a CAL suite (16). Although users often anthropomorphise computers, and inevitably take them to be callous and unthinking in criticising those users who make mistakes, all machine-generated comments offered should be framed in as tactful a way as possible to minimise the risk of alienating waivering users. This problem is not unique to computers, but the use of computers can crystalise difficulties which arise in a student through lack of confidence, but which might otherwise not be detected as early in the course. It may be particularly important to counsel mature students whose feelings of safety and security may already be threatened by the novelty of the college environment. In the long term, this additional work may genuinely benefit those students who respond, by making them more adaptive in their outlook, but schools and colleges which invest in CAL must become more sensitive to student problems of this nature.

References

(1) Preface to 'Future Development of C.N.A.A.'s Academic Policies at Undergraduate Level – A Consultative Paper'. 1983.

(2) see Some Observations on the Efficiency of Lecturing. Hartley and Cameron. (1967) 20(1) Educational Review 30-7; and Performance Decrement in the Lecture. Maddox and Hoole. (1975) 28(1) Educational Review 17-30.

(3) Notetaking Research: Resetting the Scoreboard. J.Hartley. (1983) 36 Bulletin of the British Psychological Society 13-4.

(4) Report of the Commission on teaching in Higher Education. National Union of Students. Presented to Liverpool Conference, April 1969. London: NUS.

(5) Both of which will distort the statistical accuracy of the CAL suite's evaluation package. Although the effect will tend to even out over time, it is a factor worth bearing in mind when deciding whether to amend a particular sequence. However, do not be tempted to discourage the "play" element in the students' approach to CAL systems. In fact, it is a useful trait to exploit and encourage.

(6) M.Henon. (1976) 50 Commun. Mathematical Physics 69/77.

(7) E.R.Berlekamp, J.H.Conway and R.K.Guy. Winning Ways for Your Mathematical Plays. Academic Press, 1982. pp.817/50.

(8) S.Wolfram (1984) Physica D 10. pp.1/35.

(9) e.g. handouts, see How do Students Use Lecture Handouts? Truman and Hartley. Collected in Aspects of Educational Technology 13. edited by Page and Whitlock. Kogan Page, London. pp.62–66.

(10) see note 6 in Chapter 1

(11) Much easier on the eyes. Pearce Wright. The Times. Tuesday October 28, 1986 p.28.

(12) A Small Computer CAI Course in Classical Greek. Dale V.Gear. collected in Computing in the Humanities. edited by Peter C Patton and Renee A Holoien. Gower, London. 1981. p. 275.

(13) Busing Computers – A Communitiy's Reaction. Lewis B.Miller, Timothy Roorda, Paul Lorton Jnr. collected in Capitol-izing on Computers in Education. p.256.

(14) The Drive to regulate Electromagnetic Fields. E.J. Lerner. (1984) March IEEE Spectrum.

(15) Radiation Emissions from Visual Display Units. E.A.Cox. collected in Health Hazards of VDUs?. (ed) B.G.Pearce. The HUSAT Research Group. The University of Technology, Loughborough. John Wiley. 1984. pp. 25/37. at p.32.

(16) cf. a computerised control system was introduced at one of the Royal Dutch Steel's strip-rolling plant at Hoogovens in Holland, but production fell disasterously because the operators failed to communicate successfully with the system and became demoralised. Similar problems have been reported about air traffic control systems, and were identified by the Kemeny Commission into the Three Mile Island nuclear plant accident, as one of the factors contributing to the accident.

CHAPTER 5

CENTRALISATION, DEHUMANISATION AND TESTING STUDENT PERFORMANCE

Having established in Chapter 4 that there is at least an arguable case in favour of the adoption of CAL, it is now necessary to consider two further objections to CAL in a little more detail. Hence, it is suggested that computerisation will lead to an unwholesome centralisation of authority, and that the new technological environment will be unhealthily dehumanised. But, if the new technology does spread throughout the education system, one of the opportunities for change would be in the ways in which student performance is monitored and tested. It is therefore necessary to consider what changes might be possible, and what the consequences of those changes might be.

5.1   Trends in centralisation

5.1.1 Can schools really be vocational in their teaching?

The purpose of teaching any subject in a school or college is not an attempt to make all students an expert, nor to train them for a career based upon that subject area. This is not to say that the curriculum should not be influenced by needs in the real world. All curricula change and, when the new professional practices rely upon technological or conceptual innovations, it is unrealistic of the schools and colleges not to advert to them.

However, following in the classical ivory tower tradition, many of the references will be purely academic in style.

Jobs have become increasingly specialised and training now often takes place 'on the job' or on a sandwich basis. But increasingly, employers are looking for the quality of adaptability in prospective employees, a mental facility which is not encouraged by strict regimentation of thought in the early stages of the education process. Citizens of the emerging new society need transferrable skills so that they can move more easily from one challenge to another. However, given the increasing rate of change, even if changes in educational approach are made, it is likely that society will have changed again before the first generation of students emerge from the new system. A more dynamic view of the educational process is therefore required.

It would be possible to argue that schools are simply a place where parents can send their children for socialisation and the transmission of largely middle class values; or perhaps even less flatteringly, that schools have become little more than baby sitters which allow mothers to go out to work. Such bleak perspectives would emerge from the satirist's approach of selecting one strand of reality, and inflating it to the detriment of all others. But it should focus attention on the need for the planners to consider what sort of people are going to be required in twenty years time, and to formulate a plan aimed at producing an education system which will deliver what is required. At this point the enormity of the imponderables becomes apparent. It addresses the fundamental issues of the role of the school, the family and the community in the next twenty years. If the question of computerisation is added to the planners melting pot, it is necessary to decide who will control these knowledge machines and who will program the machines. Moreover, the employment market may soon begin to require keyboard or general computing skills as a precondition of employment which will add a degree of urgency to the planning exercise.

Those responsible for the management of society should also consider the problem of increased leisure. If people are not better educated, the personal and social problems of boredom may become far more acute. One possible solution is that schools and society should move closer together, for if pupils remained integrated into the community, the educational mechanism might better attune students for life in that society. For this to be an effective solution, all would have to become better aware of the nature of the learning process. Perhaps computer support for the learning process can help, but it is not clear that present programmers understand the education process, nor is it clear that the educators communicate their skills to the programmers. However, this presupposes that a degree of programming sophistication is required in order to be able to produce CAL software. This is not necessarily the case for, like driving the ubiquitous motor car, the need is probably more for people who can operate computers and applications packages than originate

114

complex programs. Indeed, there is enough sophistication in most of the existing support packages to make modestly successful CAL manufacture a feasible proposition for non-technical teachers. The real problem lies in taking sophisticated educational decisions. "Problem specification becomes more challenging with the increased complexity of the problems which we ask computers to solve. Software production seems almost to stand still because we keep demanding more from it." (1)

As society becomes more sophisticated, individuals increasingly cede control to increasingly centralised bodies. Thus, parents have, by choice or law, abandoned home-based tutoring in favour of community-based schooling. This is not necessarily bad because professional teachers, working in economic units, can provide access to a far wider range of knowledge and skills than would be normally available for transmission in a home context. Indeed, there is a certain irony in that the capacity of the new individualised CAL teaching systems may recreate the form of individualised tuition previously only available to the wealthy and their private tutors.

5.1.2 What is the likely impact of the national curriculum?

In both the political and the practitioner arenas, detailed control of education is important because it helps to shape long-term attitudes, hence the current debates about syllabus standardisation, about peace studies and sex education. However, education is not just about information, it is also about culture and values. Traditionally, the teaching activity has been seen as the province of the professional teacher, with the interests of teachers and the interests of the state usually reaching a compromise in curriculum terms. In Parliament, Government ministers are accountable for the performance of their ministries. The difficulty which has now arisen is that whereas the cost of running the system has risen, it is not clear that resultant achievement standards on the part of students has correspondingly increased. The result of debate now seems to be all party support for the idea of a national curriculum.

The theory is that every person has an innate entitlement to learning. But because standards can vary sharply, even as between one school and another, it is only through nationally-expressed ideals that progress can be made towards guaranteeing each student the opportunity to achieve minimum competence in a wide range of subjects. Further, by expressing universal standards, it clarifies issues of financial and manpower planning. Lessons can be planned more coherently, gaps and duplications can be identified and avoided, and regional differences will be reduced which will help the progress of children who move from one geographical area to another during their schooling. If parents know what their children should learn, it makes a partnership more possible between the home and the school to ensure that attainment targets are met. A public curriculum could also act as a deterrent to indoctrination, and so the debate is as to the content of such a curriculum, and the extent to which it might be imposed by the Government without securing some sort of consent from interested parties. The difficulty is that if there is no true consensus about content, content could become a new political football to be changed with the complexion of each new Government or Secretary of State for Education.

Even if the issue of content is successfully depoliticised through the creation of independent advisory committees, there is still the problem of deciding what process of consultation should take place, and who ought to have a right to be heard. Further, it will have to be decided how quickly the new advisory committees will have to react to changes within the community. Here there will be severe problems which can only be met by more consistent in-service training to ensure that all staff are kept up-to-date with current thinking. This will inevitably increase the revenue implications for change, as will any change in books which will have significant capital costs attached to it. Presumably teachers' organisations, employers, parents' associations, local authorities and the government itself will all have rights of audience. Between them, these organisations represent the consumers. If compromises are made, some form of consensus may emerge as to what all children ought to learn. Moreover, it is to be hoped that the standards which are eventually set will reflect both national and international criteria. It would not be a constructive policy for reform if the British national curriculum was so far below that to be achieved in other Common Market countries that our workforce could not remain competitive.

5.1.3 Is this form of centralisation something to be feared?

Some might describe the creation of a national curriculum as an act of trespass on to the specialised domain of the teaching profession. But while it is true that a curriculum constrains activity and reduces choice, the end-product of this debate will do no more than provide teachers with a framework within which to devise individual lessons. Standardisation of educational aims does not require standardisation of individual lessons. Every teacher should remain free to use his or her professional judgement in the creation of suitable materials to implement each part of the curriculum.

116

5.1.4 What form of testing will be used to monitor each person's progress through the curriculum?

This is an awkward question. If the measurement is to be left to individual teachers, their standards may be too low, and not encourage the students to push to the nationally desired levels. External standards for measurement are therefore desirable. There is talk of attainment targets and regular testing at 7, 11 and 14, or some form of continuous testing such as applies in the German school system. Few parents will welcome a return to the 11 plus style of examination on a regular basis, say every two years between 5 and 16 years. There would be many objections ranging from the problems of stress, to the more insidious educational argument that the fixing of set standards of attainment for each age group tends to result in a teaching strategy whereby it is aimed to bring each pupil up to that level, i.e. the targets become the limit of achievement. All age-related tests encourage parents to compare pupils' performance and to focus on failure. That would lead to criticism of the teaching and a judging of the performance of the schools which is not the basis of a fruitful partnership between parents and teachers.

On the other hand, if children are regularly tested by nationally agreed standards, whether by examination or by some form of continuous assessment which measures how successfully each child is reaching the performance criteria specified in each subject area, and the results are directly communicated to the parents, this will have the effect of making teachers more accountable to parents for the way in which they are teaching those in their care. It will also give administrators a basis upon which to assess teachers and also upon which to base decisions about planning. Budgets can be targeted where improvements are seen to be necessary. The result is likely to be hostility on the part of the teachers. On the constructive side, the dialogue between parents and teachers could concentrate not on success or failure but on how soon, and with what work, help and encouragement the next target could be reached.

Issues of finance and recruitment, selective or comprehensive schooling, race and community relations and accountability have always been more the realm of the politician and the administrator. Curriculum development falls uneasily between the two camps, for whatever theoretical standards the state may lay down, it is ultimately the responsibility of the teachers to implement them. Education is funded from the centre but provided by the schools. To some extent, therefore, the Local Education Authorities are not a logical part of the scheme. But even if the curriculum is standardised and the role of LEAs is diminished, a whole series of questions remains to be resolved, including:

.   Will the system still be in any way responsive to the wishes of the parents?

- How can curriculum guidelines be supported by legislation?

- What will happen to the independent schools?

- Can you set a syllabus for children regardless of ability?

- What will happen if a school deliberately ignores the curriculum, or is simply unable to meet its requirements?

To think of adding computers and the attendant technology at a time of such ferment is perhaps rash, but to ignore the impact of the new communication technologies, and the liberalisation of access to information which they can achieve, would be even more rash. Caxton produced a revolution by breaking the monopoly of the clerics. The typewriter, the postal service and the telephone have given power to the individual to send uncensored messages (in this country). Computerisation could revolutionise the way in which all parts of our society stores and manipulates information, and to fail to address such potentially important factors in the national curriculum would be a retrograde step and not a positive affirmation of forward momentum.

5.1.5 Does centralisation of educational data ultimately lead to centralisation of authority?

Culture tends to follow technology. Thus, in the artistic world, music has been stimulated by increasing invention – the metal frame for the piano, valves for brass instruments, etc. In the real world, people could not consistently be housed in tower blocks until lift technology had been developed. The phenomenon of information technology has tended to produce centralisation of resources, so that the administrators of that information may achieve economies of scale. The accumulation of data in one central office permits narrow control of the decision-making process. In such circumstances, the issue of invasion of privacy inevitably arises and, with particular reference to education, it should be decided who should have access to the long-term school and college records, and how long should this data be kept? Further, upon what basis should there be transfers of information between different schools, and between different levels of schools, college, etc.? These more technical problems are compounded by the increasing problem of hackers who might find their way into otherwise confidential student data.

The computer can, of course, administer vocational tests to determine preferences, interests and abilities. The more information which is kept about age, background and performance, the more research will be possible, e.g. into whether learning ability is a result of heredity or environment, the real length of attention span, powers of retention, etc. Job matching also becomes easier because the computer can store many more details

118

of an individual's performance levels, and employers could gain a much better view of prospective employees. Further, local employers could supply educational software to local schools for those who wanted to train in relevant skills while still formally within the education system.

However, although the trend was towards ever larger machines, more recent developments have seen a shift of emphasis towards smaller machines, and better communication systems which will network different users and machines together, thus producing decentralisation and diversity. This transfers control of information assets back to the individual. "It shifts the emphasis from accessing information created by others to the creation of information and documents under the individual's control." (2) Which is the better trend? Centralisation can produce economic efficiencies and a degree of social cohesiveness, but decentralisation promotes individuality and makes room for elements of creativity and entrepreneurial opportunism. More companies are now begining to organise on the basis of home-workers, i.e. individuals who perform some or all of their employment tasks from the home environment. This is a trend which is reinforced by the increasing costs of commercial land and development. In some parts of the country, it is now significantly cheaper to fund communication costs and slightly increased travelling allowances when personal conferencing or meetings are desirable. Should this pattern become the norm, an independence of mind on the part of employees will be indispensible, and computer-based skills will become an essential precondition of employment.

In the education sector, the Government is experimenting with the delegation of more financial control to individual schools, with the privatisation of polytechnics and some colleges to the included in the next Education Bill. To some extent, this transfer of authority is made possible by the improved management capacities supported by decentralised computer facilities. Thus, although much educational data can, and will be centralised, whether at a local, regional or national level, it does not necessarily lead to centralisation of authority.

5.2 Will CAL lead to excessive standardisation of education?

Two of the major concerns in the computer education debate are that education should be seen to promote the growth of individual talent and to provide education which is consistent with the aims of an open and democratic society. In a sense, these issues beg the question because they uncritically assume that individuality is desirable characteristic, and that our society is actually open and democratic and tolerant of individuality. The problem is that pupils at school and students in Further and Higher Education are often expected to dress in a certain way, and generally to think and behave in a way acceptable to the school, college or university. It cannot therefore be said that CAL is any more likely to produce standardisation in beliefs and behaviour than the more traditional formal methods. However, Ivan Reid takes the debate a step further, "Computers are obviously far more potent than the mandatory use of a syllabus, prescribed textbook or learning resource. Not only is the clear technological possibility of curriculum almost upon us, but it will be wrapped in the persuasive values of modernity and necessity. To challenge it will be to run the risk of seeming anti-technological, Luddite even." (3)

Perhaps the question should be asked in another way. Thus, would it actually be a bad thing if, say, all children aged ten were to follow a set pattern of tuition whereby one could predict that, on Tuesday the 10th April at 1530 hours, they would all be doing computer exercise 1,271? In fact, the question would be based upon a misconception of the true power of a CAL approach, for if every pupil or student is following an individualised course of study at his or her own speed, the last thing that would occur would be curriculum standardisation. Given that all education must follow a predetermined plan if it is to be successful, the most common aim is to bring each student closer to the optimal use of in-built talents. The natural effect of this should be to enhance diversity rather than to produce conformity.

Alternatively, should it be supposed that the danger is that either the state will provide the 'standard' packages for each subject using the justification that it will reduce costs or promote uniformity of opportunity throughout the system? Even if such massive computerisation should occur, would it represent a real danger? If education is about offering support for individuals during the learning process, the planning exercise should not be concerned with the mass dissemination of information. Although it is inevitable, given the present level of technology, that learners will gather in groups to receive information, learning will always take place on an individual basis. All geographical and demographical accidents of a mixed ability group of students, or of a less competent group of teachers in any given school or college are ironed out. Thus, with a sound national CAL strategy, otherwise disadvantaged children and students will always have the same quality of access to instruction as the advantaged. Surely it is the prime advantage of standardisation that, once good software has been produced, the best quality of teaching materials can be replicated throughout the education system?

Is the danger therefore that the high cost of producing software may reduce availability given that the only way in which software can be made commercially cost-effective is through standardisation. Programs need to appeal to as wide a market as possible and consequently must address common denominator issues to achieve volume sales. If this is a disadvantage, it should be recognised that such standardisation, in economic terms, spreads the costs of production over a larger number of users. It also encourages portability both of software, and of staff and students. There are fewer disincentives for parents to move from one area to another or to opt for one school as against another because their children can pick up their studies using the same software. Staff, once trained, can be used in any school or college where material of the appropriate level is to be taught. Hardware purchasing can be in bulk and thus at a higher rate of discount than otherwise might be available, and the capital invested in software by LEAs can be most efficiently used. A series of advantages that surely outweigh the possibility of danger.

But, in producing the standardised software, a shortage of 'good' programmers may exacerbate the problems of creation and implementation, leaving government and other monied sources to distort the content of educational packages to suit their covert aims. These slightly paranoid anxieties were actually expressed when it was suggested that textbooks should be introduced into the school system. It is no surprise to see their reappearance at this time. For most practical purposes, this is probably an unreal problem and, in the same way as printing produced an explosion of written sources, the computer will probably produce a multiplicity of machine-readable materials. The potential market is certainly there. Books dealing with the same topic material are frequently written from different points of view and with different biases. Thus, a history text may either give a dry factual recital of events, or may have a thematic orientation or a political bias. From the point of view of the philosophy of education, is it desirable that students should be exposed to the full range of written materials on a particular topic or should educators censor and control access to information through library buying policies and carefully prepared reading lists? The creation of the same diversity of material in machine-readable form, may crystalise the educational debate on this issue.

5.3 Is the computer more or less impersonal than the average classroom?

More darkly, it has been suggested that there is a particular danger in the case of a computer for it may be used so as to minimise human development and interactions. The very impersonality of the machine is said to potentially interfere with a child's social and psychological development for, since by definition the machine is not human, it does not have the human capacities necessary to function effectively as a teacher. "Of course a CAI system is not a human being. It is not a good friend, a warm teacher, nor a loving parent. But once a computer has been taught how to deal constructively with individual intellectual differences, it can deal more rapidly and more patiently with these differences than can a 'live' friend or teacher or parent." (4) This crystalises the nature of the debate. The extreme human-centred lobby would emotively reject machine-based education as likely to produce zombies, creatures incapable or original thought. Those who would accept the contribution which machines can make would look to the positive virtues which can be programmed into the machine but which may not always be present or possible to the human.

The obsessive and addictive reaction of many young persons to the computer-based games machine like Pac-man and Space Invaders, has had conflicting results. At one end of the scale, folk heroes have emerged who are said to have achieved extraordinary levels of skill, while all such games encourage a tendency towards private effort and introversion. The playing of the majority of computer games is a competition between the user and the computer based upon the exciting premise, "one false move and you're dead." Movement, sound and colour are key elements in the interaction between game and player and they provide direct feedback in the player's performance from moment to moment, draw attention to critical aspects of the game, and generally seek to encourage the player to strive towards higher levels of achievement.

The player may have a degree of control in the computer-generated environment but, in the long-term, the odds against success are great. However, the player's success is associated with feelings of power which are reinforced by the sound and graphics. Added to this are the immediacy of the feedback on levels of performance – in all of the games, the player can see and hear an immediate response to the input. Further, there are unlimited achievment levels. "Such undivided attention and relentless response rates are demanded of the player even though the player never actually wins; the player can only improve." (5) The resultant blend is highly addictive. Parallelling the development of the games machine, the introduction of technology into the home in the form of television, video recorder and hi-fi sound system, reinforces a drift away from community-based social activities. The result of such excessive use of home-based entertainment may be to encourage alienation in the young, while outside the home, the use of portable sound systems reduces the opportunity for social interactions.

In the educational environment, the conventional methods for the teaching of basic skills do not match up to the excitement of the computer games, nor the sophistication of the home-based entertainment technology. Yet the same skills of hand-to-eye coordination and prediction that make, say, Pac-man so exciting are the central requirements of such skills as handwriting. It is true that every technological development has the potential to dehumanise the learning process. But, if the challenge of the new technology is not adapted to use in the classrooms, there is the real danger that the children of the future will not identify with the aspirations of the teachers and not accept learning opportunities presented in a non-technological way. The technology which is used in computer games is also available for CAL, and the question whether similar techniques could be used to enhance the learning situation, should not lightly be dismissed.

However, throughout society, the potential problem is exacerbated by the fact that much of the technology is designed by engineers without the advice or assistance of teachers, counsellors and psychologists. The characteristics which would be most useful to the world of education are not necessarily even considered, let alone incorporated into the designs of equipment. The earliest computers required specialist staff to operate it. Many of today's designers forget that non-technical individuals are likely to be using the new hardware, and make assumptions in the design and in the documentation, of technical competence and expertise which are not justifiable. Sometimes, the designers do refer to the issue of the man/machine interface, but still produce a highly technical interface because the hardware is to be multi-purpose and, to keep costs down, user friendliness is sacrificed. Thus, even to do the simple things can require advanced understanding.

Because hardware was expensive, the ethic in software design terms, was to cause the machinery to work to its optimum level of performance. Given that the machines would be tended by professionals with a high level of technical expertise, the users' actual needs were not really considered in the formulation of user interfaces, nor in terms of software function. Most machines now have substantial memories and increasingly powerful computational abilities, so there are no longer the same arguments for having to make the systems efficient. But old thinking habits diehard, and the same specialist barriers still tend to be incorporated into the modern equipment. This neglects the fundamental proposition that, in the last analysis, as Jean Barton puts it, "The answer to how the computer can facilitate the kind of thinking demanded by a computer age will not come from computer "experts". It lies at the heart of the realm where educators are "experts" - the teaching-thinking-learning process." (6)

In a sense, the answer to this question of impersonality and alienation depends upon what happens in the standard teacher-led classroom. The norm is that only the best and the worst students receive any personal attention from the teacher. With individualised teaching systems, significant personality changes have been observed as previously disadvantaged students found new confidence. To suggest that CAL may dehumanise the teaching environment is to misstate the problem. Human teachers may also be responsible for teaching which is mechanical and impersonal. In many cases, the formal lesson or lecture is a positive barrier between the teacher and the class behind which the teacher hides his or her lack of real understanding, and avoids the free-wheeling discussion situation where the paucity of information might be detected. The ideal would always be a discourse where both the teacher and the learner must be able to defend their own assertions of truth. The teacher will attempt to achieve this by constructing convincing explanations and selecting examples appropriate for the learners. Yet, in the formal class, interruptions are discouraged on the grounds of pressure of time to cover the material specified in the curriculum. It is customary to "... stress control over student behaviour and over the conditions of learning. The teacher is a manager who seeks to accomplish specific objectives as quickly and as efficiently as possible." (7) The only reasonable generalisations are therefore that there are good teaching methodologies and bad teaching methodologies, and that the system is staffed by good teachers, average teachers and some bad teachers.

It is certainly not necessary for the use of computers to produce a dehumanised learning environment. In this instance, the truth is simple. Although cliched science fiction has frequently presented models of threatening robots in future computerised dystopias, for the immediately foreseeable future, it will remain the responsibility of the humans to set the goals of education, and to create the means and the materials to be used. Thus, one of the advantages of CAL might be said to be that there is a stimulating intellectual challenge to the teacher to manage the innovation properly. The teacher will be forced to constructively reappraise existing methodology which may produce a whole range of improvements, not necessarily directly concerned with CAL.

Further, in the average classroom, one might expect the opposite to dehumanisation in that the students will be able to avoid the precise regimentation that large class teaching can impose upon the group, and will achieve a significantly greater opportunity for personalised tuition. The primary imperative of all teaching is getting to know, and then meeting, the needs of the individual student. It has long been recognised that students respond differently to criticism or encouragement, and learn more if the teacher understands their attitudes and behaviour. At present levels of availability, CAL software does not replace a teacher because it is difficult to give the computer the ability to recognise the student's needs. Although a computer can count how many wrong answers have been given in a series of test questions, or apply rules to draw inferences from which questions have been answered wrongly, (viz. author languages permit error counts and allow topics to be flagged when they have been shown to be understood), the computer is trying to make sense of mere numbers. An inanimate machine cannot look into a student's eyes and decide, say, whether there is a real difficulty of understanding, or whether the student is quickly trying to guess the answer, but it supplements a teacher in the same manner as other teaching aids.

Moreover, many teachers gain only an outline view of a student's capacity. There is therefore a greater opportunity for the

124

teacher to discover where students have had difficulty and how much effort and time has been used by each student, information which might not be available using the human-based approach. As more software becomes available, CAL could grow like team-teaching but, instead of two or more teachers to the same group, the human teacher works with CAL in the same room. However, although the computer may learn about the student users, it does not learn about teaching itself. Teachers and curriculum planners therefore have a responsibility to establish a complementary relationship between the CAL portion of the course and the material presented by the teacher, students, textbooks or other stimulus material. However, it must also be said that the curriculum is the teacher's perception of what children or students of particular ages or apparent skill levels can or cannot do. It is often the case that, allowed the opportunity, learners can achieve far more than teachers expect.

5.4 What are tests for?

In any form of assessment, the teacher should always be able to identify the educational purpose to be fulfilled by the particular method adopted. Tests are useful to determine the following:

.   Has the student learned what the teacher intended? – this involves grading the student depending upon whether the material has been mastered or not, or

.   has previously mastered material has been remembered, say, after a holiday. Either way, this will help to determine whether the material presented was too easy or too difficult, and

.   whether new concepts are treated adequately? Such tests are termed criterion-referenced and enable the teacher to provide adequate revision of topics found not to be understood or to form a more general view about the quality of the teaching and, finally,

.   how much time has it taken the students to reach and consolidate understanding?

Sometimes the test will be an informal quiz as a form of spot check. On other occasions, it will be a formal examination, in which case the test is likely to be norm-referenced, i.e. the purpose will be to rank the students by reference to their per-formance. To that extent, testing may be an amusement or it may have a fundamental effect upon a person's future education options or career. The use of tests not only assures both the teachers and the learners that objectives are being met, but it also provides a reliable basis for reporting progress to parents, employers or other interested parties. For these purposes, it is proposed to separate tests from examinations and to assume that educational tests have not the same level of finality as examinations.

5.4.1 What is diagnostic testing?

In the long term, testing is really only useful if it has a diagnostic purpose. Thus, the teacher should always clearly identify the objectives of the test. To be valid, Gagne proposes the following question: "Is the performance required during assessment the same performance as that described in the [educational] objective?" (13) i.e. there must be a 'congruence' between the curriculum objective(s) and the purposes of the test. This should facilitate the creation of whichever form of assessment is likely to provide the most useful information, setting such parameters as the number and type of questions, time constraints, and so on. These objectives should also be born in mind when writing the individual questions, so that only the desired information is elicited and not some unrelated matter.

When actually drafting the questions, it should not be an explicit aim to provide questions which are either easy or difficult. The need is to provide an accurate measure of each student's capability as specified in the course objectives. If students fail to reach standards set in the particular test, this may be described as non-achievement testing. The real aim of this form of testing is not to discriminate between the students, but to discover the limits in what the students have learned. Having drawn up the questions, it is then necessary to consider whether feedback should be given. In an informal test, immediate feedback is essential, perhaps giving a running score, and certainly identifying incorrect answers to reduce the possibility of the student believing that the computer is confirming the answer as correct by failing to comment. However, in more formal uses of the test, results may be deferred to allow review of the students' performance by the human tester.

Normally, teachers would want the ability to identify the real problems experienced by each student. It is not sufficient to simply observe symptoms. At the end of the test, the most useful information would be why the student made the mistakes actually made. One of the factors which will help the diagnosis is the consistency of the learner's responses. Only groups of questions can probe at the ability of the student to perform tasks of a given class. A single question will not produce reliable evidence because a successful response may be produced because a rote-learned answer has been memorised, and is applied without any

126

real understanding. An interdependent sequence of questions which cumulatively represent the target objectives, is more likely to produce reliable evidence, ironing out careless errors produced by a misreading of the question, and demonstrating whether the student is guessing the answers, or has actually mastered the appropriate skills.

Once it becomes apparent that the student holds an incorrect view, it must be established whether the student has a good reason for believing the given proposition. The easier method of identifying the reason for error would be to ask each student to explain the thinking processes involved in the making of each answer. However, students are frequently too shy or embarrassed to make coherent explanations, or they invent suitable rationalisations to save face, investing the teacher with judgemental qualities often quite in excess of reality. In a mechanised environment, some form of computer assessment of error is therefore useful in that it relies upon private observation. Most teachers through experience can identify the most usual types and causes of error in the materials which they teach. The storage of such errors in a comparator file will enable the computer to establish patterns of error – e.g. that the student consistently misjudges arithmetic or algebraic calculations, making the same type of computational error. Once remedial action has been taken to correct the error, and apparent mastery is demonstrated, subsequent testing is needed to show temporal dependability of mastery, i.e. that what is understood on Tuesday is still in working order the following Monday. Finally, if the skills laid down in the curriculum are hierarchical, then only when a reasonable degree of permanence is achieved in the performance of intermediate skills, can target skills be safely approached.

There will inevitably be problems of test anxiety in some students. The degree of anxiety actually experienced is likely to be a direct function of the importance of the test as perceived by the student, in the light of the self-perceived level of ability. If the testing is computerised, test anxiety may be aggravated by computer anxiety in those who are intimidated by the paraphenalia of the keyboard and screen. This is more fully discussed in section 5.7. However, at this stage, it is necessary to consider whether there is any evidence that students perform less well in the automated environment. The work of David Elwood (9) in respect of the psychological Wechsler Adult Intelligence Scale test-retest shows that there is no significant difference in results as between an automated test and a face-to-face test. This would support automation, if only on the grounds that it would save professional man hours and other associated costs in the testing process, and allow an increase in the number of objective behavioural measurements that automated testing could make available for clinical decision making.

5.4.2 Can the computer help the tester?

On a purely practical level, simple wordprocessors can be used to set tests. Banks of questions can be stored and printed out in any preset order, or in a random order, or according to some criteria of difficulty. If this is done between several teachers whether in the same school, college or university, or pooled between several contributing institutions, it gives the individual teacher potential access to questions of immense range and variety. It also reduces the creative burden on each teacher who can find it increasingly difficult to create new questions. Further, it reduces the chances of effort being duplicated and it might encourage greater collaboration between different educational establishments with all the opportunities for enrichment that would offer. The danger is that a teacher might unthinkingly pick questions from the pool without actually considering whether they were suitable for the particular students to be tested. It is tempting to believe that all the questions stored would be correct and of a high standard. Such optimism may not be wholly justifiable. There may also be security problems if hackers were to gain access to a pool of questions from which an examination was to be drawn. Alternatively, a computer can actually generate the questions - a template of the question is stored together with the numerical parameters of the elements which the machine is to generate. Within the constraints specified, the computer can then create as many questions as are required.

It should also be noted that some tests could not exist but for the computer, e.g. simulations of flying aircraft of different types as a requirement of CAA approval.

5.5 How are tests marked?

The traditional form of hand-written answer could be valued on the basis of accuracy and form of presentation as much as content. Once the use of computers is admitted, the use of spelling checkers and the computer's computational skills challenges traditional assessment criteria. For example, should there be a tranche of marks set aside for technical mastery of the computer-aided functions? This is the same problem as that faced by maths and science teachers over the use of the electronic calculator. But given that, in the foreseeable future, most routine tests will have only limited free language opportunity for the students to exploit, it would be possible to give the computer criteria against which to judge each answer and to award a mark.

However, this presupposes that the purpose of the test is norm-referenced, i.e. providing scores which will compare each student's performance with that of a group which may be the peer group, or last year's group, or any other legitimate comparator, and therefore be standardised. Given that the aim is usually to provide a more global basis of assessment, combining and integrating different skills and capabilities, the questions in a norm-referenced test will often encompass a variety of objectives and will not necessarily provide reliable evidence of the mastery of the component objectives. Thus, if the real purpose of the test is merely to identify what the student has not understood, it is gratuitous to award a mark and may actually mislead the student.

A further decision is that the computer can store all the answers given, and record whether any answer was changed. Thus, the human tester could give some credit if the right answer was originally given and then changed. This may produce a fair result and parallel the practice in written examinations, for there is never any need to rely upon the absolute of the recorded final answer.

5.6   Should the examination system be modified?

Any form of testing or examination is a delicate balance between the need to obtain some form of objective measure of performance, and the need to provide an emotionally safe way in which an individual student can provide evidence of work done. If a student has worked in a self-directed mode, and has produce unco-ordinated learning, this may be difficult to assess in the conventional examination system. That this argument should be raised in the context of possible computerisation can be worrying. It would be more reassuring if the education establishment were worried that such was the pace of student development, that examinations were proving too simple for students. Instead, more recent reforms in the GCSE mode are aimed at simplifying examinations. The recently published guide to the GCSE, amongst other things, describes the new pattern for the examination of mathematics. "Traditionally maths has been about knowing the rules to deal with numbers, percentages, areas, equations and so on... GCSE should lead pupils to see that maths can be used to solve practical problems in everyday situations... One approach is to let pupils explore their own ways of using what they know about numbers, shapes and so on, rather than insisting that results be reached by one fixed, ideal method."

5.7 How can stress in examinations be reduced?

Duncan N. Hansen (10) argues the case for variable examination testing where the computer stores an interlocking series of questions which follow different pathways to different levels of complexity or difficulty. By success or failure, the examinee 'selects' the next question, either more difficult or less difficult respectively. He concludes that such tests keep student confidence by not exposing the weaker students to the most difficult questions where failure may be demoralising. Grading is still by performance but with less anxiety to the examinee. The aim is to remove or reduce the overtly normative format inherent in the static test.

All conventional success/failure examinations have some form of time constraint imposed which will inevitably give rise to stress in some examinees. If such stress is to be kept within reasonable limits, and students are to be encouraged to "do their best", the reason for the time limitations must be understood, viz. there is the purely logistical reason that the examiner could not conveniently read or assess more material, or that students must not confuse volume with quality. In fact, it is not unreasonable to suggest that it should be an annual item of business for examiners to consider whether to take steps to bolster and support student self-confidence.

There are, however, other forms of examination. Hence, in the so-called "actual achievement" or "success-only" examinations, students can be given as much time as they want in order to finish the problems. In general, this can help to reduce anxiety and to improve performance. Arguably, this should be the method of testing to determine whether promotion to another educational level should take place, or some equally important transition is to be achieved. After all, time is the easiest constraint to alter. Alternatively, if the conventionally-timed examination is preferred, the content of the examination should be reduced so that time becomes less of a problem.

School experiences may be presumed the primary source of children's anxiety over being tested. In his research, Hill assumes that some children may be classified as low anxiety, both because of their general history of success in school, and because they have had positive interactions with adults in evaluative settings. He suggests that these children have strong motives to approach success, and relatively weaker motives to avoid failure. (11) On the other hand, those children who may be classified as high anxiety, are usually known to have a history of frequent school failure, and have often had punitive interactions with adults in evaluative settings. These negative experiences are assumed to have a precise effect. Namely, they are likely to strengthen the high anxiety child's motives to avoid failure and to gain success, but that such a child is more likely to want to avoid failure than to approach success.

The team of Hill and Eaton therefore tested groups of children with different anxiety levels. In some situations which were designated "success-only", the testees were shown the arithmetical problems they were about to attempt, and were allowed to successfully practice the method. The apparent time limit in the test itself could be adjusted by the tester so that enough time to complete each problem undertaken was always given, thereby encouraging complete success. In other situations which were designated a mixture of success and failure, a formalised test was given with the time limits adjusted to the testees' actual performance levels so that all the testees were able to complete only about two thirds of the problems attempted. The testees were monitored to determine time spent concentrating on each problem and to see whether they attempted to cheat.

The results predictably showed that high anxiety children performed poorly in comparison with low anxiety children where success and failure were mixed. But under "success-only" conditions, high anxiety children almost matched the performance of their low anxiety counterparts, going almost as fast, making just a few more errors, and cheating only somewhat more often. Thus, the disruptive effects of evaluation anxiety were reduced in the "success-only" situation. The experiment therefore fulfilled its design expectations of minimising the failure motives and, more importantly, of allowing the success motives to predominate. Hill and Eaton conclude, "The fact that high anxious children both went as fast and were as accurate as less anxious children suggests that anxious children have the specific skills necessary to perform well on basic addition problems, although they fail to do so under testing conditions involving time pressure and failure, two aspects of many achievement, aptitude, and educational tests." (12)

Such results tend to prove that poor performance is not necessarily a function of mastery, but is more likely to be caused by poor test or examination technique. Because of evaluation anxiety, many students fail to show what they have learned, i.e. they know the material but are unable to demonstrate this knowledge in the test situation. This anxiety has an increasingly debilitating effect on motivation, and self-defence mechanisms encourage students not to take the tests, or to rely on externalised reasons for poor performance (see section 2.5) If the testing situation can be restructured to minimise the debilitating motivational tendencies, the high anxiety testee can perform up to ability. One of the primary advantages of computerisation is that high anxiety students can practice more to gain in confidence as long as the structuring of the testing is controlled and patterned to actual ability levels. The computer can also privately coach the students in testing methodology and encourage the ability to cope in a stressful situation. Such an individualised program would be disproportionately expensive to staff using humans, but is well within machine capacity as long as the program is sufficiently friendly.

If the public demand greater accountability from educators, the response is often to use tests of competency or achievement. Teachers are to be assessed, schools are to be inspected and examinations revamped. The trend is to demand better results as if this proves greater learning. However, such demands simply increase the pressure in the testing situation. The more important the test, e.g. the 11 plus, the more likely is morale to be affected. Further, if students are told that the examination is difficult, this increases the likelihood of stress. Students should always be given realistic information so that more accurate expectations can be formed, and reassured that the examiner will always take account of effort and not simple objective performance. Examination or test instructions should always be simple to reduce worry about method and allow the students to concentrate on the material to be tested. Williams has found that children who are told that only a low proportion of correct answers are expected thus changing the child's expectation of success and failure, perform more successfully. (13). Similarly Zigler and Butterfield achieved higher IQ test results from children through supportive examiner comments and confirming success experiences. (14)

A practical example of computer-based progress-testing strategy is provided by the Strathclyde QL project where the tester stores questions on the VAX mainframe, the students log in using their QLs and transfer the file of current questions into the QL memory. Supplementary software in the QL displays the questions and collects the answers. These are then fed back into the VAX for analysis. (15) Although this is presently used as a form of student feedback mechanism, there is no reason why it should not be extended to formal examinations or continuous assessment.

5.8   How would computerised examinations work?

In any computerised examination system, difficult design decisions would have to be taken. Having started the examination, the student needs to have a running check available of the amount of time remaining, and the number and, where possible, the identity of the questions still to be answered. This presupposes that the student may skip questions which cannot immediately be answered, and will want return to them later. It also assumes no element of student choice in the questions to be answered. However, it may not assist anxious students to have a continuous display of time and the number of questions remaining, because this will be a constant reinforcer of the pressure. On the other

132

hand, the more procedural techniques which an examinee has to remember, the more opportunity there is for error and resultant panic. To allow the facility of switching the display on and off at will, or the student to ask the specific question, may take up valuable time.

The computer could, if there was no element of student choice, sequentially present the questions for consideration. If a question is passed without answering, after a suitable warning message, it can be returned to when the sequence of questions is exhausted. The examinee should also be allowed to return to any question and to change the answer given. It would be heartless of an examiner to force an examinee to sit through an entire examination, knowing that the answer given to the first question in the heat of the moment was wrong. The ideal would be to allow the examinee to flag any answer that was not completely satisfactory, and to return to it either when inspiration strikes, or for more thought at the end if time permits.

If the student does not ask for time to be displayed, the machine might in any event give a warning, say, half an hour from the end of the examination. This would be particularly important if time appears to be a problem, given the number of questions which remain to be answered. The difficulty in this is to determine whether the examinee should be given the maximum possible control over the system, or whether information should be forced upon the examinee. This may be determined by the extent to which the students have practiced upon the computer. But, stress in the actuality of examinations does lead to non-typical behaviour, no matter what the pre-examination practice has led the examiners to expect. The best solution is probably to allow the examinees as much flexibility as possible.

It would normally be considered desirable to allow for some human supervision of the computer's evaluation of student's performance. This might be merely at the stage of development where independent individuals might verify the software's accuracy, and the propriety of individual questions contained within the program. On the day of the examination, the operating efficiency of the hardware should be certified by the examination supervisors. However, if the questions were all of a type that are susceptible of computerised judgement, there is no reason in principle why the computer could not immediately give out a result, perhaps expressed to be provisional or subject to review. The problem is that most examiners build in the power to compensate for one bad mark in a diet of examinations if the overall average is of a pass standard. Similarly, a board of examiners may scale up the marks if student performance is uniformly poor, perhaps suggesting a bad examination standard in the writing of questions. If students were given a premature indication of performance, they might become unjustifiably disheartened and either give up altogether, or stop trying in subsequent parts of the examination diet, both resulting in an unfair assessment being made of student worth.

As to feedback on individual questions, in answering a multiple choice question, if an answer of the wrong type is given, e.g. a number instead of a letter, there should be immediate helpful advice. In any examination whether long or short, it would be possible to give the examinee helful or encouraging comments on performance, and generally to seek to counteract the tendency towards post-exam depression. But this raises the question of whether it is appropriate to distract an examinee with anything more than a brief remark. Then, if the remarks were only given if the individual answer was correct, the long silences could become depressing. If the computer makes equivocal comments, the student may unreasonably believe that success has been achieved and feel the failure all the more keenly when it is announced.

The computer could, of course, supply a hard copy of all the questions asked, but should examinees be allowed a copy of all their answers to the questions? This might be useful if the student wished to appeal against the result because the questions and the answers given could be independently validated. It also offers some security check for the student who might fear data loss after the examination. However, in any post mortem, the student might be unreasonably pessimistic about performance and become demoralised. Whether or not a student requests a print out, or is given one as a matter of course, the examiners should consider having a paper copy in addition to tape or disc copies as a security precaution against system failure. A corruption in archiving after an examination could prove disasterous. The Data Protection Act allows access to the results if they are stored on system. If no copy is taken by the examinee, perhaps the examining body should consider allowing access to the answers given if they are also stored on system?

Should all the students attend the same site for taking the examination, human staff can check the identity of examinees. The problem of cheating if the examinee may take the examination from a remote terminal is acute and cannot easily be solved without the expenditure of a large amount of human supervisory time in visiting all terminals while the examination is in progress. A final and fundamental issue is the need for an absolutely robust software and hardware system. If students are going to be judged on the basis of their machine-based performance, the machine must not fail them by losing any answers made through software error. Regular backup copies must also be taken to minimise the effect of a power failure in the computer centre. However, any system failure during the examination is likely to prove very demoralising for examinees and even extraordinary precautions should be seen to be taken to prevent the students from being prejudiced.

References

(1) Technology in the Coming Century. Arno Penzias. collected in Cohabiting with Computers. p.135.

(2) University-Industry Partnership in Computer Science. Lewis M.Branscomb. collected in Cohabiting with Computers. p.114.

(3) So far, so good. Ivan Reid. collected in Teachers, computers and the classroom. pp.184/95 at p.185.

(4) Will the Computer Kill Education? Bruce L.Hicks. (1970) 34 The Educational Forum 312.

(5) Computer-Using Special Learners. Janis Morariu. collected in Capitol-izing on Computers in Education. p.175.

(6) Literacy is not enough: The Computer as a Bridge Between Psychological Research and Educational Practice. Jean M.Barton. collected in Capitol-izing on Computers in Education. p.199.

(7) An Appraisal of Computer-Assisted Learning in the United Kingdom. J.R.Hartley. collected in Selected Readings in Computer-Based Learning. pp.30/43 at p.32.

(8) Principles of Instructional Design. Robert M. Gagne and Leslie J. Briggs. p.220.

(9) Automated versus Face-to-Face Intelligence Testing: Comparison of Test-retest Reliabilities. David L.Elwood. (1972) 4(3) Int J. Man-Machine Studies 363/9.

(10) An Investigation of Computer-Based Science Testing. collected in CAI. A Book of Readings. p.209.

(11) Anxiety in the evaluative context. Kennedy T.Hill. collected in Young Child. (Vol 2). W.W. Hartup (ed) Washington DC. National Association of the Education of Young Children. 1972.

(12) The interaction of text anxiety and success - failure experiences in determining children's arithmetic performance. Kennedy T. Hill and Warren O. Eaton. (1977) 13(3) Developmental Psychology 205/11 at p. 209.

(13) Individual differences in achievement test presentations and evaluation anxiety. J. P. Williams. Doctoral dissertation. University of Illinois. 1976.

(14) Motivational aspects of changes in IQ test performance of culturally deprived nursury school children. E.F. Zigler and E.C. Butterfield. (1968) 39 Child Development 1/14.

(15) IUCC Proceedings of the Management Conference. p.7. The QL (Quantum Leap) is a small but powerful computer made by Sir Clive Sinclair.

CHAPTER 6

THE PROBLEMS TO BE FACED WHEN MAKING A CHANGE

If the decision to introduce computers into the education environment is taken, it may be difficult to persuade teachers that the change is an improvement. This chapter therefore examines the various strategies for managing that change, and considers whether it is possible to overcome the likely resistance from both teachers and administrators.

6.1   Introduction

6.1.1 Persuading teachers to accept CAL when it appears to be a competing form of instruction is a difficult problem

To a greater or lesser extent, the bulk of teachers' professional activities are constrained by the broad guidelines laid down in course curricula and syllabuses. The test to determine the true power of these constraints is normally based on the interaction of a number of variables including the type of institution, the grade of the particular teacher and the nature of the educational aims to be met in the particular course for the identified group of learners. However, although it will be found that some staff retain a high degree of autonomy, the majority of teachers will be seen to be subject to a fairly rigorous degree of control in the selection of course content and in the specification of course aims. Indeed, it may be argued that all teachers should be accountable for what is taught and the way in which it is taught. But if the general issues of Governmental intervention in the negotiations to determine the terms and conditions of employment, and the apparent desire to promote centralisation of core curriculum development, are ignored, there is a limit to any teacher's capacity to tolerate educational interference from outsiders. At some point, the teacher's own professional judgement ought to be allowed its proper say with a view to maintaining a degree of continuity and stability. Such stability would be preserved not only for the teachers, but also for the students, for both groups have a right to expect an evolutionary, rather than a revolutionary, approach to curriculum development and teaching methodology.

A balance must therefore be maintained between the need to provide a coherent course of studies for each cohort of students, and the need to reflect changes in both the individual subject disciplines and society at large. The pace of change in any environment will be determined by the interaction of both endogenous and exogenous factors. In the industrial or commercial context, change may suddenly be forced by technological innovation. New plant or processes may produce such cost benefits that not to adopt the fruits of research may be to face bankruptcy in an ever less forgiving market place. Whereas in the education system, students may take years to progress through the system and because the commercial cost benefit approach is not generally applied, the need for change is not seen to be as urgent. A further reason for the apparent lack of a dynamic to stimulate change lies in the nature of the standard course curriculum.

6.1.2 What is a curriculum?

For these purposes, the term "curriculum" is intended to refer to a document that is no more than an approximation of an ideal. The usual course description cannot realistically seek to achieve sufficient detail of content and approach to absolutely bind all those involved in a rigid framework. If it was to be attempted, the length and complexity of a document which sought to produce a definitive course would stiffle creativity and make spontaneity unlikely, and might in itself become a barrier to communication. The drafters of any curriculum therefore hope to express an ideal approach with as much detail as is consistent with the policy of the appropriate supervisory agency – which might be a teacher in a responsibility post, a local university or a national regulatory body. The effect is to create an environment of some flexibility in which responsibility is delegated to the individual teachers to shape and direct each course for the benefit of the individual groups of students.

It is however inevitable that curricula will change. No matter how static the core discipline, e.g. as in latin, classical greek or, to some extent, the modern languages, theories of learning and styles of teaching do require the review and updating of course outlines and aims. When any given curriculum is to be modified, a consultative approach is preferable. Although it will be a slower process, it should avoid the excesses which can result from the arbitary exercise of remote authority. Thus, those responsible for masterminding the transition should take account of the comments of those who have practical experience of the course, should consider any requirements specified by existing organisations and structures, and should also seek to produce an outline scheme which is capable of being effective within a framework of human relationships, i.e. between teachers and learners. By seeking a synthesis of experience which has a tendency towards conservatism and theory which tends to be progressive, more effective change may be achieved.

6.2 What is the theoretical basis of change?

In sociological terms, the different tiers of the educational hierarchy are termed "domains". A failure to properly communicate between the various domains can cause severe difficulties. Kousez and Mico (1) have defined the term "domain" as a "sphere of influence or control claimed by a social entity... [which] is organised in functional and coherent ways that are appropriate to the performance of its primary task." Where domains are interactive, the actors in each domain resist any real or perceived threats from the other domains and seek to maintain the stability of the hierarchy. Within the education system, central government determines core policy, delegating more detailed planning responsibility to both national and local bodies, with implementation to be by the head teachers, college directors and Vice Chancellors, and their respective staff. But schools, colleges and universities are not free markets. They are arranged, to a greater or lesser extent, in a hierarchy. As students move through the system, they require the opportunity to make an orderly progression from each topic at its given academic level to the next. To achieve this desirable co-ordination, decisions about curricula are taken by headmasters or heads of department at their own discretion, but against a background of consultation with administrators or national bodies.

Yehuda Bien (2) builds on this in a discussion of the relationships which exist between schools, their principals and administrators, "Personalities tend to be in constant tension and involved in a struggle for power and control. The actors have different viewpoints, follow different norms and cannot agree on a pattern of action. A mutual adaptation develops, convenient to teachers and principals, on a non-interference basis." He argues that conflicts between the domains are inevitable, yet if people are to develop within a system, it can only occur if each individual's role is carefully defined. Once it is recognised that conflict is inevitable, those caught up in the system may concentrate more on understanding each other's point of view. Without this understanding, teachers in particular will tend to feel burdened by the experience of conflict and merely become demoralised in the face of what is perceived to be insensitive interference by non-specialists interested only in their own status and prestige.

Within this stressful context, one of the major contemporary curriculum decisions to be taken is the degree to which computers should be referred to or incorporated. George McMeen comments, "As technology outdistances education in periods of rapid technological advancement, the gap between technological invention and teacher utilisation becomes all the more noticeable. If anything positive can be said about this gap, it might be that teachers have the time to formulate a planned approach for integrating the new technology into the curriculum, as they become more familiar with that technology. But how large must this gap become before its effect is deleterious?" (3) Computers in general, and CAL in particular, have a clear potential, but present levels of activity do not suggest that the gap will quickly be closed. Indeed, without positive intervention, the introduction of any new material into the curriculum will take place in a passively evolutionary way as the material gradually seeps in from the real world, a process which tends to take about 20 years. Hence, in discussing the diffusion of Keynesian macro-economics through the American High School System, Voege reports, "The adoption period on the secondary school level was about twenty three years. This finding is in reasonably good agreement with those by Mort and Bushnell to the effect that schools tend to adopt ideas about twenty to twenty five years after they first become available." (4)

The perennial problem is that change can only occur when individuals have learned the new materials. To teach a topic, the school system must be able to guarantee a supply of appropriately qualified teachers. This depends upon higher education generally, or the teacher training system in particular, having suitable course elements available. If no such courses exist, higher education must be persuaded to change. This may be a slow process if no adequate books or other teaching materials exist, and if there is no real consensus as to course content. Further, administrators, existing teachers and parents must perceive the new subject as acceptable and, until it is examinable and produces appropriate qualifications for the increasing meritocracy in the job market to admire, there is unlikely to be much pressure for change. Further, examination boards are unwilling to commit resources to new subject areas unless there is a suitable number of candidates to make the expenditure worthwhile. So, given the complexity of the interlocking chicken–and–egg process, it is perhaps remarkable that curriculum change only takes twenty years.

However, speed is not necessarily appropriate, for too rapid an introduction of new ideas may produce thoughtless or inconsequential results. Thus, for example, teachers are going to have to be encouraged to break their rather more individualised working patterns, and to adopt a more co–operative approach. M.P.Smith deals with an aspect of the problem in a report of a follow–up study of a local primary school science project. He found that the program had only survived in those schools in which it had been initiated for as long as the original developers had remained. However, the program did move with the developers to their new schools. It may therefore be seen that head teachers and colleagues were carried along by the enthusiasms of the committed, but allowed the projects to lapse when the source of confidence was removed. (5) The conclusion must be that the support of all those associated must be positively committed if the seed is to germinate and continuity of innovation is to be maintained independently of individuals. Although he was only discussing a small scale computerisation project, M. Gene Bailey advocates a gentle approach to gain and maintain the requisite staff confidence. "The decision to implement microcomputers over a period of several months, rather than in one "fell swoop" has proved to be an excellent one. The faculty are confident and comfortable and extremely eagre to explore new ways in which the micro can be used in the classroom." (6)

6.3   Change and the formal examination system

In these increasingly competitive times, when there is increasing discussion of teacher assessment for salary determination, one of the possible measures to determine the successfullness or otherwise of teachers, is the success of their students in the formal examination system. If teachers have a proven method to engineer acceptable examination results, there is consequently little incentive to abandon it in favour of an untried method. Moreover, even without the problem of assessment, internal pressures to maintain the same successful methodology come from colleagues and those in a supervisory role, who give considerable importance to the marks and comments offered by external examiners. The curriculum in schools and colleges is, of course, closely linked to the examination syllabuses. This discourages teachers from adopting CAL unless the available software is directly relevant to examination requirements. Further, if one school or college is rich in computing resources and another is known to have very little equipment, the teachers may justify not using the computers on examination courses on the ground of this disparity. This arises because examination syllabuses must be drawn up knowing that some schools will have inadequate resources, and therefore all schools may use minimal computing input and still cause their students to pass the exams.

If the perspective of the examination boards is considered, because technology is changing at an unusually fast rate, there is a consequent problem of any technological or social syllabus lagging behind developments in the real world. The time scale for adoption of new materials on to an examination syllabus is usually at least three years, William Bott reporting a five year period between the proposal for a change in a GCE syllabus and the acceptance of a reasonable number of students as candidates for examination on the modified curriculum. (7) Further, because examiners are constrained by what is written in the syllabus, it is difficult for them to compensate by asking questions on the more modern developments. Even if some change is accepted within the examination system itself, syllabuses are rarely completely rewritten to meet a new approach. The more usual response is simply to add elements which cover the new developments. This has the effect of maintaining the core material untouched, and can be taken as an incentive to the teaching profession not to make any real change. Although this impression could, to some extent, be counteracted in the style and content of the examination papers, there is a need for examiners to reflect the general syllabus and so not unfairly take candidates by surprise; and, as already indicated, not to discriminate against those examinees who have not had the opportunity to access appropriate technology.

This constraint at the examination syllabus level is matched in the schools and colleges where courses are self-examined (with or without external validation) or are non-examinable in the formal sense. Reporting the American experience in Gary, Indiana, McKinney and Westbury report, "These teachers could not escape, at least when they turned to the ritual of course writing, from the control of the old forms..." and even when new forms were made available through outside agencies, "many teachers experienced considerable difficulty as they struggled to enact the forms embodied in these new programs in their teaching." (8) They add that awareness of the need for change, and even of the methods for achieving some measure of change, does not produce the will or the power to persuade the teachers to make any substantive change. "In older institutions there is the influence, finally, of 'tradition' to be considered. It is difficult to pin down, and severely eroded by new attitudes imported by large numbers of newly recruited staff during periods of very rapid expansion." (9)

Given the more recent patterns of employment, staff mobility has declined as LEAs have responded to falling school rolls by taking teachers out of the system. Even the universities, for so long insulated from the principles of financial accountability, have

141

now found it necessary to reduce staff numbers with a consequent reduction in the opportunities for movement. The opportunity to mitigate the conservative effects of tradition is thereby reduced because one or two staff in a non-responsibility post will find conformity to tradition the least conflictual approach. Even those appointed to positions of influence can find the level of inertia too great to move without incurring great hostility, and social and organisational considerations may militate against seeking to undermine the status quo. Similarly, the legitimate desire of ambitious parents to see their children do well in examinations to further career aspirations may produce real pressure to maintain the status quo in schools and colleges, while students in Higher Education generally expect a route to a reasonable qualification to be provided. These attitudes are a direct and realistic response to the practices in the employment market place where more employers now look for good grades, and confirm the traditional methodology which has brought success in the past.

6.4　Is the teaching profession too conservative?

All teachers have the freedom to experiment in the classroom, and small changes can be made quite easily with the minimum of disruption, and without the need to seek official approval. However, small-scale changes do not affect the overall curriculum, nor amend the organisation of education. Any change which calls for expenditure of significant amounts of time and resources must be approved by the hierarchy. One factor is therefore that teachers often perceive the cost of acquiring the hardware and software, or of implementing a CAL strategy, to be high. The real cost of acquiring computing power in the form of stand-alones has in fact fallen dramatically as against the previously high capital outlay to acquire mainframe equipment. But because costs are thought to be high and there is shortage of good software, teachers consider this money not to be well-spent and so are less well-disposed towards it.

The problem is basically one of priorities in funding. It may be put simply: should LEAs or Higher Education institutions divert existing resources to the development of computing facilities, or should this be an additional item of expenditure? Costing is not simply a matter of initial capital outlay, for the calculation should also include the revenue implications of maintenance and servicing, consumables like ribbons and paper for the printers, telephone connect time and, possibly, insurance and replacement. It is difficult to lay down specific guidelines against which to estimate the cost of implementing a CAL system because computers may be used in such a variety of ways and a large number of variables will influence the decision-making. Thus, financial planning must reflect reality in that some institutions may have equipment donated, some may borrow equipment or time-share with other users, and others may have to buy from scratch. The same imponderables apply to software acquisition. Some LEAs may be able to negotiate licences to use software throughout the educational establishments within their jurisdiction. Alternatively, hardware distribution strategies now increasingly package software in the sales deal, while other software is given by manufacturers or made available through software exchange schemes. There may be staff with particular enthusiasms which may predispose the school or college to acquire particular equipment or packages, while other staff may have no in-house expertise and be tempted into acquiring unsuitable equipment. Once acquired, suitable accommodation may be made available with little structural alterations being necessary. But, equally, major structural surgery may be required. All these factors affect pattern of use and cost. Cost also includes staff time in planning the acquisition of the hardware and software, and implementation of the overall strategy.

This issue of cost is a critical question in many school teachers' minds at a time when issues of the rate support grant and consequential money available to fund salary increases dominate the political scene. If school, college and university budgets remain the same, CAL can only be introduced if other capital or revenue budgets are cut. This would be done at a time when it cannot clearly be seen whether computerisation will lead to a reduction in, or an enhancement of, the quality of the service which can be provided. The primary elements of education costs are salaries, buildings and administration, with the elements of expenditure on such things as books and equipment small and therefore considered vulnerable. But, if the costs of introducing CAL are taken out of, say, the visual aids budget, does this mean fewer slide projectors, etc.? If it is included in the library budget, does this mean empty shelves? Given the traditional reliance on book-based learning and its apparent success, there is considerable reluctance to prune a system which appears to be of proven worth.

Equally, if the financial provision is to be approached as additional capital expenditure, the cost benefit analysis must be seen to be favourable. There are substantial problems in performing such an analysis because of the number of intangible variables which ought to be considered. But if CAL is adding to the costs of a service which is already perceived as effective and efficient, it will be difficult to prove value for money by significantly improving the quality of that service. Given that one of the elements which must be considered is staff support, it should also be said that the existing shortage of computer hardware and software actually gives teachers an excuse not to develop computer-based skills and therefore to resist the change. This attitude can be modified through in-service training, but this is expensive in staff time, and it is impossible to consider the rapid retraining of even the staff responsible for directly affected subject areas, let alone the mass of teachers currently within the system.

Moreover, if staff are to be trained out of normal school or college hours, travelling expenses and other compensations for loss of free time may have to be negotiated and funded. The willingness or otherwise of staff and their union representatives to co-operate will, in part, be determined by the overall rationale which the management adopts. One outcome of a dispassionate cost benefit analysis might be that the capital represented by computers could be used to make the revenue-expensive teachers more efficient and therefore less numerous. The computerisation of education might simply become a way for LEAs, colleges or universities to manage the education system with fewer teachers. Such a policy would lead to significant administrative pressure against change. Because of the amount of capital already invested, existing plant and equipment cannot be radically changed or replaced. Similarly, teachers cannot quickly be retrained nor can sufficient numbers of experts be recruited to allievate the difficulties. The result is that only that change which is approved throughout the system, and has appropriate resources allocated to it, can proceed, and then only slowly.

These decisions are taken against a background in which computers have been seen as the latest "flavour of the month" and there is a problem of credibility in minds of many teachers and adminis-trators. CAL itself is dismissed as a fad. Others dismiss many of the computer-based activities as frivolous and a waste of time. Thus, until the new technology proves itself or otherwise acquires respectability, claims as to its powers will be met with healthy scepticism. After all, the teaching profession, "has fallen for educational quackery in the past and is reluctant to do so again." (10) Further, teachers do not want their normal routines disrupted by suddenly finding themselves responsible for computer security or additional timetabling functions to get the most out of the new resource.

However, although there may be resistance on the part of some staff and administrators, there is growing pressure from parent-teachers associations which have raised quite large sums of money in order to make the new technology available to their children in schools. This is problematical because the most active PTAs are middle and upper class. Their efforts, albeit laudable, do produce a further distortion to the geographical and demo-graphical divide between many schools and the resources which are available to support the learning activity. Only an egalitarian and national program can counteract this tendency by placing proper facilities in all schools regardless of class and ability ranges.

A further problem in the relationship with PTAs is that teaching is one of the few trades or professions whose central activities are at some time visible to every member of a society. For given that education is compulsory, all parents have opinions on the practice of teaching as it affected their schooling, and are increasingly inclined to voice contemporary concerns. Naturally, parents are aware that children are using computers outside the classroom, albeit often only for the playing of games, and so consider that it is the teachers' responsibility to use the new technology to facilitate learning.

The efforts of parents have been partially supported by schemes like the MEP (Microelectronics Education Programme) and the MIS (Micros in Schools Scheme). These programmes are not intended to be egalitarian, but are merely introductory. A single computer in each school does not make any real contribution to the schools and LEAs where resources are scarce as against those where generous parents provide comprehensive facilities. The difficulties of such schemes are highlighted by the experience with the MIS scheme which has not really helped because it does not seek to train the staff to use the computers thus acquired, nor does it seek to encourage the development of good software. The scheme has simply proved the old adage that equipment acquired for no perceived purpose is not likely to be used effectively. A further oddity is that the DTI has not supported the acquisition of printers for primary schools. There is therefore little incentive to teach the use of word processor and database programs which would normally be considered an essential part of any computer literacy course.

Yet the MEP Micro Primer Pack includes Factfile. This is a gentle introduction to the storage and retrieval of data on a micro, and has many of the features of a commercial database. In using this program, the student needs to make decisions about the nature and structure of information. Even if the use of such programs is, in the first instance, for trivial purposes, it has been shown to significantly enhance the ability of individuals to perform classificatory tasks. Further, by learning to use databases, students are introduced to the hypothesis testing strategy. Initially, most young children look for confirmatory rather than disconfirmatory evidence of a given hypothesis, but the use of appropriate software packages can begin the process of broadening the skill range. If this is to be done effectively, teachers should be aware of the skill differentials for the various age and ability ranges covered in the courses offered, and begin training for the full range of problem-solving skills at the optimum time for each group of students. The management function of the computer can be vital in monitoring student progress in order to select the optimum time for introducing each new skill.

One of Papert's strongest arguments for the use of LOGO is that it releases the student from the tyranny of correctness. Too often, students are trained in the simple regurgitation of narrative factual information which is marked either right or wrong. But if teachers are going to gain the maximum advantage from any of the major educational software packages where stud-

145

ents are to be encouraged to experiment and research, the staff must be specifically trained in the use of exploratory teaching methodology. Thus, students need to work with random material to practice the skill of selection, and they need to find partial or incorrect solutions so that self-critical processes of evaluation can be refined. The difficulty with this strategy is that it leads to the further problem of the evaluation of student performance. If teachers are to grade work, say, on a spreadsheet, is credit to be given merely for functionality, or for the use of materials, or novelty of approach? The answer probably lies in the teacher's purpose in using the given program, but this type of issue further adds to the pressure which some teachers feel, and helps to reinforce the negative attitude which they feel towards the technology.

If such strengths as exist are to be realised, wisdom in implementation will be required. However, one of the major social issues will be that if education makes the most of computers and CAL, one of the major effects may be the more general rate of change in society. This makes the introduction of CAL not just a problem for a conservative teaching profession, but also a political issue for society at large. The more computers come to represent support tools to the performance of tasks, the more flexibility this may introduce into the work environment. Thus, if unsupervised expert systems can be left to deal with the execution of standard routines, the human assumes the role of policy maker and manager. This has immense significance in terms of social roles and in social mobility, and in the type of training which will be required to promote social survival.

6.4.1 Is the individual teacher more likely than, say, a white collar worker to resist change?

Unlike employment in the majority of commercial work environments where a team-based approach is the norm, teachers tend to work autonomously with the minimum of interaction with other teachers. Their own professional learning pattern is based on continuing experience and is non-linear. Knowledge is up-dated through new editions of standard textbooks and through periodicals. There are occasional conferences where specialists can meet to discuss the latest developments. This is not neccessarily a bad thing. Every individual teacher requires a degree of stability in core knowledge if successful predictions are going to be made about the learning outcomes from teaching input. But one of the main effects of this traditional format is to confirm subject specialists in the unassailable rightness of their view of their subject.

This isolationist and frequently non-interdisciplinary approach, which is partly a result of training methods and partly a question of attitudes, can produce highly original solutions to problems, but equally leads to difficulties of confidence when confronted by new situations. Computer skills currently represent a "shortage" area and it is difficult to recruit competent staff. The burden of making an Information Technology input is therefore increasingly likely to fall on to those whose training and disposition may not be suited to the task, either from a self-perception point of view, or at all. As a result, many individual teachers now find themselves under pressure to develop their knowledge, and undoubtedly have anxieties about acquiring computer skills. At a simplistic level, these anxieties are amplified by pressures from two quite different sources:

(1) It is increasingly likely that the younger students will already have adjusted to the new technology. A proportion of these students will therefore have a high level of expectation in curriculum terms, that computers will be systematically used or referred to; and

(2) whatever the response of the students, those administrators who have recognised the need for some innovation, but without making proper provision for it to occur, issue instructions to press ahead with the implementation of the new technology. The result is either inactivity through fear or frustration.

The more general technophobic response has several aspects. In as much as the new computer systems emulate the human teaching process, and computers have acquired a reputation for threatening jobs in industry and commerce, it is more than understandable that some teachers should fear the introduction of the new technology. It is symptomatic of the reaction of the original Luddites, and is an obviously human emotional reaction. Alternatively, the fear response may be that teachers do not want to compete with the young who are seen as more capable. There is a less flattering reason possible in this particular context, because the teaching of programming skills is not susceptible to the "one page ahead of the students" approach. At an early stage, students can naturally ask questions which can only be answered given a comprehensive knowledge of the systems or language to be taught. Given the theoretical need not to slap down questioners so that student motivation and enthusiasm can be maintained, teachers recognise the need to do more early preparatory work and are consequently less enthusiastic.

A further reason for this lack of enthusiasm is suggested by Kathleen Hennessy in Microcomputers in Education. She argues that in most secondary schools, the teachers' main aim is supervision and not education. (11) This is attributed to the compulsory nature of attendance at an educational establishment until the arbitrarily selected age of sixteen. Sadly, although the law can be used to enforce physical attendance, it cannot force those attending to learn. Teachers therefore prefer an approach which minimises the chances of disruptive behaviour, i.e. little teaching so that more attention can be given to discipline, and

147

curriculum methods and materials that might disrupt classroom order are ignored.

That the priority actually accorded education is lower than might be expected is evidenced by the fact that schools also carry out an increasing number of non-educational roles, viz. catering, sports, hobbies and crafts, welfare, etc. The school day is also divided into a rigid pattern of time slots with each class assigned to a classroom under the supervision of a designated teacher, the point being to leave no group unsupervised. CAL is therefore perceived as a danger because it undermines this supervisory role, and breaks up the normal system of the student working quietly in his or her own designated seat. In her survey of schools in the Manchester area, Hennessy reports, "No more than 15% of the teacher's time is spent in direct interaction with the class group; the average is less than 10%." (12)

It is suggested that the conventional fears of a breakdown in classroom control are exaggerated and that, in the right circumstances, discipline problems can actually be minimised through the use of individualised teaching strategies. The reasons for this are as follows:

(1) The level of personal attention which the teachers give to the student's hopes and ambitions can tend to motivate the student towards achievement of those ambitions. Also personal guidance can be given rather than the control-oriented use of sarcasm and the other put-downs which many teachers consider a necessary part of group psychology. This removes many of the sources of tension.

(2) Because the method itself is designed to promote success in learning, any success actually achieved tends to reinforce confidence in the system and to maintain motivation.

(3) If less time is devoted to group teaching, there is less opportunity for a student to engage the attention of the entire class with attention-seeking behaviour, and there is less fun in teacher-baiting, which arises from the adversarial nature of the conventional classroom environment where teachers feel that they cannot be seen to back down without losing face.

If the problem is not keeping order in schools where there is poor motivation to learn, there is the alternative problem of elitism which is enhanced by the suggestion that special technology colleges should be created. Some teachers see the computer as a further wedge between children who achieve and those who do not, given that, as a scarce resource, only children of proven ability have access or are given preferential access, e.g. for the examinable Computer Studies course which may give both students and school prestige. Other teachers dislike the threat which the computer may pose to their apparent omniscience. Now the computer can have all the answers to the students' questions, and

one of the best methods of promoting the development of students'
study skills is to encourage the research method whereby the
student finds the answer in the computer and explains it to the
teacher. This role reversal is not comfortable for some teachers.

Further, if unwilling staff are prevailed upon to enter the
field, the result can be that, given the lack of actual computing
knowledge, it can produce a distorted perception of achievement
on the part of the students. Thus, some students will outperform
the staff, producing programs of apparent complexity, and consequently be considered of ability. The fact that the same
results could have been achieved by using more elegantly simple
techniques will not be appreciated or understood. The really
well-motivated student might go on to increasingly sophisticated
levels of understanding in particular languages. This might be
considered laudable, but actually tends to guarantee long-term
skill obsolescence. "Ignorant teachers and parents alike praise
what appears to be outstanding performance in what could be an
irrelevant, or more worrying, a completely wrong pursuit." (13)

A more superficially attractive argument which is sometimes
advanced to justify non-involvement, is that the new technology
is felt to be a more natural part of the young person's world. It
is said that the young are only just begining the process of
learning about the world. They are more prepared to face the
unknown, making mistakes if necessary, so that each new experience can be integrated into the view which they are constructing
of the world about them. But the adult is more likely to have
evolved a fixed view of the world and finds it more difficult to
accommodate new and pervasive phenomena, feeling inadequate if it
falls outside the acknowledged domain of expertise.

In fact, this argument is an attempt to formulate an excuse for
the unprofessional. Even where students have some background
knowledge of the computer, there are always going to be some
students who have no liking for the computer. Such students will
only be induced to try the machines if the staff as role models
are seen to accept it. Otherwise, a form of self-fulfilling
prophecy effect sets in, viz. unenthusiastic staff see only the
disinclination of students to use the machines and are confirmed
in their prejudices, while the students see staff disinclined to
implement an interesting use of the machines, and are confirmed
in their prejudice that the computer can do nothing to help them.
It is difficult to know how to encourage the less enthusiastic
student for whom the sole attraction, if in fact there is one, is
the subject matter to be studied, but one assumption may be
safely made: the less committed the teacher is, and the more
boring the programs the students are asked to first examine, the
less likely it is that long-term interest will be stimulated.

In relation to computers, this phobic response is not as strong
among science teachers and male arts teachers. Opacic and
Roberts report that 21% of the male teachers surveyed, and 3% of
the female teachers surveyed, were actually using CAL in the

school classroom. This divergence was reduced from 7/1 to 4/1 in the science subjects. The primary reason for this divergence was the rate of referral for in-service training and the stereotypical attitudes of staff and administrators. It should be no surprise that the use of CAL was shown to be 24% in science subjects and 6.4% in non-science subjects. (14) Given that more teachers entering the profession now have formal computer qualifications or have experience in the use of computers within their discipline, and others have retrained, the examinable computer studies courses are usually staffed by competent individuals. However, with the spread of computer appreciation or literacy courses to all students, a wider range of staff need to become more aware of the technology's implications. Further, independently of the need to provide some formalised introduction to the computer, there is the educational argument that students should meet the computer naturally, i.e. where the given use is a natural part of the course taught. In this way, the student ceases to see the computer as something special, and regards it as a mere tool. If this necessary and healthy disrespect is to arise, all staff must have considered the practical and educational implications of the computer as it affects their domain expertise.

In a sense, all non-technical teachers would need some degree of remedial help but, being singled out for such assistance often reinforces a negative attitude. Adults do not like to be forced back to school because it may be perceived as damaging to self-esteem. However, it must also be said that new ideas are not needed in the implementation of the new technology. The solution to the difficulties is merely the application of existing theories of learning with which most teachers are, or ought to be, familiar, albeit that new presentational methods are available. But even if this idea is accepted, and the motivation is there to find out about CAL, the teacher still needs access to an appropriate machine, software and information, and many will react adversely to competition to gain access to the scarce resource. Further, even if training is given, there is a strong likelihood of frustration for all concerned. This frustration tends to be generated because, frequently, the teaching staff who are to implement the dreams or plans of computerisation, are given neither the time nor facilities to make implementation genuinely feasible. This creates friction as the administrators and planners take affront at what is perceived to be an unreasonable lack of flexibility and adaptability on the part of the teachers.

Morale is also likely to be affected by the comments which inevitably float around staff rooms for all learning, and some experienced, users tend to talk about the problems which they are experiencing and this has a frightening effect on non-technical colleagues. However, this is not to deny that there are pressures for change and for the adoption of the new technology. Teacher dissatisfaction with existing techniques and approaches can be an incentive to accept innovation. The counter-balancing disincentive may simply be that all change requires time and effort and, in these modern times, time can be in short supply.

6.5 Is there an optimum approach to the training of staff?

Staff need to be made aware of basic terminology so that they do not panic when computer implementation is discussed or when, in a hands-on session, the computer gives them messages in jargon. On an individual basis, staff may gain confidence in the educational approach by talking with CAL specialists. It may be helpful for teachers to meet with computer specialists, but the principal guides should be those with a good familiarity with the educational use of computers. That the computer specialists may have a detailed knowledge of business or science applications is not helpful to the teaching profession. Indeed, the ideal person to introduce to non-technical teachers would be a teacher who has already made the transition that this new cadre is being asked to make. It is also essential that the individuals charged with this early responsibility should be good teachers. They should clearly respect the professionalism of those whom they are to convince, and not "talk down to them".

Some computer specialists have a tendency, whether consciously or not, towards patronising the non-technical, and this can be a serious barrier to real communication. Equally, the sometimes Messianic fervour of the newly converted can be wearing and off-putting. A balanced and considered view is the most constructive and persuasive approach to potentially defensive professionals, if possible, levened with a sense of humour to help in relieving tension. However, whoever is to assume the mantle of ice breaker, there is always a need for a continuing in-house advocate if educational change is to be made and consolidated. "Innovations are described as acts of faith requiring considerable personal commitment often with no tangible incentive." (15) Without the emotional and practical support from a sensitive and enthusiastic colleague, initial enthusiasm will swiftly wane.

If the principle is accepted and it then comes to the reality of trying to run programs on a machine, staff may also appreciate a degree of privacy while they learn and, if it is practicable, may appreciate being allowed to take micros home with them. Again, the selection of software packages is critical to success at this early stage. The software must be seen as relevant to the needs of the particular staff and, wherever possible, the program should show a new, and hopefully, enjoyable approach to the teaching of a traditional topic so that computers may be seen as potentially contributing something different to the educational armoury. The package should also be easy to manipulate. Although the material which the software covers can, and should, be as complex and demanding as is appropriate for use by that member of staff, it must be user friendly. Sceptical teachers are easily deterred by poor menus and complexity in the operational side of user input.

Too much of the existing CAL software today is badly thought out and poorly designed. Although showing a teacher bad software may encourage that teacher to try to do better, the more usual response is that the prejudice against using computers is confirmed. Thus, while warning teachers not to become overenthusiastic because such software as is demonstrated may not be completely typical of what the market place can provide, teachers should be steered in the direction of the most constructive use of the technology. They should also be taught evaluation standards which will help to ensure that the teacher's school or college does not acquire poor software. A sensible buying strategy which produces a core stock of good educational software should avoid perpetuating the myth that computers are no good as teachers.

This must reflect reality because even after training, the majority of teachers will not assume the responsibility for producing educational software, nor will there be direct consultation between teacher and programmer. After all, it would be against normal expections for the modern teacher to write, or to be a party to the writing of, all the textbooks which are to be used in the teaching of a given course. But if the teacher cannot control the resultant system effectively, he or she will tend to bypass it. Teachers have experience in selecting appropriate books for a given course. They need to be given proper training in the evaluation and selection of software.

6.6 The evaluation of software for educational use

Retraining staff on an in-service basis is slow, and although there is an increasing amount of literature on CAL to which staff may be referred to boost their understanding, there is a shortage of direct guidance about which software to choose or which teaching methodology to adopt. The following evaluation checklist for software is therefore suggested:

(a) Is CAL a relevant and suitable mechanism for communicating the information?

(b) Is the information incorporated into the software correct?

(c) Is the computer used to the best advantage?

(d) Is the learner in control?

(e) Is there adequate documentation?

(f) Is the package flexible?

The initial practical problem is identifying what software is available. If the computer facility is to be created from scratch, it will be appropriate to discuss the matter with the prospective hardware suppliers. Acquiring machines which will not support a substantial part of the existing educational software is not necessarily a good strategy. If the hardware is already available, teachers should consult publishers' catalogues, computer magazines, other teachers, and LEA and Government support services. If descriptions or reviews of apparently suitable software are found, the next step is to discover the form in which the software is available, e.g. disc, cassette, etc., and to determine whether this form is compatible with the existing configuration?

Assuming machine compatibility, the next step is to inspect the program and its accompanying documentation. The teacher should start by reading the documentation to identify the content, and the educational aims and strategies which the software designer has used. It is equally important to seek a statement of the student knowledge required as a prerequisite to use; perhaps ideally, with a diagnostic test incorporated to determine whether students are actually ready to use the program. It may also be desirable that the program subsequently includes a checking system to ensure that students have learned the programmed material. Finally, the teacher should consider whether the software is designed to stand alone, or whether it cross-references to other materials. The more flexible the software's construction, the more utility may be found in its use.

The teacher should then study the description given as to program operation. If the evaluator is an inexperienced user, it may be advisable to find a quiet place for a trial run. Once the basic philosophy is understood, the system should be subjected to a test to see whether the operating procedures are consistent throughout, whether clear instructions given on the screen for inexperienced users, and whether these instructions can be filtered out if user is familiar with system (this avoids frustration in seeing the same things, sometimes slowly, repeated on the screen). If no screen instructions are given, it becomes more important to ensure that the user guide is clear and comprehensive. Then test for other items of friendliness, e.g. can the user change the input before the machine acts on it, can the user back track through the system to verify earlier information, does the system give good feedback, etc.?

The teacher should now be in a position to judge whether the predicated educational aims are fulfilled. But regardless whether the program succeeds by reference to its own terms, it must also be seen that what the program claims to teach is relevant to the given course and worth teaching; and, even if it does fit in with the existing course, it is still not certain that the same information could not be better taught using conventional methods. In order to assist in making this judgement, various types of educational aim may be distinguished. Thus, if the program aims to communicate a concept, the software should provide good basic definitions, identify significant attributes and distinguish key characteristics, while giving examples consistent with the students' likely experience. If the program aims to promote rule learning, the software should provide a good presentation of the rule together with appropriate examples, and then offer realistic opportunities for practice with good feedback in any testing, finishing with an integrated review of the rule.

Another possible aim would be memory training where the program content should clearly be seen to be within students' experience and, assuming that repetition is used, it should be obvious that the information learned will be of value to the students. Although memory training is a useful abstract exercise, training opportunities are optimised if the material learned is of direct utility. If the aim is simple practice, it is helpful if the subject matter has already been taught. But even then, it must be seen that the students need the practice. There should also be consistency between the way in which the practice is organised, and the structure of what has been taught in the classroom. If revision teaching is included in the package, the overall program should be judged on whether it fits in with the needs of the target class(es).

If the program appears to have merit, it is advisable to try it out on random students to observe how they use it. The instructions which seem clear to the teacher may not seem so clear to them. Even if the instructions are apparently understood, it should also be seen that they do what is expected of them throughout the program. Then consider the more intangible qualities of the package: does the program capture and hold the students' attention, and is the program compatible with the preferences of the students, e.g. in the pace of presentation, repetition of instructions, level of difficulty etc.? This will help the teacher to recognise what teaching management and supervision is going to be involved in implementing the program into the course.

It is appropriate to insert a comment upon this general approach of existing software evaluation, which has been the basis, inter alia, of the MEP. By concentrating upon the use of current software, it is true that the process of breaking down prejudices against the use of computers can be begun. However, if this is the sole theme, teachers will not gain an insight into the design criteria which underpin the software, nor will they come to understand the true potential of the computer. There will therefore be no basis upon which the novice can judge whether original or innovative ideas can be implemented by competent programmers. This may become a drawback. Most teachers could judge whether a text book could make a valuable contribution to a course, and then either write it or draw up a specification for an author to work from. As computers become more pervasive, the development of similar software design skills among the teaching profession may become more necessary.

6.7 The content of an introductory course for teachers

As a first step, it may be enough to aim at establishing mere confidence in the operation of existing packages. But, even so simple a statement conceals a difficulty. Many of the software packages which some teachers are expected to master are now coming from the business environment, viz. spreadsheet and data-base systems. Indeed, independently of curriculum requirements, teachers' own superficial knowledge of the jargon may lead them to expect an introduction to this type of software. Such software was not designed with education in mind, so the introduction to teachers must be very supportive and demonstrate how they may be used in the teaching environment. Further, many of these packages require considerable effort to achieve proficiency, and may not be appropriate for their students to learn. It is therefore vital that the designers of these introductory courses select realistic examples of software utility. Thereafter, workshops may be useful where teachers can exchange experiences and, by sharing common interests, aspire towards both real enthusiasm and more general competence. Obviously, these workshops can be short, with minimal hands-on experience, if the teachers have ready access to micros either at work or at home.

In a model course, there should be two or three staff for each computer. Individual computer use can lead to a feeling of isola-tion and overdependence on the tutor, while more than three prevents a reasonable period of hands-on experience. People learn from each other and this sharing situation forces the faster learners to clarify their own thinking for the sake of the slower. The slower therefore gain encouragement from the success of the faster. Moreover, the enthusiastic student full of half truths who may be a problem in full class discussions, is helped to recognise the limitations in his or her knowledge by the dynamics of small group learning. Small groups encourage greater frankness between students, and provide an environment in which people may grow more aware than on their own. Bostock and Seifert suggest that, wherever possible, an informal atmosphere is created where the teachers are encouraged to co-operate with each other. This should minimise the risk of the teachers perceiving computers as unfriendly and difficult machines. Further, the course should not end with any test or certification, stressing that its function is to enable the teachers to continue to expand their knowledge afterwards. (16) This should reduce the stress which might otherwise arise from a threat to self-esteem. If staff are lacking in confidence and equivocal in their motivation to learn about computers, any form of testing may be counter-productive.

Hardware robustness and reliability is vital at this most sensitive of stages. Any machine failure, no matter how trivial it actually is, can prematurely alert teachers to their inability to repair the damage or to recover from the disaster. Quite apart from the waste of time if input has been lost, enthusiasm may wane before the psychological point of technology acceptance has been reached. One of the better training strategies is for each teacher to role-play a student and, with no preconceptions, to directly experience the learning opportunities which CAL can offer. If the innovator is able to make convincing material available, a practical demonstration of this nature may be helpful and convincing.

If the micros are kept in the school or college, the workshops may have to be longer to permit practice. However, if staff are to work at home, or if development is to continue after formal training has ceased, it will bolster confidence if telephone help lines are available, where skilled advisors can assist staff when they get into difficulties. It is too easy to become demoralised through a sense of incompetence. This risk can be minimised if sympathetic help is available within ordinary hours. Staff should also be encouraged to maintain self-help groups where mutual support can be offered. If electronic mail is available, staff should be encouraged to use it for this purpose. Once the introductory workshops and the practice sessions have been completed, a period of gestation is useful.

Teachers cannot be expected to change work patterns, revamp teaching materials and integrate existing or new software into their courses overnight. Time is essential if reasoned choices are to be made. However, the mind must be focussed on the task. A balance must be struck between a positive but reasonable deadline, and a premature and unsatisfactory emergence into the classroom with an incompletely thought out strategy. The deadline set must be real to move the teachers to action, but administrators must maintain realistic expectations for the first years of implementation. To expect instant success is to foster demoralisation when impossible targets cannot be met. Those responsible for the management of change must ensure that a suitable amount of time is made available throughout the early years for development of the CAL system. This requires a reduction in class contact hours if it is to be done properly. This also assumes that the staff are motivated to change. The current pay scales and the system of rewards and incentives give very little encouragement for what may be a major investment of time and energy by the staff involved. In the past, it was accepted that much of the reward of the professional teacher was the intangible pleasure in communicating to willing learners and a high status within the community. As a result, comparatively low salaries were accepted. The modern teacher must be recruited from the competitive job market and the good graduate has a tendency to more mercenary concerns.

6.8   What is the American experience?

In the IBM Secondary School Program, the teacher training was based on extensive hands-on practice. To achieve this, it was felt essential to have sufficient hardware and software so that no-one was required to share equipment, or to feel rushed to accommodate others if software packages were to be passed round. Topics were formally introduced, but the overall course momentum was maintained with helpful staff available throughout who had clear goals and objectives in mind and could guide the teachers through the program. It was found to be problematical to give even experienced teachers wholly unstructured time to practice whatever computing skills they wished. Any assumption that all course participants are capable of acting as self-directed learners, can set appropriate goals, and will create their own activities, proved unjustified. When the subject matter is new and liable to cause an anxiety-based response, giving specific software assignments and projects was felt to be essential. The teachers themselves were encouraged to interact and to form special interest groups where collaborative work could take place. Overall, the theme of the training program was planning for implementation. This referred both to the development of lesson plans for the use of various software packages, and also to institutional planning for curriculum adaptation.

The final recommendation to emerge from the IBM Program was that the training should be during the summer where there is reduced distraction from work. It was felt that the trainees could devote more time and energy to the in-service course because they were free from other responsibilities. If this cannot be arranged, the scheduling of the training should, as far as is possible, be isolated from outside distractions. (17) Change is a personal process and deserves proper management care, for individuals must change before the institution may follow. Revolutions require passion, evolution requires co-operation. By involving the staff and giving them a degree of control in the learning process, understanding followed by training may be effected. Making involvement voluntary wherever possible may also help, because a free choice usually means greater motivation and commitment.

There is another, more positive side to the lack of confidence which some teachers feel about learning about computers. It reminds them about the learning process itself. Too many teachers have forgotten what it is like to learn. This experience should help them to empathise with their students. In the IBM program, 59% of the teachers surveyed reported more, or a little more, rapport with the students. (18) This may be due, in part, to the fact that some students know a lot more about computers than the teachers. In such situations, the resourceful teacher has to work more collaboratively with the students, if for no other reason than to learn from them. If people are reluctant to try anything because they are afraid of making mistakes, they will not make as good a rate of progress as those who say, "I wonder what would happen if...?" Those who jump in at the deep end and then look around tend to make good progress. Indeed, all learning environments should encourage people to make mistakes and to experiment, for if people get something right too quickly, it may be dismissed as uninteresting and nuances may be overlooked.

6.9 What should the teachers be able to do after training?

The teacher will have established enough technical expertise in the use of the hardware to be able to exploit the available CAL software. There should also be sufficient understanding of the merits of software to be able to evaluate new programs for possible acquisition. For those who are to teach some programming, the range of skills is more diverse. Ignoring the need to acquire an acceptable level of technical ability, the teacher must retain a degree of open-mindedness when approaching a class of students. Many young children can teach each other how to program, and the way in which they communicate understanding is rather different to the way in which a teacher would attempt the same task. Thus, teachers should aim at collecting as many programming projects as possible which help to make the true power of programming and computers apparent to beginners.

It is also necessary to develop a jargon-free way of talking about computers which does not frighten off the non-technical. There is a further salutory lesson to learn in that there is rarely one right way to solve a programming problem. Different people are likely to find equally valid solutions to programming problems, and to develop viable strategies for learning or exploiting knowledge learned. Teachers must therefore concentrate on examining the results of labour, and if functional but non-standard, merely point out that there were other (perhaps better) ways of producing that same result. It is not a constructive teaching strategy to damp down creative explorations, and to regiment academic performance.

However, perhaps the most important issue to try to understand is the nature of the resistance which prevents many adults and some children from experimenting with mathematically-oriented materials. Once this resistance is understood, viable teaching strategies can be devised to try to combat it. Teachers often have no further to look than their own learning resistance for an insight into other's problems. This will be particularly important when introducing students to spreadsheet and database packages. In fact, the data manipulation facilities of the packages are interesting and stimulating challenges in their own right, and anyone who enjoys the use of computers is likely to respond favourably to spreadsheet and database systems regardless of inherent mathematical skills. The best strategy is therefore to approach their use with relevant practical examples which inevitably have some numerical base, but only incidentally so, e.g. the names and addresses of friends and their telephone numbers which can be sorted alphabetically or by telephone number, or classified by street, etc.

6.10   Must CAL itself change to enhance learning skills?

Many students do not want to learn in the way schools currently teach. One reason for this may be the learning styles of the members of a given class. A student learns in a way that depends upon his or her individual cognitive style. Pask and Scott (18) distinguish between serialists who learn by simply linking a series of items together, and holists who learn as a whole, forming more complex knowledge structures. Serialists are more intolerant of irrelevant material, whereas holists can assimilate logically irrelevant data which is inserted to "enrich" the curriculum, and can use that data to manipulate whatever he or she was originally required to learn. Indeed, serialists can fall into serious difficulties if they fail to distinguish the wood from the trees, and consequently try to assimilate masses of sparsely related or irrelevant information.

Experimental data suggests that if the teaching program matches the cognitive style, effective learning will result, but is less likely to do so if there is a mismatch. Most teachers select a single presentational style and, since this will tend to have a bias towards one type of student, a mismatch is highly probable. This can only be circumvented by testing the students to determine learning competence, assigning students to groups based upon that testing, and matching the teaching style to the group profile. The testing used by Pask and Scott was based upon a free learning task which was unbiased, i.e. it could be attempted either by serialist or holist strategies, and which required each testee to externalise his or her mental processes as an observable stretch of behaviour. This technique is algorithmic and can therefore be automated in a CAL system. Once the students have been classified, teaching strategies can be slanted towards tutorial groups with a given sort of competence. This is not to say that humans are not adaptable. It is acknowledged that it may be possible for an individual with any sort of competence to learn in the end whatever the teaching strategy. However, the experimental results clearly show that the rate, quality and durability of learning is enhanced if there is a match. The serialist will therefore benefit from the routine linear CAL approach, whereas a holist will receive greater assistance from a multibranch program which contains both enrichment material and overall concepts.

Hartley, Sleeman and Woods (20) describe a medical diagnosis game which can be used to match teaching strategy to an individual learner's competence. This matching is achieved by comparing the learner's efforts with various models stored in the system. The result is to identify trends towards certain identified types of errors. If such systems are exploited, and the CAL suite has alternative remedial or teaching materials which will either repair error or seek to reduce the possibility of similar error in future subject matter, the best path through the suite can be selected for each student.

If no effort is made to classify the student's cognitive style, the values which the system represents may well prove to be out of step with the perception of the students. No teaching system, CAL-based or otherwise, can realistically hope to make the motivation of the student more real if materials of relevance are not seen seen to be available. It may also be suggested that should the right presentation be made, the educational diversity which the computer can bring to the classroom can further motivate the student to learn. The sad but intriguing feature of this proposition is that it implicitly assumes that students are by nature lazy and not inclined to learn. If natural curiosity has been stiffled, this must be a reflection of the environment whether in school, or in the community.

Research is therefore required into the different cognitive styles found in students so that the practices of teaching in general, and CAL programming in particular, may change and become more effective. CAL programming techniques must become more aware of learning motivation and, as indicated in Chapter 2, explanations of motivation depend upon assumptions about free will. Many feel a need to be competent to maintain self-esteem and peer group approval. People therefore seek the optimum challenge to be overcome. If the challenge is too easy or too difficult, people will be deterred. If there is no external reward, emotions and other internal consequences must be seen as rewards. But, curiosity, the satisfaction of grasping new points and the enjoyment of the search for information, are emotional drives which could be stiffled by too rigid a CAL approach. Thus, CAL must allow individuals enough intellectual elbow room, and encourage experimentation and research. However, in considering the effect of CAL upon the student, it must not be forgotten that the programming exercise also forces conscious conceptualisation of the problems to be solved or the exercise to be performed, and this must also improve the understanding of the programmer. As to the larger-scale planning task, the analytical exercise required will produce an improved awareness of both behavioural and social issues. This is immensely beneficial to the teacher qua educational programmer.

6.11 Conclusions

The introduction of CAL from scratch is expensive both in hardware and software production. Although set-up costs can be reduced by joining a network, this means higher operating costs through telephone linkages, and sacrificing part or all educational control over the style of presentation and content of material, and consequently may not be considered appropriate. If schools are not to be discriminatory through geographical accident, i.e. the accident of having an LEA with the capital to produce an effective system, or a generous PTA, a properly thought out national plan is required. At present, there are poor lines of communication between teachers and parents, and relations are strained between teachers and administrators. Each group has different criteria by which to judge the success or failure of any venture into computerisation. Added to this is the tension and the threat of violence in inner-city areas which are often the most deprived in terms of schooling provision. If the teaching in these areas is already impersonal, the use of computer technology could merely compound that impersonality.

Children's motivation is often a direct reflection of teacher enthusiasm. If the children have a poor self-image and little initiative, this is probably a result of poor teaching. Attitudes are not taught. They are acquired from other people. Teachers have the capacity to convey either positive or negative attitudes through their personal relationships with the children. The teacher is a model for the learner. Derek Blease confirms this in a limited although significant study. "If an individual child encounters [such] expectations from a teacher, or better still, a group of teachers, which are consistent over time, it is possible that the teachers' perceptions and the child's own self-image will become more and more alike. In other words, if the conditions are right, the child will come to see himself more and more as his teachers see him. This [is a] self-fulfilling prophecy effect". (21) This is a socio-political problem and social planners must fairly confront the whole picture if non-

161

devisive progress is to be made.

In all probability the key to the solution of this increasing disparity must be the definition of a meaningful role for the teacher to play in a class which uses self-teaching aids, whether these be computers, television, programmed texts or other material. This will involve a complete change in the concept of the teacher both on the part of administrators, policy makers and teachers themselves. If large numbers of students are all proceeding, each at his or her own speed, it is obvious that the teacher cannot be the sole source of the study material. The consequence is that the new teacher will have a role similar to that of a doctor. The primary concern will be the diagnosis and correction of each individual student's difficulties. In other words, the teacher will have to be less discipline-oriented and more student-oriented. Overall, the teacher will achieve a multiplicity of functions: demonstrator, teacher/lecturer, problem setter, arbitrator, decision maker, challenger, collaborator, question asker, idea extender, observer, admirer, encourager, time provider, model learner and policeman.

Teachers and administrators must therefore both admit that there are problems, some common, others particular. Those who are prepared to co-operate and change must be given proper recognition and encouragement and all co-operation must emphasise action rather than the machinery for decision-making. Often the traditional pecking order must be overcome. From the point of view of the administration, key personnel must be identified and encouraged both at an administrative and at a teaching level. Awareness and proficiency must be developed so that proper planning for utilisation may take place. Although some people always view the new as an exciting challenge, many are hesitant about, or even fear what they do not understand. This is particularly the case when staff fear that their jobs may be at risk. Staff must therefore be involved in the planning process to prepare them for the transition to an electronic system. The administrators must also show themselves to be interested in the new system as implemented by the teachers. Staff may become dispirited if they encounter problems which the administration seem to have no interest in solving. All new systems involve practice whether as a manager or as a worker. Administrators should therefore be directly involved in the learning process, preferably alongside the teachers, so that all will gain a more realistic expectation of what the computer can achieve, and will come to recognise the degree of commitment and expertise necessary to get the best out of computers in education.

One would not expect a person to change the method of personal transport from a bicycle to a car without some form of training. Time must therefore be made available for each new development to be assimilated in the least hurried and least pressured way possible. Even though future savings of time may be achieved, time in the initial stages is of fundamental importance. In determining the training policy, there are a number of central propositions:

- one should never train just one person if continuity of effort is to be maintained in each educational environment

- training should never be on a "once and for all" basis, so by always seeking to update skills, the risk of complacency and a plateauing of performance are minimised

- training must be planned given the ultimate configuration of the system. The educational targets must be set – how many students, where are they, what administrative locations fits in with this institutional framework, architectural considerations, networking and communications, etc.

Teachers often give long hours of extra effort for the general good of their students, and some enthusiastic teachers have spent many years struggling to make progress with CAL. Sadly many administrators have failed to recognise that if real progress is to be made, proper allowances must be given to those staff so that development work may proceed. If staff cannot easily switch roles from teacher to advisor, retraining may help to reduce the scale of the problem, but a change in salary structure will probably be necessary to bring in people with the appropriate skills. In this process, it is entirely possible that new jobs will emerge, e.g. educational technologist or some comparable para-professional class which will maintain the machines and guide use while freeing the teachers to concentrate on their new tasks.

Unless students, parents, teachers and administrators accept that new relationships must be created between student, teacher and administrator, little use will be made of the new technology. CAL individualises the teaching environment no matter what the educational level. The traditional teacher prepares lessons, sets group assignments, and generally arranges for participation and projects. Homogenous teaching is the resultant norm. If teaching is individualised, this means, for example, that children will be ready to move to the next grade or school at unpredictable times because they will achieve levels of understanding at their own speed. Whereas progress through the contemporary school is by exposure to information on a formatted yearly course basis, and expectations about examinations and entry to higher education are based on the concept of the academic year, progress could soon be on the basis merely of mastery of relevant information and concepts. School entrance and exit criteria may have to be re-evaluated and the "normal" ages for entry to different stages of the educational system may have to be changed. If individuals have the ability, each generation's Ruth Lawrences should neither be stigmatised nor lauded as the exceptions in a system where all progress when ready. A natural corrolory to this is that, given that educational achievement may come more quickly, there will have to be enhanced social development effort by the teachers to ensure that the socialisation function of the schools is properly pursued.

References

(1) Domain Theory. An introduction to organisational behavior in human service organisations. (1979) 15 Journal of Applied Behavioral Science 4.

(2) Resistance to change in education. An analysis of domains of power and control in educational systems. Yehuda Bien. Research in Education. No.35. p.34.

(3) The Impact of Technological Change on Education. George R McMeen. Educational Technology. (1986) February. p.42.

(4) The Diffusion of Keynesian Macroeconimics through American High School Textbooks, 1936-70. Herbert W. Voege. collected in W Reid & D Walker. Case Studies in Curriculum Change. Routledge & Kegan Paul, London. 1975. p.229/30, the other references being to Now we're lagging only twenty years. Margaret Bushnell. School Executive, LXXVII (October 1957). pp.61/3. Principles of School Administration. Paul R. Mort. McGraw-Hill, New York. 1946. pp.199/200.

(5) Curriculum change at the local level. M.P.Smith. (1971) 3(2) Jo. of Curriculum Studies 158/62.

(6) A Structured Approach to Microcomputer Use in an Elementary School. M.Gene Bailey. collected in Capitol-izing on Computers in Education. p.13.

(7) Education in Great Britain and Ireland. A Source Book. Robert Bell, Gerald Fowler and Ken Little (ed) Routledge & Kegan Paul, London. 1973. p.94.

(8) Stability and Change: the Public Schools of Gary, Indiana. 1940/70. W.Lynn McKinney and Ian Westbury. collected in Case Studies in Curriculum Change. p.41.

(9) Negotiating Curriculum Change in a College of Education. K.E.Shaw. collected in Case Studies on Curriculum Change. p.58.

(10) Learning and Teaching with Computers. p.218.

(11) A Systems Approach to Curriculum Development, the Manchester project for Computer Studies in Schools. Kathleen Hennessy. collected in Microcomputers in Education. pp.15/30 at p.17.

(12) ibid at p.22.

(13) Myth of the Learning Machine. p.84.

(14) CAL implementation. P.Opacic and A.Roberts. collected in Teachers, Computers and the Classroom. pp.60/78 at pp.64/67.

(15) Learning and Teaching with Computers. p.219.

(16) Adult Computer Literacy: Analysis and Content. Stephen Bostock and Roger Seifert. collected in Microcomputers in Adult Education. pp.1/17 at p.9.

(17) The Electronic Schoolhouse. Hugh F. Cline et al. pp.39/61 particularly at p.57/8.

(18) ibid at p.123.

(19) Learning Strategies and Individual Competence. G.Pask and B.C.E.Scott. (1972) 4(3) Int J. Man–Machine Studies 217/53.

(20) Controlling the Learning of Diagnostic Tasks. J.R.Hartley, D.H.Sleeman and Pat Woods. (1972) 4(3) Int J. Man–Machine Studies 319/40.

(21) Teachers' Personal Constructs and their Pupils' Self–Images. Derek Blease. (1986) 12 Educational Studies 255/64 at p.255.

CHAPTER 7

DESIGNING THE CAL INPUT TO THE CURRICULUM

In this chapter, the practicality of design must be examined. Based upon the ideas of Piaget and Gagne, a series of rules are suggested which should help both the teacher and the computer programmer to produce better educational software.

7.1   How do teachers prepare teaching materials?

Any teaching theory that is used to produce a CAL suite must be explicitly formalised. If this cannot be done, instead of being embarrassed, the educator should use the exercise to learn and to identify research topics. If precise theoretical definition ultimately proves impossible, the educator must approximate an education model. This need for an explicit model makes CAL programming significantly more demanding than class or lecture preparation because the teaching models have to be made operational. The theory is to be directly translated into action which can be viewed and analysed independently. This is a far more rigorous form of evaluation and validation than conventional teaching materials face. Lectures have an ephemeral quality about them, being continuously adjusted in the face of the immediately observable, rapid comprehension or stubborn incomprehension, whereas every word rigidly preserved in a CAL program may achieve significance.

The ideal would be that the programmers make the computers act like experienced teachers. But, in default of a natural language facility and an innate understanding of the materials to be taught, the computers will simply repeat the same preprogrammed phrases. However, at a purely mechanical level, a form of mimicry can arise so that, if the teachers would show the children a picture at a particular point in a lesson, the computer can do the same. The resultant system should then be tested against groups of children and, through a process of revision, an effective presentation should be arrived at.

As a simple starting rule, the programmer should avoid undemanding linear (i.e. non-branching) programming techniques based upon simple written materials (see section 4.3). This is bad educationally through its strong tendency to produce a simple catechism or mechanical pedagogy which dulls student motivation.

7.1.1 In the creation of a course of lectures, precisely what must be specified?

The sequence of learning events must be specified on a lowest common denominator basis for the group to be taught within a time framework, i.e. the method and logic of instruction must be identified and the content related to it. This homogenised approach may be converted into individualised education by specifying educational goals (goals suit an individual when, for example, courses are chosen for vocational reasons – in elementary education, the goals tend to be the communication of core knowledge, but as the student proceeds through the education system, it becomes increasingly necessary to identify goals for individual students), individual capabilities (i.e. those abilites which an individual brings with him or her to the instruction as a result of prior schooling or experience) and instructional means (i.e. what is taught and how it is taught).

In the non-computerised system, it is the differential decision-making quality which individualises the teaching. Such decisions require a variety of information about the individual:

. It is first necessary to decide what criteria of competence should be applied, e.g. test grades or teacher judgements of quality.

. Any testing will necessarily take account of the background of the student. The student's written record of previous performance will sometimes be available. If not, initial testing will have to take place to determine where the student should start in the course. It can also be important to distinguish between long-term and short-term background, i.e. it can be more important to review immediate performance criteria in comparison to the longer-term background to pick up changing trends and patterns in development (or lack of it).

. The teacher will now have a yardstick against which to monitor how quickly the student proceeds in the learning, but in a non-computerised environment, the teacher's subjective impression of the student as slow or fast, responsive or inattentive, is rarely documented in detail.

. At this point, the teacher can begin to consider what instructional means are available to teach the given topic - this will normally be catalogued in the teacher's head or in an otherwise informal way.

In a computerised system, all this information can be stored and continuously up-dated, (the ultimate form of continuous assessment, given the setting of adequate decision points and criteria of measurement), so that data for each decision can be supplied in a summarised form to the teacher upon demand. This can make the human decision-making process more accurate. The data can also be supplied to the student to permit the student to participate more fully in the pre-decision discussions with the teacher.

The computer can also make the learner more self-aware by providing him or her with more information about progress and failure. The constant demands on modern teachers may mean that they do not have time to explain and discuss the most recent results with each student. But a student relying upon a CAL system which supplies proper feedback, can be given more guidance by the system and, thus, become more confident of progress. Hence, an intelligent CAL suite can advise a student on possible remediation or on the options for future progress, suggesting a range of possible routes to an understanding of the next topic which will exploit the full range of presentational media. However, if the qualities of responsibility and adaptability are to be encouraged in the student, a view must be taken as to the power of the machine. It might be argued that overdirectiveness on the part of human teachers stiffles initiative, and that a student, working alone with the help of a machine, will develop the necessary skills. But this denies the rigidity of programming which may be as directive as the human with no in-built capacity for compassion if, say, the student is seen to have a bad cold or otherwise be under the weather. A balance should therefore be struck whereby excessive reliance on both the computer and the teacher should be discouraged.

The end-product should be a CAL-based course which teaches the user how to learn as well as communicate information. Thus, if learning or problem-solving strategies are relevant, the system should have the ability to coach the student in the appropriate methodology. With the development of databases and retrieval systems, the question arises as to the extent to which the individual student should impose his her own structures on the learning experience. It is clear that young or inexperienced students will require help and guidance to develop study skills in the new environment, but older students should be encouraged to become more self-sufficient. The rationale for this approach is that, with the learner in control, the course can be better suited to his or her needs rather than the needs of the teacher. The problem in this approach is that, since the information is often divided into small segments, the learner will find it difficult to grasp the whole unless syllabus structures are made available to show the relationship of each part to the whole.

Without such a map, a learner might find it difficult to navigate through the course, making rational decisions about direction and method of study. This approach also allows the teacher to see the subject from the student's point of view since the computer will keep records of each student's decision. If consistent choices are made, this may, through a process of rewriting and redefinition, lead to more satisfactory teaching programs. If a student starts at too advanced a point in the course, it is easy to see what earlier path ought to be followed in order to arrive at the point of difficulty with appropriate background information. However, teachers must be brave enough to allow students to advance into the more difficult areas. On many occasions, the students will benefit either because they rise to the challenge or because, through failure, they then better understand the need for earlier principles in a proper sequence of learning.

With this approach the teacher's time can be reserved for the more subtle and difficult educational decision-making. The computer can, of course, be programmed to make suggestions based upon previous decisions with similar students. The teacher can then decide whether to accept the recommendation. A teacher may give one child easy problems to perform because that child needs his or her confidence building. Another child may be given deliberately difficult problems to work on as a stimulus to a clever, lazy but proud mind. These points might be a natural part of a sensitive teacher's role but a machine cannot see how a person is feeling and act accordingly. However, with the information which the computer can supply the teacher, adjustments in emphasis in the teaching system can easily be made so long as initial flexibility has been built into the system.

However, attempts to humanise the computer's response are often rather patronising and seen as fake. An analogy would be the telephone answering machine which is efficient, but rarely personal and often found to be intimidating. Resistance to the idea of using machines is broken down through familiarity of use, and with acceptance comes the recognition that although the medium is mechanical, it does not mean that it cannot be useful. One possible danger in humanising the interface is that the sheer controlling power of a machine that may greet a child by name and judges his or her performance, might make the child submissive towards the machine. Indeed, Piaget suggests that a child's thinking is dominated by animism, i.e. the attribution of human qualities to inanimate objects. Some young students have been seen to talk to computers as if they can understand, and error messages from the computer are sometimes taken as personal criticism. But long term and rational use of essentially polite systems, should show that the computer is merely a tool, useful only if directed by a person.

One of the recommendations to reduce the level of anthropomorphism is to suggest that other students who have mastered the topic, should be assigned to help the individuals in difficulties. Group work could thereby be constructively used, subject to the teacher's knowledge of the temperament of the student(s) available to fulfil the role of teacher. Some might be resentful of this function and perversely not help the weaker students. Other more introverted students may become better integrated into the class by having to verbalise helpful explanations. Group discussions, debates and interactions between students may be freely allowed in the classroom, or the students may work two or three to a terminal, taking turns and advising each other on strategy. It is a simple matter of matching the machine and room layout to the given group of students. Whatever decisions are made, group CAL would seem to have advantages for learning, for totally isolated instruction may ignore human learning needs.

7.2 The general rules for designing effective CAL

It must be re-emphasised at this point that CAL is not an educational panacea. It is but one of many possible presentational media available to the teacher. Thus, CAL should only be used where it is educationally justifiable and not merely for its own sake. If a rational decision is to be made in favour of CAL, this necessarily involves an appraisal of the entire curriculum and existing teaching strategies. Given the range of skills to be called upon, the subsequent creation of appropriate CAL software may be better done by a team comprising subject-based specialist, programmer, graphics designer and educational methodologist. It must be acknowledged, however, that it is difficult to get such teams together and to enable them to produce software of significance. Woodhouse and McDougall believe that such teams should be attached to curriculum development groups where longer-term commitments may be made. This involves organisation and a proper financial base. (1) But whether it is attempted by one or many, it is suggested that the following rules for the preparation of interesting teaching materials which may include CAL represent the most constructive approach:

Rule 1

Adopting the principles laid down by Gagne, the educational and behavioural objectives to be fulfilled should first be specified

The resources available to meet those objectives should also be identified, together with those circumstances which impose constraints on educational planning. In general terms, the planners and administrators must decide how students learn the things which have been specified, from whom they learn such things, where the resources can be found and whether the use of those resources in that way is cost effective. If this general evaluation appears favourable, the detailed objectives or goals form the basis of a curriculum and for the individual courses contained within it, each course being divided into a hierarchy of the various concepts and skills which are to be learned. For each lesson, the teacher should categorise the types of learning outcome which are to be achieved. The best way to design any instructional material is to work backwards from the expected outcomes. Thus, various target skills will be identified as curriculum objectives. To achieve these objectives, intermediate and supportive skills are frequently required. The hierarchy of component skills is identified at each level by asking what simpler skills the learner would have to possess in order to progress to the present level, and thence towards acquisition of the target skill.

It is not necessary to take the process of analytical simplification ad infinitum because, sooner or later, the teacher will identify material with which the target students are already familiar. Gagne (2) has specified the categories of learning outcome as a series of capabilities which are defined in terms of the following classes of human performance:

(a) Verbal information, i.e. knowledge which is stored in the learner's memory and which can be recalled as words or sentences.

(b) Intellectual skills are those skills which help to make the individual competent, i.e. which permit the learner to carry out symbol-based procedures, and it is customary to distinguish five subordinate types, viz:

.   Discrimination, i.e. the process of distinguishing between phenomena, whether concrete or conceptual, and being able to recall the points of difference.

.   Concrete concept, i.e. when the learner is able to identify instances of the property of an object, of an event, or a spatial direction.

- Defined concept, i.e. where the concept is identified by demonstrating the rule which defines it.

- Rule, i.e. learners acquire a rule when they can demonstrate its application to one or more previously unencountered instances. It is a "relation", i.e. it relates two or more concepts.

- Problem-solving, i.e. where the learner encounters an unfamiliar situation posing a question to be answered by applying known rules.

(c) Cognitive strategies that the learner applies to the cognitive processing activity and so govern each individual's own learning, remembering and thinking behaviour.

(d) Motor skills, i.e. the movement of muscles with a view to accomplishing purposeful actions, e.g. riding a bicycle, using a computer keyboard, etc.

(e) Attitudes, i.e. internal states, more usually inferred from observations than made explicit, which influence the choices of personal action which the learner makes. Every individual formulates a range of attitudes towards events and circumstances in the immediate social environment, and these emotions may modify behaviour given the strength of the feelings generated. One of the functions of education is supposedly to inculcate socially acceptable attitudes, e.g. being kind and considerate to others. Similarly, if learning is to occur, the student must have a positive attitude towards the subject matter to be learned, and have a willingness to either co-operate with the teacher or to work within the educational environment provided.

Gagne argues that any society must perform certain basic functions if it is to serve the needs of its members. Most of these functions require human activities which either contribute to the functioning of an individual within society or to the functioning of society itself, and all must be learned. It is therefore legitimate to identify it as the responsibility of society to ensure that these functions are learned. However, because society has become complex and subject disciplines diverse, it is not helpful to specify educational outcomes as, say, studying English, Geography or another identified discipline, because bare academic headings conceal a multitude of individual component elements. Instead, one should refer to activities made possible by learning, e.g. using English to communicate in a particular way, navigating by using a map, etc. Thus, the classes of capability identified above, are the basic physical and intellectual skills observable in most human performance categories. (3)

When considering a given lesson or group of lessons, it should be apparent that the learner should be able to perform certain tasks when the learning sequence is complete. To classify the task in terms of the list given, the planner must identify the mental processes and capabilities required in order to perform each given task. Once the learning outcomes to a given lesson have been classified, and therefore the real purposes of the lesson have been listed, the teaching strategies to be used can be more clearly identified. In this context, the term "teaching" is taken to mean the presentation of a series of displays that stimulate the learner so as to make learning more readily occur. A further practical point is that it is impossible to confront all the objectives at the same time. A realistic sequence of topics and teaching strategies must be devised which will both build up the hierarchy of skills in a logical fashion and hold the learners' interest.

Gagne and others hypothesise that the teaching process is comprised by various "events of instruction" which begin by gaining the attention of the learner and stimulating alertness. Without capturing the learners' interest, the immediate attitude of the learners may be such that the learning event of reception is either unlikely or likely to be delayed. These events in total represent a set of communications to the learner aimed at moving the learner from one state of mind to another, i.e. moving the learner from the present state of knowledge to achievement of the target skills. Any or all of the events of learning can be initiated by the learners, e.g. when reading, performing experiments or discussing a topic. The normal expectation is that learners will become more proficient at self-instruction as they gain experience in learning skills. The result is that lessons will tend to be more teacher-centred for the young or inexperienced students. For older, well-motivated students the environment can be more student-led.

Having determined the learning outcomes, it is necessary to select the most appropriate presentation mechanisms whereby each learning event is to be accomplished. The medium might be a verbal exposition, supplying written material, discussion, watching a video, using CAL or some other equipment-based method. At this stage, the planners will determine what materials already exist, and will appraise the suitability of that material for inclusion in the course. It might be that a particular book deals with the subject matter, but does not have quite the right orientation, or that software does not have quite the right learning objective for the particular course planned. Alternatively, it may be decided to create new materials. At one level, this decision will be based on a balancing of costs, the availability of resources and the probable effectiveness of the new materials. In more practical educational terms, it will be determined by the size of the group to be taught, and whether the use of the material or device is likely to prove detrimentally disruptive - the disruption could affect the administration of the school or college, or the pattern of learning experience to which the students are exposed, or simply the classroom organisation. If a piece of equipment is to be used, it will be important to consider the range of viewing and hearing distance for the use of the given device, its robustness and reliability, whether staff need to be retrained, and the ease with which it is adaptive to the learners' responses.

If it is decided that the use of a computer is desirable, then in the case of a CAL suite, the first event must obviously cause the learner to look at the VDU screen rather than at the keyboard. By then telling the learner of the various objectives to be fulfilled in the prospective lesson, a sense of structure and context is communicated and expectancy created. The degree to which this is done must vary with the degree of familiarity which the learner has with the structure of the overall course. In many cases, where the degree of familiarity is high, this step will not be essential in any detail. However, whatever the level of overall appreciation, the contextualising of information in individual lessons also serves the purpose of stimulating recall of prior learning and guides future learning. Information is then presented and performance is elicited which will lead to reinforcement through feedback. The teacher and the learner may then assess performance and, in a generalised summation at the end, the teacher can seek to enhance retention and consolidate the learning transfer.

Where CAL is not to be the exclusive teaching mechanism, the full context of the curriculum must be studied and adequate attention must be given to the formulation of introductory teaching materials, and the provision of suitable follow-up classes, discussion opportunities, tutorials, etc. Without this integration, the CAL software is unlikely to make its full impact. Although this approach would always be the ideal, it is doubtful that every teacher goes through the process for the formulation of individual non-computerised lessons.

The design of any individual lesson or lecture is not linear but evolutionary. The teacher must first decide what the students are to know, understand and be able to do, both at intermediate points during the lesson, and at the end of the lesson. The reason for this distinction is that many intermediate skills are enabling skills in the sense that mastery is required before proceeding to the acquisition of the target skills. In essence, this planning exercise will be determined by the actual needs and abilities of the target student group.

The teacher will now have a list of points, some of which are fundamental to the particular subject matter, some of which reflect aspects of the topic that students always find difficult, and some of which reflect particular interests of the teacher. This will normally represent more than can conveniently be packaged into the given time slot so the process of compromise and goal redefinition takes place in a cyclical or iterative manner. A part of this process can be to consider what other teachers include when they teach the given topic. Although every teacher has a right to his or her perhaps idiosyncratic approach, time is also at a premium and there is always the risk that, after the expenditure of effort, the teacher has merely reinvented the comparatively square wheel.

At this point, the real art of the teacher is required. "It is far easier to decide what to teach, that is, to define the purpose of instruction, than it is to decide how to teach it well." (4) The authors suggest brainstorming as a way of creating a pool of interesting ideas for the teaching of any given concept. The interaction of subject specialists either amongst themselves, or with interested colleagues, can cause a significant reappraisal of approach and methodologies, and this is bound to have a constructive outcome as long as there is the willingness to change. Depending upon the nature of the subject matter, it will then be necessary to distinguish between the sequence of skills which the students must learn, and the relationship between the different substantive elements within the concept to be taught. Once this has been done and reviewed in the light of the actual students' needs and abilities, with consequential amendment as necessary, the teacher is now ready to make rational decisions about teaching delivery systems.

However, many teachers find themselves in the situation of having a perfect strategy but inadequate means. In such situations, the only solutions are to have flexibility in the initial planning, or if the strategy is to be rigidly adhered to, then to make do with a second best substitute. The more well-established the needs identified, the more likely it is that suitable delivery systems already exist. If new needs are identified, it is highly unlikely that materials will exist in a form which immediately can be utilised without substantial amendment, or the materials are expensive. This lack of available materials can be a disincentive to innovation because, where the school or college must develop a delivery system from scratch, time and cost (both real and personal) can be disproportionate to the results achieved. But such additional expenditure can always be justified if the original strategy was well conceived, subject to be need to carefully monitor the economics of the exercise.

Thus, it may be decided to implement a system based upon one of the primary mechanisms for communicating concepts to students, namely the tutorial, both computer-based and human-led. A tutorial is three interacting elements and if a computer is to lead the student(s), it must have the information to be taught, know who is to be taught and know how to teach it in a variety of different ways and at different academic levels. A human-led tutorial is a discourse and does not depend upon single questions and answers. Thus information is presented or problems outlined; this gives rise to questions and answers which are judged by the tutor resulting in feedback and remedial effort; tangential information may be introduced if conditions are right; comparative or interdisciplinary connections may be made subject to an overall control of direction and timing. Pattern analysis is therefore essential if the computer is to emulate spoken forms, e.g. taking advantage of situations to introduce additional information, spotting an error and repairing the damage, etc. The danger of the computer is that CAL software writers are seduced by the nature of computer hardware, viz. "the nature of the computer which encourages a mechanistic, detail-oriented education, focusing on "correct" or unambiguous answers..." (5);

Most of the modern CAL systems are teacher-centred, i.e. the software simulates the teacher rather than allowing the user to become the equivalent of a researcher. Thus, in a spelling program, the child is shown a picture, say of a cat, and responds by pressing the button marked CAT or by typing the word out. It would be better to allow a child to type words into the computer and to show the child pictures appropriate to those words. The more sophisticated the program, the more complex the pictures could become to reflect sentences input by the user. "In this way the computer lends power to the child, in his learning, by amplifying the effect on the immediate world around him of his use of the written word." (6) Although the longer-term implications of this suggestion would rely upon the development of a natural language facility, the short-term matching of nouns to pictures is already technically possible.

For design purposes, the term "needs" reflects the discrepancy between the way things "are" and the way things "ought to be". These decisions as to what the students should be learning and how well, will affect the translation of the technically feasible into the actual treatment of the material. Thus, a verbal ex-position, perhaps supported by the use of an overhead projector, would differ from a paper-based presentation, and both would be unlike a computer-based approach. Given this review, a strategy should now emerge that the conceptual material will be presented using the separately designated methods, and that skills will be communicated and practised in the way thought most appropriate and effective, the effectiveness or otherwise being judged by a testing mechanism used at predetermined times.

The assessment of "needs" is not, and cannot be, a precise science. At present, the Government is concerned at the lack of defined educational performance standards and suggests regular testing against national age-related criteria. The proposal is that progress through the educational system should be determined by such tests. Even if consensus could be reached about the standards to be applied, it is not clear that every gap between those standards and actual achievement should be taken as a need to be cured by education or training. Often the gap can be better closed by other changes in society. The problem is that the needs which a Government may identify as reflecting society's general concerns, are not necessarily the needs of individuals. Moreover, the rate of social change is increasing, and unless all needs are regularly reviewed, and consequent changes integrated into the education system, the sense of alienation felt by sections of the community is likely to increase.

Rule 2

Always aim for the simple explanation and avoid verbosity

In this, the designer should make sure that the content is consistent with the curriculum, and appropriate to the various skill levels of those likely to be using it. Thus the reading ages of the target user group should be catered for, and screen layout should take account of the different levels of perceptual skills (see 5 below). Teachers may use spoken language in an idiosyncratic way either through the use of a dialect style, or consciously for effect, but it is suggested that programs should always aim to use standard English and should seek to avoid the creation of trivial material. The designer should always look to create material which covers a reasonable quantity of subject matter at a variety of instructional levels, if possible, cross-referenced to existing textbooks and other teaching materials. The writing strategy for this material should be to draft an outline of the topics to be communicated. This outline should remain as a coherent text and not be broken down into the individual frames of information until all the information to be communicated has been identified. The next step is to gloss the outline with a priority being accorded to each point, indicating whether all students should be given that piece of information or only those who fail to demonstrate comprehension of earlier points. The information should now be broken down into screen sized bits of information. This is best achieved by flowcharting the material into a teaching schematic.

Rule 3

Offer a variety of explanations, bearing in mind the need to provide accurate information

The danger in being asked to provide highly portable software which may be used in a wide variety of different institutions, is that the common denominator level of presentation actually selected, may result in an oversimplification of the teaching materials. The designer must always maintain academic standards suitable for the target group.

Rule 4

Use colour, graphics and complementary documentation to add or maintain interest through a diversity of educational stimuli

On a standard VDU, screen displays will either be text or graphics. It is usual to describe the screen display as a "frame" or a "window" in which, or through which, material is seen. The student may move through the frames at his or her own speed, or it is possible for the computer to cause the user to be moved through the frames on a time basis or, in the event of a delay, to prompt the user to make an input. The problem with time is that it is not user friendly, i.e. it takes no account of individual student's capacities to read or assimilate information, nor of the fact that the student may be distracted and wish to restart at the same position.

Moreover, it is important not to use colour and sound merely for their own sakes. The musical fanfares of success or failure may initially be amusing, but can be distracting to other users and boring in their repetitiveness. The constant sounds of failure may also breach the essential privacy of the learning experience, and cause embarrassed demoralisation in the unfortunate user as continuing failure is communicated to the peer group. But equally, the facilities are there and should be exploited to make the computer more than a mere book. Consequently, it is necessary to take an intelligent view of these facilities so that the most educationally constructive uses may be found.

The designer should also think carefully about vocabulary and sentence length, and the standard devices of highlighting and underlining. In this, it should be borne in mind that material displayed on a screen is of a transitory nature and lost when the next item is displayed. The need to provide the option of a hard copy of the whole or part of the materials should always be addressed. But if the screen displays are strongly based in a graphics environment, it should be remembered that even sophisticated plotters cannot guarantee to reproduce the screen displays.

CAL works by breaking down information into small and digestible bits. It is therefore necessary to use imagination and creativity to allow students the opportunity to reassemble the bits into a true level of understanding. In this, it is never safe to assume that users will accurately read screen-based information. Comprehension questions therefore assume an importance, causing remedial instruction to be repeated until user competence is established. Good design involves accurately predicting user response. In "Learning Versus Readability of Texts" (7), John T Guthrie concluded that there is a direct correlation between

readability and comprehension, and hence the chances of learning
were enhanced if the vocabulary and sentence structures were
within the capacities of the target group. It is further important to make sure that there are no spelling or grammatical errors
to avoid confirming the users in error through repetition, and to
maintain user confidence in the software.

The use of graphics can help to explain concepts that might be
hard to explain conveniently in screen display form, or they
create images which may assist retention, or simply help to
increase attention span or improve motivation. It can be useful
in graphics to show trends and results on a graph, pie chart or
histogram, or to represent parts of a piece of machinery. Such a
use reduces the need for long textual explanations for, in
general, people can absorb information better visually than
orally, and it is important to recognise the power of imagery in
thinking. Visualisation is also an effective aid to problem-
solving.

"Instrumentation to cultivate, activate and interact with the
learner must be based on whatever human behaviours are involved
in learning. Inevitably effective technology is shaped by these
behaviours." (8) John H Martin argues that the more a person's
senses are involved in a behavioural act, the more efficient the
learning will be. For all its initial attractiveness, television
is seen as essentially passive. He advocates the use of multi-
sensory and multiple involvement – kinesthetic, tactile and
vocal. Thus, with the use of graphics and interactive video, a
stimulating learning environment can produce effective results.
A broader range of response stimuli is probably desirable. An
oral capacity should be encouraged and display functions should
be enhanced, e.g. video tape and discs – tape and discs can store
the same material, but discs access it faster and display it with
higher quality and are most robust – tape/slide facilities, etc.
The traditional method of communicating with a computer has been
the standard keyboard and this has shaped design expectations.
The designer should remember that the new generation of machines
will permit mice and touch screen interfaces, graphics pads,
etc., and adapt design to these new methods. These other interface methodologies also avoid either user frustration in rejection through typing error, or the tedious task of building up a
synonym file to cover the multiple possibilities of a misspell-
ing. To further enhance the friendliness of the system pending
the outcome of research into natural language interfaces,
wherever possible, it is appropriate to select an author language
which will facilitate the evaluation of the text which the user
has input.

However, Martin's view contains two implicit assumptions. First,
that the child must always be active if the child is to be
stimulated to learn. Second, that an unhappy or bored student
cannot learn. Neither proposition is really sustainable.
Passively watching television can be enjoyable and the programs
may contain interesting materials which cause learning to occur.

It is clear that activity per se is not a precondition to learning. Research is therefore needed to determine what role pleasure plays in the education process. Perhaps enjoyment actually does enhance the memorisation of material. It may be true that students resist learning if they are bored, but both these propositions simply define the role of the teacher as the demonstrator of the relevance and interest of the materials to be communicated. If motivation is always external to the student, then in any learning activity, the student is passively acceding to the teacher's blandishment or threat in assimilating the subject matter of the lesson.

The truth is that the best learning probably occurs when the motivational drives are internal. Thus, if a child wishes to learn the art of roller skating or trick riding on a BMX bicycle, endless practice, and many falls and injuries, may be engaged in before the desired mastery is achieved. If there is no interest in the prospective task, there is less willingness to invest the effort in what is perceived to be boring and repetitive practice. To grow, a person must feel the stimulation of success. This success may be a form of peer group competition to see which of the group can achieve mastery of a particular skill or there may be more personal satisfactions in meeting and beating a challenge. Whichever rationale forms the basis of the motivation, each success brings more confidence which can sustain work of an initially less interesting nature.

Rule 5

Relate explanations to any practical situations relevant to the students' own experience and to contemporary events

This helps to reinforce memorisation by creating associations in the students' mind and can improve motivation through the demonstration of more immediate relevance. The CAL writer must also consider what knowledge or information is likely to be held by the users and seek to confirm existing knowledge, remove error, and build on the established base. If possible, teaching should be demand-led, i.e. the request for information should come from students who have perceived the need to know.

Rule 6

Always ask for a response which is directly relevant to the material immediately under consideration

To minimise the risk of user passivity, the students should regularly be asked to make some form of response, but the designer should avoid asking questions which simply call for copying from the screen. The software must also be robust so that it will not fail if the wrong or unexpected responses are given.

Rule 7

Vary the type of responses which the students are expected to use and require the most active response pattern possible from the student

In situations other than the giving of helpful instructions or of confidence boosting messages, it is not constructive to simply require the student to press Carriage Return in order to access the next step in the program, arguing that such an action is still more active than turning a page in a book. Even if such a statement were true, it is an abuse of the computer's capacity to respond to different types of user input and not as useful as a book in as much as the user cannot quickly flip back through the pages to check on an earlier point. The whole point of CAL is that it is to be an active learning experience. The more input a user is required to make, the greater the opportunity for error. The more errors, the greater the chance for the system to fulfil its role of teacher and guide. The system should not accept incorrect responses. Although these could be ignored, the best pattern is to give a message indicating the nature of the error and allow another opportunity for input. A user, however wayward, timid or disabled, should be patiently guided towards ultimate success.

"Autonomy tends to be discouraged in handicapped individuals. Children whose activities are unusually limited, who are watched over and protected, who for years cannot do what they see their peers doing, who are treated as patients, invalids, babies, incompetents, or bystanders learn to be passive. When the handi- capped child gets older, this passivity is often enhanced by depression, upon realising that he or she will never be like his or her parents. Motivation is the basic educational issue for these children." (9) Here the computer's ability to enhance performance becomes particularly important. It is also useful because it gives the child an opportunity to succeed at tasks which previously have been impossible. Thus, the child who cannot hold a pen can still be taught to type, etc.

Rule 8

Provide immediate feedback reinforcement

In the human interface, the teacher responds to the student by smiling encouragingly, frowning, or some other visual signal. Such clues allow the student to move forward confidently, or to reappraise the line being taken and thus avoid embarrassment. Computers cannot read expressions nor predict what is going to be said. The answer is therefore to give immediate feedback once the input has been made.

Rule 9

Incorporate regular tests which the student may take at his or her discretion

It is important to allow the student the opportunity to undertake regular tests of progress, but in order to minimise the risk of damage to self-esteem in the event of failure, the taking of the tests should not be compulsory (students should be allowed to choose the time when they are ready to take each test), the feedback and remediation must be supportive, and it may be appropriate to assure the students that the results of informal tests are not retained by the software.

Rule 10

Be user friendly

The working software should give clear instructions both to the teachers and to the end users. This includes good documentation which takes nothing for granted, e.g. the ability to switch on the machine, load programs, etc. and good screen layout. If possible, build in the capacity for the teacher to modify the content to suit particular course requirements or to meet changes in the curriculum content. Modularity in the design can assist the teacher to customise the software so long as there is a control mechanism which permits each teacher to select or deselect units for student use. Quite apart from this advantage, the writing of software in a modular form is the approved style because it reduces the amount of information that the programmer must bear in mind at any one time. This should also result in fewer errors, and more effective error detection. It is also helpful for the designer to give details about the structure of the software, the target group and level(s) of content, and an indication as to the length of time study is likely to take. The educational design philosophy should be indicated, together with an idea of how the teacher can test to see whether the particular learning objectives have been met.

Rule 11

Validation at all points in construction is useful

The designer should never tell the validator in detail what is to come. The objective viewer should come with no preconceptions and feel free to comment and to note problems. Prototyping and pilot testing are important stages in CAL software design. A prototype is a quick approximation of the finished product for, upon seeing the implementation of what seemed a good idea, the designer can often make a significant reappraisal based upon something more than intuition.

If the programming is done by an independent programmer, it can also give the educational specialist an insight into the real capacities of the computer. However, unless the initial process of design produced clear and precise performance criteria, it is difficult for the educationalist to judge the actual program's effectiveness. All experienced designers expect imperfections in the first versions of the program, but without a good system design, it is difficult to determine when work of sufficient quality has been produced. The iterative process of design, programming, evaluation and new design specifications can produce highly effective results, but is costly in terms of time and effort. Without clear initial guidelines, a law of diminishing returns applies as less and less substantive improvements are actually achieved in each iteration.

It is always necessary to have the completed software vetted by subject-based experts who can then vouch for the accuracy of the content and teaching methodology. However, if the writer is not completely familiar with the subject matter and wishes to minimise the number of revisions, early consultations are in order. That software has been vetted by people of appropriate authority also enhances the marketability of the product.

7.3   More detailed rules

7.3.1. CAL packages can either be command–driven or menu–driven

The menu presents the user with a number of choices at each node and is well suited to the inexperienced user because it eliminates the need to remember long lists of possible commands. The drawback is that it is slow in comparison to the command–driven form, both because it takes longer for the screen display to appear, and because it can take the student longer to read and assimilate the menu material. Further, through inexperience, a user may have to move through several menus in order to achieve a given effect. Even when experience is built up, it may be that the same menu–grinding approach is continued with no short cuts possible. This can be extremely tedious. On the other hand, the only time the user is presented with instruction in a command–driven form is when it is requested. This is most convenient for experienced users but can take longer to learn. The best solution is therefore to provide a mixture of the two. In the first instance, the learner can use the menus until familiarity with the commands is established, and then switch to the command–driven form.

7.3.2 At the begining of each computer tutorial, a title page is useful

This should set out the nature of the topic to be covered and indicate the general approach. The designer should also consider whether any motivating material is useful – a humorous introduction may be funny the first time but pall on repetition, and musical recitals or animated graphics may unreasonably slow down access to the substantive material and ultimately annoy. Following the title page, it may be a good idea to tell the student of the learning objectives to be achieved. The issue is whether the statement focuses the student's mind only on the objectives listed, and means that there will be less attention paid to important but peripheral matters. To leave the user to make up his or her own mind is to allow a mature reflection of all issues raised whether specifically or non–specifically intended. Other objections are more pragmatic, e.g. too much for young or inexperienced students to absorb and, in any event, it may not be appropriate for them to have this more detailed information. It may be hard to write.

7.3.3 Clear and accurate instructions should also be given at the begining

All users should have a clear indication of how to go forward, how to go backwards, how to get help and how to leave the program. A way back to these instructions should always be allowed because people may not opt to read them (if a choice is given), or may read them superficially and not remember. The user, whether staff or student, should be allowed to leave the program at any point during the run. Equally, because it cannot be assumed that each student will have the time or the inclination to finish the tutorial, a restart facility is a good idea so that the student can return to the point left. This avoids the frustration of having to work through the program again from scratch. It is always useful to be able to pick up and put down a book. The computer should be capable of working in the same way.

7.3.4 People learn better when new information can be related to existing information

A tutorial should not review prior knowledge in detail, but should make reference to prior knowledge. In educational theory, the Gestaltists try to generate the opportunity for students to perceive patterns in, and relationships between, different pieces of information, while Cognitive Psychologists try to encourage reflective thinking and problem-solving skills, by exposing the students to previously acquired knowledge. It also enhances the overall process of memorisation and helps to consolidate understanding, particularly in those students who are serialists (see section 6.10).

7.3.5 The use of a pretest may be desirable

The designer should consider whether it is appropriate to provide an introductory synopsis of the knowledge which is to be relied upon. If a synopsis is built in as a possible sequence, some designers have a pretest to determine whether the existing knowledge is either good enough to permit using the immediate tutorial, or too good to make it worth the student's while. In the former case, the synopsis can then be used. Otherwise, the student can be referred to another program altogether. It makes sense not to waste a student's time if the tutorials are not in some predetermined sequence. Equally, the use of a pretest would be a redundant section if it is known that all students will need to use the program. The very existence of the test may also be counter-productive in that it make the students unreasonably apprehensive about the material to be studied. Some students may even consider that they have a vested interest in always failing the pretest (see section 2.5). The designer may therefore reach the conclusion that it may be better to have the pretest as a separate program so that teachers can make their own decisions, perhaps using the pretest for other purposes. Incorporating the pretest without the option to exclude its operation may give teachers who have not been consulted with a view to approving the idea, a disincentive not to use the program.

7.3.6 Presenting information through text

One of the justifications for keeping text short is to increase student interaction. Self-evidently, the more frames a student must access to acquire the information, the more active the student must be to initiate the move from one frame to the next. Whether complex information is also better presented in short sections depends upon student age and levels of concentration. This will be determined, in part, by whether the students can read a longer time without loosing interest or becoming confused. It is important to challenge the students, and even if concentration is thought to be weak, longer text may be appropriate if interspersed with pictures or sound. With short pieces of information, users may be able to get through programs more quickly. But if students are advanced, information may be better assimilated in a more coherent form, and small dribs and drabs may be annoying. Regardless of ability, students must be able to perceive a clear flow of ideas, and not view each segment as a discrete box. It may therefore be useful to refer backwards and forwards between frames.

Systems limit the amount of text which can be displayed through the number of characters in any given line, and the number of lines which can be displayed on the screen at any one time. In the West, people read from left to write and top to bottom. It is usually sensible to add new text to the screen in this way. The designer should always avoid scrolling text because all people find it difficult to read text in motion, and usually forget what the first line was after it has disappeared from the screen. It is also more difficult to distinguish new information from old, and so hard to determine from where to read when text suddenly stops scrolling. Similarly, text should only be erased when the user indicates that it is no longer required unless time constraints are being used - anything else is distracting and irritating to users.

7.3.7 Text format

The screen format should always adopt the convention that lines do not end in the middle of words, and that paragraphs should not start on the last line of a page display. Text should be distributed evenly over the whole screen or centred. Text in upper case is more difficult to read than normal text. If it is necessary to create emphasis, this should be achieved by drawing a box around the relevant text to separate it from other elements displayed. One of the major design issues is whether the layout should be varied. Constant change can make the activity more interesting, avoiding visual boredom and retaining attentiveness. Alternatively, visual consistency might be more important to keep users confident and comfortable with the conventions adopted, i.e. where to look for new information, how to answer questions, etc.

Pictures capture attention more than text, so it is important only to use pictorial presentation when the information is particularly significant and the image highlights something in the text. Some graphics are visually excellent, but bad educationally because they distract from the important material in the text. Consequently, authors should suppress the creative instinct unless it represents the primary method of presenting information, and will add an analogy or mnemonic, or make the information more memorable. In any event, it is a good policy to avoid excessive detail in the graphic. No matter how impressive the end-product may appear to be, the time taken to generate perfection is often not justified. Line drawings are usually sufficient, in successive overlays if necessary.

7.3.8 The program should say just what is required and no more

In general, text should be lean and summarised. In design terms, it is better to start short and let it grow, rather than start fat. This is because, if the text does start full and the program is only partially successful, i.e. upon pilot testing, it induces only some learning, the designer will not know which bits to cut out and which bits to change. Overall, the validation process will probably be more straightforward if a minimalist writing style is adopted. In any event, students may learn more from a summarised text.

A typical textbook contains about four hundred pages of text, but no teacher would seriously expect the student to learn all that material. The question is what the student is expected to remember. Some of the information will be factual, some will be aimed at communicating skills. Research tends to suggest that recall is enhanced by the logical structuring of the information, rather than by the reader's perception of importance. (10) It seems that readers implicitly recognise the importance of central points. This might be taken as an argument for omitting any detailed information from the text because identifying the points as minor or subordinate consumes processing time. Further, if students have difficulty in distinguishing the main points, re-call can suffer or the less important points may be memorised.

On the other hand, the full text can be a valuable resource because the detail provides illustrations and expansions of the points, and these may reinforce understanding of the main points. It also gives a feel for the argument structure underlying the field. Although specific arguments may not be remembered, the lines of debate may be recreated in the future if the overall framework is grasped. Further, the main point might be unconvinc-ing without the detail. However, although these details have the potential to add to the memorisation of the main points, the question of effectiveness remains. It is accepted that the detail may imply the main point, but the reverse is not necessarily true. To discover whether the inclusion of detail is advantageous to memorisation or not, Reder and Anderson have conducted a series of experiments. (11) Information was presented both in text form and in summary form, and students were tested as to recall immediately after study and after a delay of one week. The summaries were approximately one fifth the length of the full texts and were about 1,000 words long. A series of comprehen-sion questions were then devised, all of which could be answered from the summary. Their experimental data suggest:

. that learning material from summaries is at least as good as reading the original text

. that people's ability to recognise important facts about a topic after studying it, regardless as to the delay between study and test, is superior when the information is learned from a summary

. that new information is learned better if information learned earlier on a related topic was learned by reading a summary

This ran contrary to their initial expectation which had been that the embellishments of the text would aid retention since they would provide a redundant coherent structure. It must there-fore be assumed that recall is based upon first accessing the main points, and then moving to the detail. These experiments do not show that the students have a better appreciation of the topic by reading a summary. Indeed, all they may show is that some students are unable or unwilling to identify the main points and only skim the detail in a full text. However, analysis of the data reveals that the results are general to all levels of academic ability.

7.3.9 Problem of response time

When the computer keyboard is being used, one of the decisions to be made is whether the response to the touch of the key should be instantaneous. Clearly, long delays will lead to a loss of concentration and motivation – indeed, machine abuse is becoming a more real problem as users expect fast response times and grow impatient – but equally, some find an immediate display a little threatening. John Heaford reports that most users are now conditioned to expect a response rate of better than 2 seconds and that anything over 4 seconds is unacceptable. (12) On the other hand, a student is entitled to one or two seconds relaxation between the completion of an exercise, or the absorbtion of difficult material, before concentration is required again. This assumes that time is adjustable as a variable. Sadly, on a mainframe system response time can be significantly affected by the number of on-line users. If delays are to be expected at certain peak times, formal educational use should perhaps be deferred, or some form of scheduling or timetabling introduced to spread the load more evenly. However, if students or staff are being introduced to real-world phenomena, artificial delays should be built in to models of full systems so that the full sense of user frustration can be experienced.

7.3.10 Graphics and colour

The use of graphics can enhance student understanding where spatial or quantitative issues are involved, while dynamic graphics allow the display of processes and procedures. Sound is not so well developed. Most machines can do no more than produce a range of primitive electronic tones, and the development of music and voice synthesis is technically demanding or virtually impossible, depending upon the nature of the given machine.

Colour on its own, and changes of colour, attract attention but both can be overused and lose their effect. As a positive device, colour adds an extra dimension to an otherwise bland screen. The contemporary environment is filled with colour – television, newspapers and magazines, and the new architectural and design standards, all now make an innovative and creative use of new reproduction, paint and plastics technology to provide an interesting environment. If the educational environment is monochrome, it may fail to compete for the students' interest.
Colour also better reflects best practice in graphics design. Even simple colour coding can make graphs, pie charts and histograms easier to understand where multiple variables are involved. But an overuse of colour coding should be avoided because students can easily forget which colour relates to each variable and become confused. It should also be remembered that some students are colour blind. To cater for this contingency, there should be

189

an element of redundancy in the use of colours, their use being perhaps merely as a back-up to cross hatching or some other unambiguous signification system. In any event, some combinations of colour are easier to see than others, even given ideal lighting conditions. Further, colours should never be used in a perverse way, e.g. red for "go", and green for "stop", etc.

The more difficult the tutorial or complex the information, the less the student may want to interact. The main student desire may be to extract meaning and to establish salience. There are a variety of prompts which may be used to assist the student. These include simple underlining, changing the size of letters, inverting the colours, e.g. black on white, changing the typeface, using arrows and drawing boxes, or isolating a key point on an otherwise blank screen - other information may be distracting from that point actually shown. Most computers also offer the facility of blinking - ie words flashing on and off. This is very wearing on the eyes if persisted in so, once the point is made, the word or phrase should stop flashing.

7.3.11 The function of questions

The program must always demand interaction. This is usually done by asking questions. This forces attention, forces the student to practice knowledge, gives data by which to assess how well the student understands and remembers the point at issue, and facilitates switching from one frame to another. For this purpose, informal questions should be frequent. This particularly aids comprehension and recall if significant quantities of information are being given. Questions can be dichotomous, multiple choice or more open ended. Questions which require a simple true/false choice are unreliable because of the problem of mere guessing. For this reason, the multiple choice format is the most common form. Thus, the designer can number alternatives, use identifying letters, or require the student to move the cursor to the desired answer or, if a touch sensitive screen is being used, invite the student to point to the preferred answer. Numbers are the easiest approach because unfamiliarity with the keyboard may make letter searching too slow, but both are prone to error in pressing the wrong key. The simple movement of the cursor is the most foolproof system. In designing multiple format questions, the incorrect answers must have some degree of plausibility so that the student does not simply eliminate the obviously wrong answers, and four or five alternatives should be given.

The type of question can be varied by requiring student input in completing a sentence or identifying incorrect words in a definition. It is not possible for a computer to deal with a free language answer in an essay form, although short answers may be required (limited to no more than four or five words, this permits the author some chance of predicting the likely words and minimises the chances of mistyping). In completion questions, the problem is to decide how many words should be entered, where they are located in a sentence and how significant each word is to be. The general rule is that only important words should be blanked out, and not too many per question because otherwise the entire meaning may be lost. It is also better to have the blank near the end of the sentence. These latter forms reduce student guessing and more truly test comprehension.

In general, questions should not merely restate the textual information given. New examples, situations or descriptive terms should be used to ensure that the student is not merely recalling information, but being asked for the substance of the concept. From a purely grammatical point of view, it is better to avoid the negative form of question, which students frequently misunderstand. Further, questions should not deal with mere details because this may attribute the wrong level of importance to the point in the student's mind, and distract from the more major points. Finally, any questions posed before the disclosure of information can be rhetorical, and be aimed at stimulating the student to search for the answer by demonstrating the need for the knowledge. However, this should be used with some circumspection where the target group are lacking in confidence and self-esteem.

When the answer is given, various possibilities arise:

. The author may simply judge the answer as given to be correct; thus, if the answer is 49 or option (c) then the student will either have made the right selection or entered the correct amount.

. Or it contains an expected error; thus, the usual arithmetic error is known to produce the result actually entered or, because of conceptual difficulties, students often mistake option (b) as the right answer.

. Or it may contain an unexpected error; where a numeric is required and the answer entered bears no resemblance to the predicted answers both correct and incorrect, the answer may simply be deemed wrong or the student could be asked to write the methodology to a file for later evaluation by a human tutor.

. Or it is partially correct; thus, the term is misspelt or a synonym of not quite the right accuracy is used or, say, the decimal point is in the wrong place.

. Or it is neither right nor wrong, e.g. input of user's name, or it is a response of the wrong type, e.g. letter instead of number.

In a tutorial, students should be allowed time to reflect upon the material and their answers. They may also wish to consult

additional materials such a notes or books. The general setting
of time limits is probably not a good idea, for some pauses may
be occasioned by the fact that the student does not know what to
do. After a period of inactivity, it may therefore be useful to
ask the student whether help is required.

7.3.12 The computer can be used to generate problems, solutions, associated remedial routines and remedial materials

This is done through algorithms and the process has several
advantages in that, in numerically-based subject disciplines, it
is possible to create a virtually unlimited resource of instructional material, it is unnecessary to prestore instructional
materials, and it is more adaptive to individual students because
it allows the student to attempt as many problems as needed to
attain the educational objectives of the program. The first step
is to parameterise the various components in the given problem.
This includes the data for the problem, criteria of difficulty,
the performance criteria necessary to define success, and the
expected behaviour of the students. This latter element, as Gagne
would describe, is rule-governed and it should help to determine
the order of problem presentation. Gagne postulates that learning
is a hierarchical activity and that skills should be acquired in
optimum order to fit into a total perception.

The individual parameters must be generated in a particular order
and will be selected randomly from a pre-selected range. Some
variables will be independent of the others, some will be dependent upon others. When created, these values will be fitted into
the problem template. Some problems can only be solved by the
application of a single rule. Others may involve the selection of
an appropriate solution strategy. To some extent, this may be
controlled both by the class of problem and by the values
assigned to the variables. All these features generate the
problem. Palmer and Oldehoeft describe a system to generate
problems on analytic geometry, specifically testing whether the
student can construct the equation of the line, then, given a
point and the equation of the line, can construct a line through
the given point which is parallel or perpendicular to the given
line, then, given any two components of a parabola (directrix,
focus and vertex) can find the remaining component and construct
the equation of the parabola, and so on. (13) It is, however,
clear that this system could be adapted to most concepts in
maths, physics, chemistry, emgineering and those disciplines
where tasks and skills are based on absolute data and are well
structured.

The computer must also calculate the answer to the problem and be
able either to test student performance at each point of
difficulty, or to give the students a step by step explanation of
how to arrive at the correct answer if an error is made. If the

student achieves well from the outset, or responds to the remedial explanations, the system must be able to generate problems of greater difficulty or to move on to the next class of problem. Thus, the computer must have good rules for assessing the level of difficulty and must know what achievement criteria, i.e. the number of partial or complete successes in a sequence, justify passing on to the next level of questions. The result should be that the student is drilled more thoroughly on the elements not well understood. Successive failures will, of course, result in the human teacher's attention being drawn to the need to offer assistance.

In dealing with Nuclear Magnetic Resonance, which is one of the mechanisms whereby chemists study how atoms are joined together to form molecules, Sleeman has constructed what he terms a problem-solving monitor, written in LISP. (14) He began by considering the type of interaction that would go on between a teacher and a single student. It seemed unlikely to him that this would consist of a simple question/answer sequence. It seemed likely that the student might make assertions about the problem and that the teacher would allow him to talk until he came to a contradiction and then help him resolve it, or tell him immediately whether his last assertion was correct. In designing the monitor, he assumed that the student was familiar with the algorithm but needed assistance in extracting the essential information from that presented. The monitor selects a problem for the students to solve and then observes the various student assertions as to the equivalent form of the spectrum, which group and which peak form the head of the molecule, which group is the next in the chain, and what is the structure of the molecule.

If the student solves the problem by deducing the nature of the molecule, this will prove familiarity with the algorithm. Should there be an error, there are a series of what he terms Socratic features, viz. the three commands Summary, Help and Explain. Summary gives a synopsis of the information which the student has collected about the current problem. Help indicates how the student might set about trying to solve the problem, and Explain tells the student why incorrect assertions or hypotheses are inadmissible. To meet these objectives, the computer has to have an algorithm which can build all the possible and permissible permutations given the molecule so far specified, the remaining atoms available, the spectrum still to be explained and the spectrum which corresponds to the molecule built. Any program which purports to teach in an intelligent manner, must have the ability to perform the task itself and to provide hints and explanations on request. The goal is to permit the program to impose a structure on the student, i.e. it gives the student physical data and asks the student to make deductions about the structure of the molecule which would give rise to such data; by monitoring the student's performance, and matching student behaviour to the algorithm, the computer can guide the student into the correct line of analysis.

7.4   Conclusions

"My own perception is that you should only bring the computer in as a part of the total educational content of each subject studied, that the computer should never the segregated in any sense from that which should be the main focus of study, namely, knowledge." (15) Whereas the traditional chalk-and-talk approach an fudge the educational issues through the inherent flexibility of the form, the best practice of computerisation must always start with an express analysis of educational aims and objectives of each general course element. Only if a proper justification for the use of CAL has been formulated, should the author then move on to the more mechanical side of software production, knowing exactly what educational outcomes are to be expected. Hence, computerisation for its own sake is likely to be educationally bad because it will not have a clear direction either in content or in design. If such is the case, no amount of invention, say, in the use of graphics or of colour, will conceal the hollowness of the shell.

References

(1) Computers: Promise and Challenge in Education. 117/8.

(2) Planning and Authoring Computer Assisted Instruction Lessons. Robert M. Gagne, Walter Wagner & Alicia Rojas. (1981) Educational Technology. September. pp.17/26.

(3) Principles of Instructional Design. Robert M. Gagne and Leslie J. Briggs. particularly Chapters 3, 4 & 5.

(4) Computer-Based Instruction. Methods and Development. p.289.

(5) Cognitive demand of CAL. Jean D.M.Underwood. collected in Teachers, Computers and the Classroom. pp. 25/37 at p.26.

(6) Microcomputers and special education: survey and prospects. Peter Goodyear and Annette Barnard. collected in Microcomputers in Education. pp.61/73 at p.69.

(7) Learning Versus Readability of Texts. John T Guthrie (1972) 65 Journal of Educational Research 273/80.

(8) John H Martin's report contained in Joseph B. Margolin and Marion R. Mirsch. (ed) Computers in the Classroom. An interdisciplinary view of trends and alternatives. Spartan Books, New York. 1970. p.89.

(9) Computer, Education and Special Needs. p.125/6

(10) B.J.F. Meyer and G.W. McConkie. What is recalled after reading a passage? (1973) 65 Jo. Educational Psychology 109/117.

(11) Lynne M. Reder & John R.Anderson. A Comparison of Texts and Their Summaries. Memorial Consequences. (1980) 19 Jo. of Verbal Learning and Verbal Behavior 121/34.

(12) Myth of the Learning Machine. p.215.

(13) The Design of an Instructional System Based on Problem Generators. Brian. G .Palmer and Arthur. E. Oldehoeft. (1975) Vol.7. No.2. Int. J. of Man—Machine Studies 249/71.

(14) A Problem—solving Monitor for a Deductive Reasoning Task. D.H.Sleeman. (1975) 7(2) Int. J. of Man—Machine Studies 183/211.

(15) Personal Thoughts and Prejudices. Michael Slade. collected in Computers and the Law Teacher. edited by David V Marshall. North Staffordshire Polytechnic, Stoke—on—Trent. 1983. pp.76/80 at p.79.

CHAPTER 8

COMPUTERS AND THE PROCESSES OF SIMULATION, MODELLING AND GAMING

Up to this point, the main assumption has been that the educational use of computers has been restricted to an inter-active question–and–answer form. It is now necessary to consider the other main possibilities, namely that the computer supports a model of a phenomenon, or that it is used for simulation purposes or for gaming.

8.1 What is a model?

A model is a concrete or theoretical representation of a real system which provides an analogue of that system, and which allows for the possibility of using that analogue for the purposes of prediction or experimentation. Some models are entirely deterministic, i.e. they are mere demonstrations of fixed phenomena. Others are non–deterministic and depend for their operation upon random elements within the program, or the specification of parameters by the user. A practical researcher might use a physical model, say, to determine the aerodynamic drag factor in the design of a new motor car, and this might obviate the necessity of building a real machine with all the expense that would involve, including time in a wind tunnel. The saving in expenditure would become truly significant if the model ought to be continuously variable to determine the optimum shape through practical experimentation. It is true that costs could be maintained within reasonable bounds due to the fact that neither the real nor the computerised model needs to be a complete replica of reality. To be useful, the model need only have the features immediately relevant to the user. Hence, the real model to test wind resistance need only have physical shape, it does not need an engine under the bonnet nor the elegant dashboard displays which an end user might expect. However, if the model can be mathematical, it may be used to produce an interactive representation of the processes involved. Such models are infinitely more flexible than physical models and will tend to be cheaper, even though substantial computing power may be required to support them.

8.2   What is a simulation?

The process of building and using a model is termed simulation. A simulation may therefore be seen as a representation of some process or activity which allows a student to experience some of the elements of the real world. This may involve the student taking on a role which is unfamiliar, e.g. in driving a car, and designers have the option of incorporating a gaming element which may enhance the motivational quality of the simulation. The model underlying the simulation is usually a simplification of reality in that details may be omitted or changed, but the resultant system should nevertheless imitate or replicate an aspect of the world. Hence, in designing a driving instruction program, the monitor screen could be made to show a view of reality in terms of road conditions and all the dashboard gauges and instruments (whether through the use of graphics or video). However, in engineering terms, this model may have too much noise, i.e. too much redundant information is given, and this excess both makes it more difficult to identify the most significant elements of information, and obscures the simple processes required to meet standard situations and hazards. If the designer neglects to simplify down to the bare essentials, the student may be confused by this excess of information and fail to identify the primary constituent elements of the problem. To that extent, the use of simulations has the capacity to improve salience.

8.2.1 When should simulations be used?

The decision to use simulations should not be taken lightly. It must be seen to be educationally appropriate to use a simulation in the particular learning context. At some ages and in some subjects, it is more beneficial to handle the real object or to perform the real process than to use a simulation, computer-based or otherwise. This is not to downgrade the interactive quality of simulations, for the student is usually more than a mere spectator and will normally be required to make input to the model after deciding upon some strategy.

As with the decision whether to use CAL outlined in Chapter 7, so the teacher must decide whether a simulation will communicate precisely what is needed in the best way to be assimilated by the target group of learners. Hence, vocational training courses may require direct real-world experience. Alternatively, given that each simulation will tend to be a simplifed version of reality, the less confident students can be gently introduced to problems and their solutions, and can safely explore and build up a picture of that part of the world before being exposed to the full reality. However, in making the educational value judgement, it must be recognised that the use of simulations does not necessarily support any direct educational aim. The student may simply be put in a position where learning is to be through experimentation with the model, so that rules of cause and effect may be determined. To that extent, simulations are distinguishable from tutorials because the students learn by performance rather than through a Socratic discourse. It is an aspect of discovery learning, allowing the student the opportunity to develop the skills of hypothesis-testing, logic, inductive and deductive reasoning, and extrapolation.

In some senses, the use of any simulation may be best suited to the teaching of problem-solving or decision-making skills. Thus, students with a good level of understanding will be able to explore each model in a systematic way, varying one parameter to determine the effect upon other variables. But it is not clear that younger or less experienced students can benefit from simulations in the same way. Older and more experienced students may have the confidence and the ability to manipulate the model to gain the most insight into the processes and procedures involved. Where there is less conceptual ability, the student explorers will need significant prompting if the maximum benefit is to be derived from the experience.

Under normal circumstances, no programming expertise on the part of the student will be called for in the manipulation of the simulation, and the user interface will permit, indeed encourage, such a positive investigation of the relationships between the variables. In extreme cases, however, where there is appropriate expertise, and there are adequate precautions taken to protect the original software's integrity, the students might be allowed to amend the program to more positively investigate cause and effect. This overall approach of experimentation leads to a critical educational advantage. Many mathematical models qua models are outside the ordinary manipulative competence of the students using manual means. But, with computer assistance, their importance can be directly investigated. Other phenomena, such as nuclear reactions, could not safely or conveniently be handled in an ordinary educational environment. Yet, through computers, detailed reactions can be observed. The graphics capacity of the computer is essential in this. Further, simulations are significantly less expensive than many real-world experiments which may involve the use of valuable chemicals or equipment. Experiments can also be run quickly one after another, whereas in the real world, many hours of preparation might be required before each repitition. Finally, the use of the computer avoids the frustration of an experiment being ruined and data lost through faulty equipment or preparation or, indeed, through poor technique.

8.2.2 Why do computer-supported simulations tend to be more useful than their manual counterparts?

One of the primary features of even the smaller capacity computers of contemporary technology, is that a large number of variables can be controlled and manipulated in a computer-based simulation. Moreover, the monitoring of user responses can be effected unobtrusively without interruption to the participant's involvement or concentration. Hence, the dynamic nature of the simulation and the speed with which requests and responses may be handled, retains the attention, interest and involvement of the participants. Further, a computer can handle more complex areas of knowledge and reach a closer match to reality than is possible using manual methods. This would allow considerable scope to the designer in the creation of a more realistic setting in which the student is to be presented with the model.

Simulation programs, because of their self-directive qualities, tend to be popular with learners. This is a mixed blessing. Learners can be strongly motivated to explore the model which may enhance the learning opportunity. But, given the amount of work sometimes necessary to fully explore the model, it can take up a lot of a group's time. This has serious implications for the conventionally-based teaching curriculum if a given amount of material has to be covered in formal lectures or classes for the purposes of an externally moderated or assessed examination.

The teaching staff must therefore take care only to schedule simulations when time is properly available. However, should the teaching environment have the necessary degree of flexibility, there is no reason why simulations cannot be widely used. More-over, if it should be required, the motivational qualities of the simulation can be signficantly improved by turning the simulation into a game, a step which, in turn, may improve student perform-ance. Finally, simulations can also be a useful testing mechan-ism, it being so much better to see whether a prospective pilot can fly a simulated plane without crashing, before allowing access to the real thing.

8.2.3 Is it possible to produce a taxonomy of simulations?

The first step is to identify the primary characteristics upon which computer simulations are to be classified. These features will include:

. the complexity of the rules

. the extent of the structure

. the use of graphics

. the degree of interaction

. the extent of competitiveness

. the underlying functions and assumptions

Measurement and assessment of these factors should allow the identification of four major classifications:

. educational

. experimental

. evaluative

. predictive

However, it will be relatively unusual for a program to fall exclusively within one classification.

To a greater or lesser extent, all computer simulations will make use of graphics and visual displays, and structured questioning may play a part. Hence, a drill and practice engineering program could be accompanied by a dynamic visual simulation of the subject-matter to be tested which can either lead the user to the right answer, or retrospectively demonstrate the nature of the error made. Alternatively, the user may change the value of variables in the model and observe the differences in result. Such programs can be accompanied by a form of computer coach which comments upon the different values which the student has adopted, and may suggest other testing strategies which will demonstrate different results. But if the model is being used to explore entirely new phenomena or new data, and so no pre-programmed coaching can be built in, the computer may still supply a partial commentary to support the predictive or evaluative functions. Such a simulation might be used for entirely commercial purposes, e.g. to attempt to predict total market share based upon a trial regional marketing campaign, or it might be educational to demonstrate the methodology to business or management students. However, by bearing the suggested framework of classification in mind, the best simulation can be selected from existing software, or designed to match the particular need.

Moving from the broad categories of a taxonomy, there are several different applications and functions for simulations. A physical simulation is where a physical object or process is displayed, allowing the student an opportunity to use it or learn about it. There are laboratory simulations where the student is given pieces of equipment and allowed to perform a range of experiments. In either a gaming or training simulation, the user will be given more direct experience. Thus, in a simulation of flying an aircraft, the user may see a simplified view of the instruments and a view through the cockpit window. Such simulations may be used to demonstrate the procedural content of particular skills, as opposed to allowing practice of procedures, i.e. the student or trainee learns about how a process works so that the relevant skills to operate it may be acquired, or it may involve both, so that the student or trainee not only learns about the physical object, but also about the procedures for operating it. Finally, diagnostic simulations present the student with a problem to solve, and allow the student to learn the procedures necessary to solve it, e.g. medical diagnosis and attempted therapies and treatments, car maintainance and repair, etc.

One of the more recent examples of a medical simulation has been produced at the University of Liverpool. It is based on the authoring language MICROTEXT, and runs on a BBC micro. The major design requirement was that the student's responses should be made without external assistance or undue menu prompting, against a time base which shows the deterioration of the patient. The clinical simulation reflects the natural sequence of an emergency within a hospital environment. The patient must first be resuscitated and the condition investigated with a view to formulating a diagnosis and devising appropriate treatment. This treatment should not only take account of the immediate symptoms but also provide against late complications. Tests on this software at both undergraduate and postgraduate level have shown a significant improvement in performance in later multiple-choice question examinations. (1)

These simulations are most effective where the topics are of a more absolute nature and susceptible to algorithmic analysis. There are, however, limits to the fidelity of such simulations and, sooner or later, students must be allowed access to training

on the real thing. Moreover, fidelity in programming terms costs
money and so, for example, the capital invested in many flight
simulators now approaches the cost of real aircraft, although
they are not as expensive to operate per hour as the real aero-
plane, and they can simulate fire, storm and other dangerous
phenomena which it would be inexpedient to risk in real life.
This is not to devalue the expenditure in producing realistic
software. Many skills depend on an intuitive feel for the machine
or the situation. Sophisticated simulations which replicate the
physical as well as the intellectual activity in question, can
prepare a student for the real experience in a way that no paper
and pencil expercise could. The design must therefore strike a
balance between simplicity, which makes the model initially more
accessible to the target group, and complexity which may be more
real. This dilemma is accentuated by the fact that reality will
always be potentially confusing to the target group, as well as
being more expensive to produce in programming time.

8.2.4 What other functions do simulations perform?

Situational simulations are usually role-playing, i.e. they rely
upon each of the participants acting out a role within a pre-
defined scenario. Their purpose is to reflect and investigate the
attitudes and behaviours of people in different situations.
Process simulations allow the student to select the values of
various parameters at the begining of the run and then act as a
form of window on the world, giving the student an insight into
the changes which would result. Economists might use this to
demonstrate different forecasting techniques, say, for the gross
domestic product in a model of the economy. The learning results
from the repetition of the simulation a number of times with
different values and a comparison of the results. Such a simulation will either be a speeded up, or a slowed down, version of
reality. Some phenomena literally happen too fast to see with the
naked eye, while others take years and it would be impossible to
maintain an objective perspective. To that extent, perception and
conceptualisation can be significantly enhanced by adjusting the
time base.

8.2.5 Why are simulations more motivating than conventional learning aids?

Simulations are motivating because it is more interesting to fly
a simulated aircraft than merely to read about it. It is more
interesting to try to save a patient, or to repair a car, than
merely to see sequence of photographs or a video about the
process. In a conventional teacher-centred course, it is often
the case that a significant amount of introductory material will

have to be communicated before any real understanding of a practical process emerges. Even with the most charismatic of teachers to make the presentation, this can be very boring and demotivating. But a simulation can introduce a topic and pose questions which can then be answered by the teacher using the more traditional forms of communication. Students are more easily motivated once they accept the need for the information. Equally, it could be dangerous to allow inexperienced individuals to experiment with expensive machinery, or indeed, to allow them to run a business just to facilitate training in accountancy or marketing. Real-world experiments might rely upon the use of expensive materials and equipment, and it would not be possible to fund school or college laboratory work in new areas of knowledge. Although simulations are not, and cannot be, the real world, they still represent an approach based upon learning by doing and, in general, this produces a better and more efficient transfer of skills from the educational environment to the real world.

8.3 How effective are simulations as learning aids?

Stanley Roscoe asserts that the process of measuring the degree of effectiveness in the transfer of training is incremental, i.e. it deals with the degree to which the learning of one task is facilitated by the prior learning of another. Any saving of time is therefore a function of the degree of similarity between each successive task, and the extent to which the first interdependent task has been recently practised. He postulates that if there is a relative incremental saving in learning time for each new task, the learning method can be seen to be increasingly cost effective. He based his experiments on the methods used to train aircraft pilots. The main reason for selecting this training situation was that he considers flying to be a criterion-referenced task, i.e. basic competence can be measured by absolute standards.

The focus of the experiment was the amount of time which each trainee spent in the simulator, an activity which was approximately one third the cost of dual instruction in the air. Independently of the revenue implications, the Federal Aviation Administration (FAA) had implicitly recognised the effectiveness of ground-based training by legally requiring eleven hours of simulator training in some FAA-approved courses. Roscoe set out to test whether the savings were real up to the eleventh hour, acknowledging the obvious truths that the effectiveness of any training device depends upon how well it is used by the trainers, and upon the timing of its introduction into the training time-table.

The working hypothesis was that the incremental transfer effectiveness of any device may be expected to be a series of negatively decelerated curves associated with successive phases of a training curriculum. He and Kingsley Povenmire tested the performance of students enrolled in the private pilot course at the Institute of Aviation at the University of Illinois. All the students were to be trained in a Piper Cherokee, but different groups received amounts of time in a Link GAT-1 ground-based simulator varying from no time to eleven hours. Estimates of the tranfer effectiveness of the GAT-1 were based on the relative amounts of flight training required by those students who were recommended for certification as private pilots.

The first major finding was that when the GAT-1 was introduced, there were significant savings in the time taken to reach the prescribed performance criteria. The speculation is that the instructors' enthusiasm for the trainer communicated itself to the students who responded favourably. However, as the novelty wore off for the instructors, and they became less tolerant of the machine's lack of robustness, the students apparently did not gain the same benefit. It is therefore reasonable to conclude that the effectiveness in the use of any training device will be enhanced if the instructors are educationally ingenious in its use and confident in the outcome. A further element was probably the weather. In a perfect test, both simulator and aircraft would be equally available as a resource at any given time. The decision as to which method to use would therefore be determined exclusively by educational need. But because the weather might prevent flight, the simulator might be used at a non-optimum time.

Analysis of the data showed that the trainer was most effective when used for between five and seven hours. The final conclusion, which should apply to any educational situation in which simulations are used, is that the GAT-1 was an effective aid to the learning experience because it was highly comparable to the real-world experience. Given the then level of sophistication in the technology, it can be said with some certainty that it is not necessary that that the simulator should be a complete replication of reality. Indeed, a part of the efficiency lies in either making time more amenable to the experimenter, or in removing distractions from the elements considered the most important. However, no matter how effective the model itself may be, to optimise the learning transfer effectiveness, sound educational use had to be made of it, rather than decisions based upon mere expediency. (2)

8.3.1 What is the true value of the interactive role-playing simulations?

Role-playing simulations are quite common and can serve a variety of educational purposes. In an introductory vein, the younger student can either be required to assume the role of a mountaineer (Everest), diver (Mary Rose), or archaeologist (Expedition to Saggara), or to confront a real-life problem of a more scientific nature, e.g. Slick! (oil polution), etc. With due consideration being given to the decisions to be taken at each stage of the scenario, these simulations can take quite a long time to run, and can completely absorb the interest of a young player. However, to be most effective, it must be clear what the user is to do, and what happened must be made absolutely explicit so that, in any later debriefing, the player can meaningfully discuss why it happened.

Such simulations are distinguishable from the so-called adventure or fantasy games where there is little or no direct contact between the subject-matter and reality. Thus, Granny's Garden is a children's adventure game which takes the players to the Kingdom of the Mountains and asks them to find the king and queen's six children who have been kidnapped by a wicked witch and hidden in various places. The rescues rely upon solving puzzles, e.g. one child has been changed into a broom and hidden in a cupboard. Such games should not be dismissed as educational tools simply because their subject-matter may appear frivolous. Adventure games are good for developing language use. They also teach the skills of deductive reasoning and hypothesis-testing, because players must use existing information and resources to solve the problems posed for each character.

A more pertinent question is how best to exploit the students' interest and enjoyment for explicitly educational purposes. With young children playing the games, it is probable that the ideal approach is play with groups of children. Stephen Moss suggests that the optimum group size is six or seven, with the group members using some form of consensus or voting system to resolve decisions about action (3). Because of the players' inexperience, teachers will have the responsibility of supervising these groups, but they must have the confidence to allow children to talk their way through the problems, even though they may ultimately fail completely, and even though there may be nothing written down and nothing to mark.

Burton and Brown believe that the revolution in personal computing will bring with it extensive use of increasingly complex games which can provide rich, informal environments for learning. (4) They argue that properly constructed games can lead to the formation of strategies and knowledge structures that have general usefulness. The difficulty is that the gaming environment is often unstructured and, without some form of supervision, students of all ages and experience may make errors. Thus, any student may form an inaccurate understanding of the underlying game structure, or not appreciate the limited nature of the strategies formed, or not actually realise that mistakes are being made. Yet one of the major attractions of any simulation/game is that the student appears to be in control, and any substantial interference with this component element is likely to damage the attractiveness of the game. The student must be free to make mistakes and to observe the results. The role of the teacher must therefore be to strike a balance between mere observation, and critical interventionism and overdirectiveness. With sensitive handling, role-playing simulations can be a highly effective learning environment where players can learn as much from failure as from success. This learning will not only relate to the subject-matter of the simulation and its component skills, but should also address issues of socialisation. Players of all skill levels should be encouraged to be self-critical in success, and mature and balanced in the face of apparent failure.

8.4   Can the computer perform a coaching function?

An alternative to the supervisory activity of the human teacher would be the incorporation of a tutoring mechanism or coach in the program itself. One advantage of this development is that it would assist the human teacher to maintain a more general role within the classroom environment. But the same problem exists for the programmer as for the human teacher, because any coaching system which is incorporated, must not be intrusive enough to destroy the fun. Further, if the coach continually points out mistakes and their remedies, the student may become resentful and see the computer as a nagging critic, or is not encouraged in the development of skills of self-reliance to recover from error through constructive thought and analysis.

The design of any in-built coach will usually incorporate the means to determine whether, at each decision point, the student has made the best move or decision. From this negative information, the coach must attempt to guess the reason(s) for any failure or suboptimisation. If it is apparent that one or more key issues have not been understood, the coach can present an explanation of the general concept, accompanied by a better move. In this way, the student can immediately see the usefulness of the information and be more receptive to the learning exercise.

However, there is both a positive and a negative side of the coaching role for, in addition to saying the things that the student does not know, the student should not be told things already known. This minimises boredom on the part of the players, and potentially encourages their respect for the perceptiveness of the system. Further, the coach should be designed so that the tenor of its remarks will only be seen to give positive encouragement. If this is not feasible, all reasonable steps should be taken in the drafting of comments and remarks to minimise the risk that the players will only see the system as a critic. Indeed, whenever appropriate, the coach should encourage the student, e.g. when the optimal move has been made based on an issue where the student is known to be weak, the possibility of some congratulatory comment should be considered. But all comments should be relevant, memorable and not meaninglessly repetitive. So, for example, the system must be absolutely sure that a real weakness has been diagnosed in the student before anything is said. The expectation should therefore be that the coach will not speak until a significant amount of corroborative data has been acquired. This would be consistent with the general proposition that too fussy a coach will antagonise the students by continually butting in, particularly if the prime reason for error is mere carelessness or inconsistency (a strategy remembered one move, may so easily be forgotten the next).

In subject domains where there is a direct link between the student's belief and the results observed, e.g. elementary arithmetic skills, the cause of error can often be located quite easily. But in those areas where there are several ways of solving a problem, it is more difficult to diagnose error or misconception. The reason for this difficulty is that the student must not only take steps to solve the problem, but must also select those steps, i.e. generate a plan to achieve the solution. The task of the coach is therefore one of plan recognition. This is the inverse of planning. A planner uses facts known about the problem area to devise a plan that is intended to achieve the goal. A plan recogniser starts with the sequence of actions and tries to reconstruct the plan.

If human teacher or computer is to impute a plan to a student, there is an underlying assumption that each step actually taken is intended in some way to contribute towards the solution of the problem. The coach must therefore have a record of all possible goals and sub-goals, and the various strategies which might be adopted. By examining each step actually taken by the given student, and then comparing it to both the expert and non-expert possibilities stored, the structure of the evolving plan may become more apparent. A direct match between actual and stored strategy may be found which will pinpoint a particular misconception. If there is ambiguity in the action which might suggest several possible methods and/or goals, the coach must await more data in the hope that the plan will become more clear.

One coaching strategy is to hypothesise one or more misconceptions and to try to construct the plan using individual errors or combinations of errors to see whether the student's answer can be replicated. If all attempts to diagnose the source of the error fail, the computer should ask for clarification. In most cases, this will involve taking the student through the correct method step by step, asking for confirmation at each point. If a discrepancy is found, this will either match an existing stored misconception, or represent a new error which the programmer must build into the coach if it appears likely to recur. The problem in the more complex areas is that, without a natural language interface, it is usually impossible to get the student to explain precisely what the plan was, although the user can always be invited to type an explanation into memory for later human evaluation. (5) But, even if the plan is immediately diagnosed, the coach must have criteria against which to judge the system of beliefs and misconceptions which caused the student to devise that plan. Some errors are more acceptable than others, and any lack in the flexibility of computer responsiveness may bracket the understandable error with the unforgiveable error in the student's mind. This can be demoralising for the inexperienced student who has yet to gain a sufficient overview of the material to be able to make a valid judgement on the point.

If the student is in any sense playing against the computer, i.e. a gaming element is incorporated into the simulation, the design expectation should proabably be that the computer should adopt optimal strategies so that, whether as a winner or as a loser, the human player can learn by observation and experience. Further, if the player becomes convinced that the machine is playing down to him or her, the simulation/game may appear patronising and lose its appeal. However, the converse difficulty is that if the student always comes out second best, interest may be lost. In some simulation/games, it may be possible to discriminate between several levels of skill. In such an eventuality, it may be thought better for the student to have an opponent only slightly above his or her level. This will tend to keep the game element more evenly matched while still providing examples of better moves. In playing the game 'How the West Was Won', Burton and Brown report research evidence that students playing the coached version of the game appeared to enjoy it more than the uncoached version. (6) However, this should not be uncritically accepted as an endorsement of the coaching method. One suggestion of difficulty is that the students may become interested in a metagame to cause the coach to speak, i.e. non-rational strategies are deliberately adopted to force the coach to appear.

8.5 What is the best design for a simulation?

In designing a simulation, educational decisions must be taken about the nature of the simulation to be constructed and the level of realism which is required. Some situations can be very precisely simulated, while others are necessarily simplifications of reality. The express educational aims to be met must therefore be clearly born in mind when making the selection of the elements to be incorporated into the model, and when deciding the degree of accuracy required to show their attributes. It should now be recognised that the effectiveness of the learning experience is not necessarily enhanced by maximising the amount of detail, because this may distract from the simple message which is to be communicated. But real-world skills depend upon being able to filter out distracting noise and to tune into the pure signal. If such skills are to be incorporated into the simulation, then this must be a conscious decision.

The designer must then decide whether the user is to be actor or reactor, or both. Until the level of interactiveness between the user and the model has been fixed, the detailed working of the model cannot be determined. In part, this will be based upon the identification of the student perspective. If the aim is simply to allow passive or semi-passive observation, perhaps by way of introduction to the given process, the presentation will differ considerably from a role-playing simulation where direct involvement of the student is to be required. In the former, the student will be given an overview, whereas in the latter the student must act and react to the immediate stimulus material in whatever role has been adopted.

In those simulations which do involve high student input, the issue of feedback is also something which needs to be carefully considered. In the real world, the actor does not always get convenient messages which inform him or her of the current situation. A necessary part of the actor's expertise is the ability to diagnose the situation from the available evidence. Thus, the simulation should aim for realism of feedback unless specific learning objectives require, say, that warning messages should be given, or that the results of actions be more particularly emphasised. If in the real world, feedback would be delayed, then it is a good idea to delay feedback. If the reaction would be immediate, then immediate feedback should be given. In this way, the experience given to the student is closer to reality and may be more interesting. However, this view might be modified for those learning the use of the simulation, where artificial feedback may speed the learning process by averting the more obvious mistakes. It depends upon the learning objectives to be met in each case. But as a general rule, in a model being used as a test situation, only naturalistic feedback should be given.

8.6 What are educational games?

Games are similar to simulations, but usually contain an explicit
element of competition by always having an opponent, even though
that opponent may be the machine, or the player him or herself.
Simulations teach by presenting a part of reality for student
consumption. They may be inherently entertaining, but entertainment is not one of their necessary component elements. Games may
simulate reality, but their primary purpose is to present the
student with entertaining challenges. Any simulation can be turned into a game by adding a scoring system, or by comparing
results as between different individuals or groups.

8.6.1 What makes a computer game a success?

Some card games, or games of skill and/or chance achieve their
motivating effect by the amount of money which may be won or
lost. A game which has no real skill element could otherwise
become repetitively boring in a relatively short space of time.
In an arcade, visual and auditory signals greet success or failure, and help to maintain or enhance the fun of the gaming situation. This will be so even though little or no skill on the part
of the player may be involved. But in the true computer game, the
game's skill levels can also be manipulated in line with the
player's actual performance levels. The play need not become
boringly simple, for while some elements will always be mastered
with varying degrees of ease, others will remain to represent the
challenge; motivation being maintained by the sensation that the
computer is only marginally better than the human player at any
given instant of time. The design challenge is therefore to
maintain both the reward of progress and success for motivation
reinforcement, and the continuity of challenge. One possible
strategy allows the player the ability to select the level of
difficulty. The player may therefore protect the ego in moments
of weakness by forcing the computer to perform at low skill
levels. Alternatively, the machine may unilaterally keep track of
performance and adjust to each player's current skill levels.

In the arcade setting, such games often incorporate a fantasy or
science fiction element. A game is often found more challenging
if the player is dealing with unknown elements. Further, the
incorporation of self-evidently non-real factors signals the
novelty of the situation, and should further stimulate curiosity.
The desire to know is a powerful motivator, and must substitute
for the simple greed which may motivate players to continue at
the intellectually undemanding fruit machine, or more extrava-
gantly, at the roulette tables or playing poker, chemin de fer,
and so on. This does not mean that a computer game must not have

stakes. Rewards must always be present, but they need not be material.

Some games are a challenge because the ultimate scoring potentials are unknown, and this stimulates curiosity and levels of expectation. People are motivated by the desire to achieve mastery and by the entertainment element, and may learn despite themselves. Whereas the scoring of points is often on an arbitrary basis, some games have intrinsic qualities which make them useful learning devices. The arcade style of game is acceptable in the school or college as a psychomotor game. These games will tend to use joy sticks or paddles, and combine intellectual skills with motor skills. These skills will usually be simple physical manipulative skills or predictive skills, which may or may not depend upon memory enhancement. Thus, by playing a game, the player learns what the various challenges are, and in what way they may or may not represent a danger. Very accurate memorisation is frequently an asset, and through practice, the powers of prediction and recall can be significantly improved.

Where games have an educational purpose attributed to them, the practical danger in their use is that the user may never really grasp the full educational point. If the game is merely perceived as fun, the problem may be that the player latches on to a limited strategy and sticks with it because it is apparently a winning line. This will be unfortunate because the player will never develop an overall appreciation of the principles involved. It may be that the player only actually performs one simple calculation rather than the ideal more complex evaluation, and it would take an observant teacher or a computerised coach to push the player to the next skill level. This problem is compounded in that, with most scoring systems, there is nearly always the illusion if not the reality of progress, and unless players are taught to be self-critical about their achievements, their learning is likely to plateau at one of the lower levels.

The goals of the game must therefore reinforce the educational objectives and ensure that success only really comes about through the application of skill, rather than by chance. This must be the better educational approach even though it must be acknowledged that a proportion of luck can increase the challenge. True skill in the long-term ought to prevail whatever happens in the short-term, but the uncertainty which chance can introduce, may stimulate the formulation of damage limitation strategies, and other similarly useful real-world survival skills. If the game is pure skill and a student cannot master the requisite level of aptitude, motivation will often be lost. There must come a point when even the most dedicated of individuals admits defeat in the face of consistent losses. However, the fact that sometimes luck helps out and produces a win, can help to retain motivation over a longer period of time during which true skill mastery may be achieved. A further consideration is whether the game can be designed so that losing is not merely defined in terms of absolute criteria, but so that the teacher can always point to some success in skill mastery or goal achievement. In this way, the weaker student's morale will be safeguarded over a longer period.

Every game has goals whether it be the scoring of points or the solution of problems, and each game takes place within a rule framework. Because of their intrinsic nature, games depend upon competition either between player and machine or between players, and the game may be affected by luck or time elements. The quasi-conflictual challenge is what has to be overcome to reach the goal. However, because games, like simulations, incorporate a fun element and take place in essentially non-threatening environments, they provide a physically (and often emotionally) safe way of enacting dangerous reality, e.g. war games or stock exchange games. It must also be recognised that many games use violent forms of competition as their primary motivator but, in the educational context, their use should be sparing in that the apparent fun element might completely obscure the learning objectives, even if it is considered desirable to appeal to the student's more violent tendencies.

As with pure simulations, games are often attractive to students as learning vehicles, and it can make them efficient communicators, because the students are less easily distracted and tend to concentrate more. If the teacher advises on strategy, this may make the teacher seem more approachable and help to break down barriers. However, because of their strongly competitive nature, failure can be demoralising for the less confident students. Teachers should be aware of the problem and ensure that proper support is given while learning the play, group students on a mixed ability basis so that the stronger students may help the weaker, or allow a degree of privacy to the players to minimise peer group pressures.

8.7   What is the best design for a game?

In designing games, decisions must be made about the level of realism to aim for. It is usually the case that the more realistic the game, the more complex the rules and the more difficult it is to play. Thus, in board games connected with war or conflict, only a nominal understanding of war would be required to play a game like Risk (a Waddington's game), whereas actual models of campaigns or battles focus on real constraints, e.g. distance which can be travelled in different time periods, fire power, etc. So among those which draw from World War II, Battle for the Pacific (designed by Avalon Hill) starts with Pearl Harbour and then allows the development and execution of strategies by both sides. Real levels of ship building and munitions manufacture are adhered to, with delivery of materials being taken at historically verified times during the play. Victory criteria are established whereby if Japan, as a player, out performs the historical Japan, Japan is the winner; if the same historical result is achieved, the game is a draw; the player representing America only winning if the game victory margin is greater than in the real world. Such games cannot be played unless the players learn a reasonable amount of history, and have some familiarity with the military strategic options for the personnel and weaponry available for manipulation. Once learned, the players practice their knowledge in the gaming format.

In the classroom, if the game represents a sufficient attraction, the prospective players will learn the relevant knowledge so that they may play well. By playing well, the students are testing their knowledge and understanding in a more thorough way than by a conventional test or examination. However, the more complex the rules and the more demanding the pre-game learning, the more difficult it may be to motivate the students if the game itself is weak. In such a situation, the designer should consider simplifying the information to be incorporated, and seek to accentuate the fun element in the game to sugar the pill. The problem which then arises is that the student may simply enjoy the competition without really concentrating on the learning aspect of the game. Instead of simplifying all the aspects of the game, it can be more effective to concentrate on particular elements or groupings of elements, than to seek to produce something with the comprehensiveness of reality. The problem here may be that the further the game moves from reality, the less information may be transferred from the learning activity to the real world. Alternatively, the student may find it difficult to understand the proper context for the topic or topics referred to in the game.

In all games, the players need information upon which to base their strategies and their decisions. If complete information is not given before the game, information must be supplied during the game. Sometimes, giving a hint can help to solve a problem, and can lead the student to feel more confident because the right inferences were drawn. Too much help, and the student does not develop self-reliance. Too little help, and the player may be outfaced by the apparent difficulty unless the human teacher has been monitoring progress and steps in to offer assistance. One design possibility is to provide for play in a number of cycles, with the teaching of new techniques and strategies inserted between each cycle. The student may therefore understand the difficulty and see the need for the particular technique, and then be given an opportunity to try its effect upon the resumption of play.

In any interpersonal gaming situation, there is the element of bluff and misinformation. Introducing some uncertainty in the accuracy of machine-supplied relevant additional information can be a useful element of realism. However, the computer should never be allowed to cheat in the ordinary game role. (It could be a useful characteristic if the computer is acting as a model of a student for teacher training purposes, but rarely otherwise.) In general, the program should always use consistent and verifiable rules for the basis of its actions, and the substance, if not the detail, of these rules should be communicated to the players before the game starts. To that extent, the computer should always play fairly. Striking a balance between these different design constraints is the art in creating good educational games, and proper attention to these issues should permit the games to be successfully incorporated into a teaching strategy.

8.8 What hardware is necessary for simulations and games?

In the non-educational context, a dedicated machine will be provided which, by virtue of its specialised design, can deliver a good product at an economic price. The education market tends not to buy single purpose machines, (with the possible exception of wordprocessors to support busy school or college administrations), but looks for flexibility to get the maximum utility from the capital expended. Hence, the selection of hardware depends upon what the range of intended use is to be. In this, it must be recognised that use for gaming or simulation work is but one possibility among many but, in taking the hardware decision, the availability of suitable software can be vital. If a reasonable number of computer simulation and gaming packages can be supported on a particular machine, this may help to justify acquisition of that machine because an effective use of an expensive resource can be shown.

In modern times, the purchase must also fit in with the overall budgetary cost constraints of the particular institution. Even though more discretion is being given to schools and colleges to allocate resources, budgets are now more tightly controlled, and all expenditure must be more positively justified. To some extent, the use of computers to support more formalised learning is accepted through the commitment of Government funding, but the use of computers for the playing of games is considered more controversial. Two battles may therefore have to be fought:

. to acquire a suitable computer

. to acquire simulation and gaming software, or to be allowed to spend time in developing such software

However, any finance committee's first consideration is likely to be the physical performance characteristics of the computer with respect to speed (bearing in mind the increasing problem of machine abuse if response time is slow), and the capacity and power of the computer's memory and processor. It should be honestly recognised that hardware which depends upon floppy discs or, heaven forbid in these high technology times, cassette tapes, is impossibly slow and tends to lack storage capacity. Buyers also need to ensure that the computer is both robust and reliable, and is supported by an appropriate maintenance agreement. The secondary considerations are likely to be the configuration and portability constraints. The purchasing body may need the equipment to be physically portable so that, by moving the equipment from one site to another, the largest poss- ible number of users may gain access to a scarce resource. In addition, the hardware must be compatible with any existing equipment and software.

In general, software development has tended to lag behind hard- ware development, but there is no shortage of games and simula- tions aimed at the business executive. "Indeed war and business are two fields where conflict is institutionalised and simulated conflict training is necessary and well catered for." (7) Thus, when buying hardware, it is advisable to consider which of the many computer-based games and simulations are of interest, and to try to match the prospective machine to the largest number of those programs. Marginal cost calculations can make it appear advantageous to functionally share space with an overall service system, but response times on some big systems slow down with large numbers of users, and communications can be slow to remote mainframes because, with older communications kit, only low baud rates are achievable.

Further, a big computer can be using the metaphorical sledge hammer to crack a nut because a lot of CAL material in general, and simulations and games in particular, does not need sophisti- cated computational power, although it is useful to have a big memory and it is easier to update the quality of the service to multiple users. The more realistic answer may be a Local Area Network (LAN) like ETHERNET which allows otherwise stand-alone equipment the luxury of shared access to courseware libraries and central collection of performance data. Moreover, the staff can more easily monitor student use or communicate with their stud- ents through a messaging or electronic mail system. The existence of such systems also allows the students to continue game-based negotiations outside the formal classroom context, and to practice both the direct face-to-face bargaining skills and the (perhaps) more formal electronic messaging medium.

Computers also need to be surrounded by the paraphernalia of printers, keyboards and screens. If the games or simulations are to be used by groups of students, it may be appropriate to use larger screen display systems so that all participants have a reasonable opportunity of seeing the machine output. Similarly, some programs may call for multiple access either through key- boards, or through joy sticks, paddles or comparable devices. Suitable communications devices must be obtainable. In those simulations where greater sophistication of decision-making is achievable, some machine-generated output may come in the form of graphs, histograms or pie charts. This requires a printer capable of generating that form of output at a reasonable speed. If this form of output is only achievable at a snail's pace in some far flung outpost of the computing empire rather than in the gaming environment, it will be too disruptive to the otherwise smooth running of the game/simulation to wait for bearers to bring this precious product back to civilisation, unless the decision-making format allows for such delays.

8.9   Conclusions

The use of simulations and games is a well-established way of providing essential variety of learning experience for students. The monotony of a school or college timetable which is predominantly large group teaching is a significant cause of alienation of the part of those attending. The belief that students must be regimented into teacher-led activities still has currency even though education theory looks for different forms of challenge and stimulation in the learning environment. The fear seems to be that the entertainment element of simulations and games will somehow trivialise the subject-matter to be communicated, whereas the fun element can play a vital part in maintaining interest while either introducing the need to under-stand a particular technique, or practicing and reinforcing tech-niques already communicated. But, as with the more conventional dialogue systems, it is still absolutely essential to define expected learning outcomes before devising or using a computer-based simulation or game. Without clear objectives in mind, the very triviality which critics would always seek to find in the use of learning devices with a gaming element, will be only too apparent.

References

(1) System Design Features for Clinical Simulations. M.J.Taylor, W.A.Corbett, P.R.Edwards and J.R.Coughlan. collected in Trends in Computer Assisted Education. pp. 97/105.

(2) Incremental Transfer Effectiveness. Stanley N. Roscoe. (1971) 13 Human Factors 561/7. A Little More on Incremental Transfer Effectiveness. Stanley N. Roscoe. (1972) 14 Human Factors 363/4. The Incremental Transfer Effectiveness of a Ground-Based General Aviation Trainer. H. Kingsley Povenmire & Stanley N. Roscoe (1973) 15 Human Factors 534/42.

(3) Computer simulations, adventure games and language development. Stephen Moss. collected in Teachers, computers and the classroom. pp. 96/104 at p.103.

(4) An investigation of computer coaching for informal learning activities. Richard R.Burton and John Seely Brown. collected in Intelligent Tutoring Systems. pp.79/98 at p.79.

(5) as in the experimental system described in ACE: A system which Analyses Complex Explanations. D.H.Sleemen and R.J.Hendley. collected in Intelligent Tutoring Systems. pp.99/118.

(6) supra at p.98.

(7) ICT Executive Game: A Case Study in Management Game Development. Michael Harrison. (1984) Vol 14 No.2 Simulation/Games for Learning (Summer) pp.55/69 at p.55.

CHAPTER 9

COMPUTER-BASED
TRAINING (CBT)

Up to this point, it has been assumed that use of the computers
has been restricted to the purely academic environment, but there
is no reason in principle why computers should not support
industrial training. If it is accepted that computers support the
learning function, then computerisation may be of value in any
context. This chapter therefore examines the practical and
economic worth of CBT, and particularly considers the role of the
computer-supported simulation or game for management training
purposes.

9.1   Introduction

Across the world, both manufacturing and service industries are
increasing their competitiveness by incorporating more computer-
based facilities in manufacturing processes, the resultant end-
products, and customer services. However, for all this apparent
commitment by industry, some industrialists argue that the level
of investment in IT technology in fact requires a supreme act of
faith. They would consider it impossible to put a value on
any alleged qualitative improvements in control, faster processing and more accurate information. This tendency must be seen
against the most recent work of Professor Kit Grindley, author of
the 1987 Price Waterhouse review of DP spending (1), who reports

that both private and public sector IT budgets have been cut for the second year running.

This slow-down in implementation has probably arisen because an increasing number of commercial firms decline to make investment on the basis of mere faith, denying that the standard cost bene- fit analysis techniques can be applied to the decision whether to computerise. In fact, the decision can be so justified but it has to be supported by an in-depth study of the organisation to identify the elements most critical to the success of the busi- ness. If it is found that IT is relevant to any of these critical elements, the degree to which computerisation may affect that element must be determined. In part, this will involve calculat- ing how much time is spent on each aspect of the organisation's primary functions. Should it appear that employees spend only a proportion of their time doing work which is directly profitable to the organisation, while otherwise undertaking administrative tasks that could be machine-based, the organisation could in- crease its earning capacity by allowing the computer to do those tasks. Thus, a sales representative could spend more time selling the organisation's products if all enquiries and orders were logged into a portable computer. Then, instead of the representa- tive having to spend time in the office writing up orders or sending out standard brochures, the computer could be handed into the office each evening for a dump of data from which all rele- vant documentation could be drawn up and sent out automatically. Alternatively, the data could be transmitted by telephone to the office, say, from the representative's hotel or home. In both cases, the use of the representative's time and skills would be more efficient.

The problem with this approach is that it forces organisations to change the focus of their business so that the new technology can be used to reduce or remove unnecessary activity. Given that most of the organisation's revenue overhead is likely to be staff costs, the saving will almost certainly be in jobs. Such proposals not unnaturally meet with hostility from threatened employees, or indifference from complacent executives whose training does not predispose them to think strategically or in terms of information systems.

To apply the new technology effectively requires a good understanding of the nature and power of computers qua machines, and of the new software packages. But there is not enough time to wait for trained recruits to be produced by the education system if Britain is to remain competitive. In a report entitled 'Changes in the Employment of IT Staff' and commissioned by the Department of Trade and Industry, the IT Skills Agency has reported that major commercial and public sector organisations are finding it difficult both to keep specialised staff, and to recruit the numbers of staff they need. Yet they are planning to increase the numbers of employed IT staff (some expect an increase of as much as 45% by 1991), and to reduce the number of contract staff. It is therefore clear that too many organisations will be chasing too few trained and competent staff. Current statistics show that about 25,000 individuals are recruited to the IT profession each year, but the recruiting agencies and employers report a shortfall of 16,000 unfilled posts given current demand.

With staff turnover in the IT sphere running at 15%, it should not be surprising that retention problems were reported by 57% of all those organisations surveyed, and by 67% of those in the public sector. A rapid turnover of staff can have many consequences. It can:

.   disrupt delivery schedules

.   inhibit the development of proper and consistent standards

.   damage customer relations.

The level of salaries (including perks) and pressure from competing employers were the factors most usually identified as the main causes of the responder's difficulties - the problem being accentuated because of the Big Bang in the City of London. (2) However, no matter what the immediate short-term cause of staff mobility, it is not economically feasible for organisations to spend their way out of the problem by recruiting new staff. Quite apart from the salary spiral which the additional competition among firms would cause, the existing problems of poaching would almost certainly grow as the hard core of competent staff are pursued by increasingly desperate employers. In fact, the only way to alleviate the existing shortage of trained manpower and to communicate a proper understanding of computer technology, is through increased in-service education and training.

The rapidity of change also means that the training must be on a regular basis. "Poor or obsolete technical skills and poor general IT awareness hampers not only the supply side; there is evidence to suggest that the demand side is constrained because users do not have the knowledge to exploit IT fully." (3) Industry must therefore acknowledge that major and continuing capital investment is required on the training side. It is perhaps significant that hardware manufacturers have already recognised the deficiencies in many of their prospective, and indeed existing, customers, and have begun to develop courses which are to be sold alongside their products, e.g. Tandem has announced a Faststart scheme for its UK users to boost the number of staff familiar with its systems, with training at rates subsidised by Tandem. Sadly, industry itself has failed to recognise the genral need for training. This may be evidenced in the case of new recruits where, inter alia, the National Computer Centre's own Youth Training Scheme has had a poor response due to lack of financial support.

This lack of enthusiasm has been compounded by the Manpower Services Commission which has made significant changes to the

National Priority Skills Scheme (NPSS). Until 1987, the MSC
identified and published a series of categories under which
industry training organisations such as the COmputing Services
Industry Training Council (COSIT) and employers could apply for
grant aid. As a matter of practice, all aid was made available
with the minimum of difficulty. These categories and associated
guidelines have now been withdrawn, and the full burden of
initiating the proposals and of justifying the allocation of
funds has been transferred to industry. As a result, grants for
computer training from the NPSS have been discontinued. The
reason for this decision is the criticism of the Audit Commission
which suggested that the MSC was subsidising training programmes
which might have been arranged in any event, and that the
subsidies were made available without proper scrutiny of the aims
of each application. Given that industry itself is not strongly
self-motivating, this leaves COSIT with a role which may actually
be unreasonably demanding.

9.2   What is training?

The main justification commonly advanced for distinguishing
between the activities of teaching and training is the somewhat
obvious observation that they tend to take place in different
educational contexts. It is further said that teaching is not
necessarily directly related to vocational requirements, whereas
training relates to specific tasks within the real world. Such
assertions are then used to support a motley variety of propositions, e.g. that it is more acceptable for training to be based
upon criterion-referenced drill and practice programs. Yet, in
the last analysis, these distinctions are spurious. Training and
teaching are both essentially the same process in that they seek
to promote learning, and they should really be judged by the same
educational standards. In the context of this book, the primary
training concerns would be taken to be either specific training
aimed at promoting the introduction of information technology
into the workplace, or the support of the general in-service
training function with computers.

In the case of the former, new forms of technology are appearing
in the workplace with increasing frequency, and most of the
innovations have the capacity, either directly or indirectly, to
improve local productivity and overall profitability. However,
although computers and robotics have made real improvements in
the performance of physical processes, management organisation
has not kept pace. One of the reasons for this slow development
is that, typically, computers are introduced into general offices
by a policy decision taken at a senior level within the
organisation, rather than by decisions at office level. This

means that the managers required to learn about the computer have had no influence in the changes in office practice which the introduction of the technology will cause.

This quasi-political dimension may lead some managers to resent or be anxious about learning. Further, one of the ways in which the technology may be used to improve performance is by giving the senior managers accurate information by which to judge the performance both of departments, and of individuals within those departments. While this may be welcomed by some members of the administrative hierarchy, it is a source of acute anxiety to others. Consequently, as in the education world, there is significant inertia and conservatism in the hierachy of decision-making where institutional delay makes changes irrelevant or outdated. But because of the increasingly hostile commercial environment, even the most ardent of anti-technologists is forced to acknowledge that simple delay cannot really be defended, so a variety of strategies have been formulated to mask the true nature of the process. Hence, the production of policy statements by individual departments, and the busy work and reports of committees and study groups may give the appearance of positive activity; but all of these things are actually a substitute for action. Similarly, other managers use vague threats of difficulties with the unions in resisting the making of changes.

Thus, if effective change is to be introduced, there must be consideration of two key factors:

The human factor Whenever plans are being drawn up, the needs of each person who is to directly interact with the computer must be considered. Any lack of involvement in the planning processes often leads to resistance on the part of those who must implement the scheme, and proper consultation is essential at all levels if smooth transitions are to be achieved from the manual to the automated system. There is also the real possibility that through the consultation mechanism, considerable efficiencies can subsequently be built into the system. Senior managers are frequently distanced from the actual processes of the business and lack the detailed insight of those responsible for operating the paper-based systems. At the support staff level, if, say, secretaries and clerks comment upon the need for, and design and layout of, any new documentation, significant savings in printing and administration costs may be achieved by removing or redesigning antiquated paper systems, preserved only through tradition. Similarly, junior and middle management may be able to suggest powerful information manipulation possibilities which previously would have been unworkable using manual means, but which now can enhance the decision-making of the firm.

A further issue is that the new generations of networked computers can produce a decentralisation of the power and influence previously enjoyed by technical staff. Roles

222

within the business must therefore be redefined if staff morale is to be maintained. At all points, consultation is necessary to promote knowledge and understanding of the changes, and training and adequate working conditions are essential if implementation is to be achieved with the minimum of disruption. The final impact of the changes can be constructive through increased job satisfaction and better personal development on the part of all the staff. However, without proper planning, the more likely consequences of automation are increased monitoring and social isolation, little autonomy, and less commitment and more alienation. Although it has been the trend to talk only of the benefits of automation, the machines' performance is only as good as the humans who manage them, and the firm ignores its human resources at its peril.

The management factor The management of new technology is difficult both because of the man-management problems of overcoming the already mentioned institutionalised mechanisms to resist change, and also because more information is suddenly made available to the managers about the state of the business. The power structures of the business may be altered since authority within a business stems from access to information. The more privileged the information, the more power and influence exercised by the holder of that information. But the normal lines of authority may become meaningless if information can be seen and analysed by any employee with access to a terminal. One view of this state of affairs would be that the more individuals who can contribute to the decision-making, the better the likely decision made by the organisation because of the diversity of insight and view that can be melded together in each decision. However, the more usual result is that the computers generate an increased bureaucratisation.

It does not matter how good the technology is, if the social issues have not been properly considered, the emerging system will be less efficient as too many willing employees consider the same problem. The management problem is further complicated by the fact that computer designers are not necessarily trained to design systems taking account of the human's needs. Their criteria tend to be cost oriented. Computer science courses should therefore include organisational theory, human resources development, psychology, and other similar topics. Pending this curriculum review, current managers should seek to mitigate the potential user unfriendliness of automated systems with good management planning.

If it is assumed that a business has taken the decision to automate some or all of its functions, the resistance and anxieties of line managers cannot quickly be dispelled in a short training course. This will rapidly become apparent in those cases where the initial decision to import the technology has been taken unilaterally, and the attendance at training sessions is made compulsory. In fact, the more arbitrary the actions of senior management, the more likely is resistance on the part of the key managers. For these purposes, the key managers are those in the middle to senior grades, where they will have responsibility for offices of between twenty and forty people. In their present roles, which will give them reasonable status and prestige, they will be accountable to nominated senior managers in a clear hierarchy. Most are educationally qualified and their ages will range between thirty and forty five years.

At a practical level, small organisations do not generally have the resources to engage in internal training, while large organisations can find that staff are resistant to in-house trainers. All staff tend to view outside trainers with suspicion if they do not seem to have command of the detail of the immediate office environment from which the trainees have come. But, assuming that the training staff can overcome initial distrust, there are certain advantages to be gained in using a training environment physically separated from the normal office buildings. If the managers are taken out of the work environment, it can reduce the sense of personal assessment and measurement which, in turn, may encourage greater confidence and more co-operation. The organisers of any such training should seek to promote an informal atmosphere which will help to minimise the natural stress reaction. It also helps to promote group solidarity which is an advantage if the mood of the group is positive. However, the longer the course, the more disruptive this is to normal work patterns and schedules.

These key managers require a generalised introduction to computer technology in the management environment. If the course is narrow, the benefits will last only as long as the specific hardware and software packages are available, and it will not lay the basic foundations to support the longer-term integration of the new technology into the office environment. Any training course should start with the recognition that good management is a human skill based on thoughtfulness, self-criticism and a willingness to see other people's problems. A computer course is no different from any other training course and so it should reinforce and encourage those qualities in relation to the use of computers. However, it should also have a more specific focus on the use of computers as a support to problem-solving in the management context. In this way, the middle managers may be shown the best practice possibilities which should make them better able to relate to their senior managers' needs. Training for these purposes will be through a combination of talk and experience. If lectures are to be given the teacher/manager ratio should not generally be more than 1:15, i.e. a compromise between cost-effectiveness and a necessary degree of personal attention for the trainees. If the trainees are going to share a computer terminal, not more than two should sit together, as the competitiveness which is often encouraged between managers in the work place may inhibit co-operative learning.

The material to be used in the hands-on experiential part of any course should, wherever possible, be taken from the organisation itself, e.g. current forms, information structures, and so on. So for example, database training exercises might be based on personnel information drawn from actual personnel records, albeit with sensitive information deleted. The value of computerised systems can then be discussed with more understanding because its relevance has been directly demonstrated. Generalised financial information can also be supplied by the organisation to the trainers, and the managers can then be given direct tuition in the use of computers as a support to management decision-making.

9.3 CBT and general management training?

Quite apart from the difficulties in human acceptance of computer technology at large, delays in the implementation of computer-based training techniques for general staff training may arise for a variety of reasons. Hence, albeit that hardware and software costs have been falling in real terms for some time, there are still significant economic commitments to be made and justified. Then, even allowing for hardware of appropriate power being available at the right price, there may be technical problems in the lack of availability of good software; and there are the inevitable socio-political arguments whereby CBT has only just reached acceptability as against traditional training methods. This is actually a perverse reaction because CBT has a proven track record, and is no longer seen as a gamble by those organisations which have installed state of the art systems.

The dynamic which motivates the implementation of all training programmes is the need to improve the efficiency or effectiveness of the trainees. Just as it is now recognised that a uniform and co-ordinated design approach to the colour and style of premises, displays, packaging and stationary can improve an organisation's public image, so standardised training can also help both to build an image through the way in which staff interact with the public, and to promote the smooth running of a large and otherwise disparate organisation. In the overall framework of human resource management, CBT techniques reduce the normal resource requirements. Thus, there is a reduced need for centralised training centres and fewer training staff can maintain the same level of service. Alternatively, the training body can achieve a higher throughput of trainees with the same unit of resource.

As in the academic environment, better quality instruction can be given on a one-to-one basis, but this is not considered economically viable in the normal commercial organisation. Yet it is more often achieved in a training situation which exploits CBT rather than the conventional manual training methods. Equally, training on the actual job may be dangerous or expensive and so computer simulations are used - e.g. the training and competence testing of commercial air pilots. Here training is on a hands-on basis without actually risking an aircraft, or taking a capital-intensive asset out of commercial operation. Given that training time can represent money thrown away by the training organisation, cohort training can become expensive if the pace of the training is set at the speed of the slowest trainee in a group. Thus, the individualisation of training achievable through the use of CBT allows the better trainees to achieve competence and enhanced earning capacity far more quickly than might otherwise have been the case. This would be particularly important where there is a significant skill-disparity between the employees to be trained. This feature will also minimise the risk that the over-qualified trainee might quickly become bored and lose motivation.

Because of differences in educational background and work experience, different trainees may find different parts of the course either easy or difficult to understand. There can be compensation for such inequalities through pretest facilities. The results of such tests would then be used to allow some trainees to enter at more advanced levels in the course, or left as background data which would simply let the computerised system skip over sections obviously understood while providing more intensive remedial assistance wherever it is seen to be needed. Alternatively, all may be required to work through pre-attendance materials (e.g. as in the case of staff joining Tandem UK) so that all recruits attend initial training sessions having a guaranteed minimum competence. A further advantage to CBT facilities is that those recruited may be more rapidly inducted into the organisation. Thus, instead of a would-be trainee having to wait for a place to appear on a course, or for the next course to start its cycle, training can be more efficiently made available so long as access can be given to a suitable terminal or stand-alone machine.

Once staff have joined the organisation, there are also fewer problems about scheduling absences from work to attend central training facilities. This is particularly likely if the employees are already working on a computer-based system. It is more convenient to train them where they work. Without this flexibility, employees may be trained in an aspect of the business even though there is no direct need for it, merely because a place is free on a manual course. Such training is often wasted because, without the stimulus of implementing the training, information is often forgotten. At a more prosaic level, CBT is also more economical because there are significant

226

savings in transport and accommodation expenditure to bring staff together in a regional or central facility. The disadvantage, if such it be, is that the organisation sacrifices the socialisation element in the training programme, which may be considered one of the benefits of the course, and denies individual managers the opportunity to get to know each other.

The employer must therefore balance need in each case. Because of the law of supply and demand, human tutors in given subject areas may not readily be available or command high fees. It can also be inconvenient to take experts to remote sites for training purposes, or to take employees from such sites when on-the-job training would be the preferred approach. However, no matter what economies are achieved either through reduced training time because of the individualisation in training, or through reduced dead salary time because performance can be improved on the job, CBT is actually more tiring than conventional lectures because more intensive effort is required on the part of the trainee. Long periods of concentration are tiring and potentially counter-productive. Computer-based training is therefore more effective in short bursts.

Home-work schemes and training at home have also become more cost-effective now that communications technology is more reliable. It also has the advantage that disabled people, who might find the conventionally designed office environment difficult, can be trained and then work productively at home. Not only is this provision of employment opportunity socially desir-able, it will also assist employers to comply with their legal obligations. Overall, because CBT is more popular with trainees, there tend to be lower drop-out rates, so each organisation should get an improved return from the investment in training. Further, keeping pace with changes in technology and practices within the organisation is achieved more easily by using a centr-alised software review and distribution agency. But whereas the education world has a reasonable prospect of achieving portable CAL software which teaches the core curriculum, industry has the problem that each set of training requirements may very well be unique to individual organisations, and each organisation may therefore have to bear its own costs of production.

9.3.1 What has industry actually achieved in the CBT field?

The uses of the computer in industry training have proved to be many and varied. At one end of the spectrum, large organisations like Barclays Bank have implemented major CBT schemes. Thus, after researching the then available software, Barclaycard acquired IBM's Interactive Training System in 1976 to help in the reorganisation of clerical work from large functional sections to the integrated workgroup concept. Only the training centre at Northampton could have coped with the retraining problem so, with the help of CBT, training was given on local sites saving #120,000 in 1977/8. With this success, Barclaycard have gone on to create a library of training programs to deal with on-going training and staff development. Their progress has not been without its problems and one of the present unsolved difficulties is that when training takes place in a remote centre, a supervisory role is placed upon staff who do not necessarily have the background or expertise as training officers. (4)

Similarly, until 1977, the Customer Equipment Service Division (CESD) of Eastman Kodak used traditional training methods to prepare staff to service Kodak products. Given the product range and the speed with which the technology was being upgraded, a severe training problem emerged, given that Kodak then operated in forty five different countries. The computer seemed the answer because of its capacity to deliver consistent training on a worldwide basis. Further, many of the more complex repair functions could be demonstrated in a step-by-step fashion using the graphics facilities. It was hoped that this would lead to an enhanced understanding on the part of service engineers, whether as trainees or otherwise, and therefore a better overall service offered to Kodak's customers. The company eventually selected the Apple II micro and recruited a team to use the Apple Pilot authoring language, working on the basis that it would be best to have in-house production capacity. Although outside specialists may have greater programming expertise, the company itself knows the products better and can more quickly communicate the essential information to its own staff once they are integrated into the organisation. (5)

Sometimes, the CBT project is the result of a co-operative venture between industry and academia. Hence, CAVIS is an interactive video system providing text and video in a branching system. It has been developed by the West Sussex Institute of Higher Education and the Training Division of BP. It reflects the perceived need to offer a presentational mix in a single package. The problem with work books accompanied by video cassettes or tape/slide presentations and texts, is that there is a cumbersome quality about them. By combining video and computer technology, the best medium for the presentation of a concept can be selected and controlled by the computer, thereby giving much needed flexibility to the educational designer. (6) On other occasions, the development is by an entrepreneurial concern which seeks to exploit the market for CBT systems. Thus, Advanced Training Technology Associates have developed a system called TASTE (Technology ASsisted Training and Education) which is based on the education theory called the 5 ring model produced by Hartley and refined by O'Shea. The claimed advantage of the TASTE system is that it pretests the learners to determine which cognitive style is most compatible with each learner. Having performed this matching operation, information can then be presented to the learner in a manner most likely to be assimilated quickly.

9.4 CBT and gaming/simulation techniques?

Every game is based upon a set of rules. These rules will define the basic elements of the gaming situation, and:

.   allocate roles

.   regulate the methods of interaction

.   specify the criteria for evaluating the final position

Among the many virtues of operationally based management games which Ingolf Stahl has identified are that gaming clarifies concepts and provides a useful brain-stroming device. It also allows the development of heuristic skills and provides a test-bed for new ideas. "Gaming is the only science which uses humans not only as an end but also as a means." (7) Given that management games explore both social and economic reality, the educational rationale is to provide skills which will be of use in the business context, an environment which draws its dynamic from the interaction of people both within a given business and as outsiders dealing with a business. For this purpose, some real-world functions have to be provided by the umpire/referee figure to simplify and limit the number of active roles within the model. The actual roles for each participant will be defined in the gaming scenario. The extent to which the game succeeds will then be determined by the degree of identification between each player, the allocated role, and the declared objectives of the game. Hence, no matter how well the roles may be defined in the opening scenario, if the players are not interested in the problems posed and the possible strategies to resolve them, there is no motivation to play the game.

If the players are motivated to actively participate, the core model underpinning the game or simulation may be institutional, whereby only the situational environment is provided, leaving the players the freedom to formulate their own strategies and to make their own behavioural assumptions. Assuming that there is strategic interdependence between the players, so that the activities of one affect the fortunes of the others, the players must make choices which manipulate the model at a human level and which might, for example, be either integrative or distributive. Such exercises are described as "play" because the player is not necessarily aiming to optimise his or her own position, nor need the goals conform to strict cannons of commercial rationality. This can lead to valuable insights both on the part of the players and on the part of the game designer(s). In fact, gaming is an excellent way of teaching the teachers. There can be a dangerous gap between the academic theorist and the practitioner because their training and experience may lead them to make

229

completely different assumptions about the nature of practical problem-solving. By inviting academics to design and run simulation exercises and games with practising managers, the extent of the perception gap can at least be appreciated if not bridged.

However, from the players point of view, the aim of gaming is to encourage policy formulation and to permit a dress rehearsal for reality. It has an experimental quality about it but, when training, the organisation which is supporting the training exercise must address critical issues of human resource policy. It must, for example, be decided whether the organisation ultimately requires a conceptual approach from its staff. Unless and until such questions are answered, proper decisions about the training cannot be made. It might be argued that lower and middle managers need only to understand the current operational system. It is not intended that they should gain profound insights into the management philosophy which led to the development of those systems. Such a view would, of course, be contrary to the strategy of academic management education which is more interested in abstract ideas, but it has profound intellectual and financial implications. Hence, it is easy to train someone how to complete a given set of pro forma documents, but it is not so easy to train people how to design good documentation. It also raises the difficult question as to whether, if games are a simplified form of reality, they suitable for the training of higher management.

Such debating points are often approached from an oblique angle. Games, it is said, can have an element of entertainment. This does not have a residual effect, but is intended to support the game as it is played by making the experience more enjoyable. The implicit or explicit aim of the game may be to introduce or demonstrate specific principles known and understood by the game designer, or to induce a shift of attitude on the part of the players. If the game is to be played by senior management, it must therefore be seen that the concepts and ideas to be communicated are appropriate for the particular managers who are to play, and that they are communicated in a way which is consistent with their status and responsibility. If it is a choice between communicating a point economically, and leading someone gently by the hand through an enjoyable discovery exercise, the latter may need to be carefully justified if key staff are taken away from their tasks for longer than necessary.

Alternatively, the game may have an experimental quality where the aim is to test the model itself either for research purposes, or to support specific decision-making. To that extent, the purpose is to increase knowledge to the point where better forecasts can be made as to probable outcomes. Thus, the model need not represent an existing feature, but can be a prototype of future reality. The players should therefore either be the real-world decision makers, or should be in similar positions because they are more aware of the social norms or accepted implicit rules of the situation. Students or volunteers could be invited to play but they are likely to act in a more random fashion, or to engage in gaming for its own sake, i.e. try to win at all costs instead of adopting more integrative postures which might leave some good will on the part of the losers. But busy executives cannot be expected to spend, perhaps, many days in playing a game unless they are absolutely sure that they are going to get something valuable out of it. Hence, the involvement of non-serious players or gaming elements may be counter-productive. Whatever the aim of the game, business people also tend not to take the playing of games seriously if they include a fun element, and they tend to be resentful if invited to make time available during the working day.

In this, there is an interesting point of contrast because the playing of games for training purposes has long been recognised as indispensible by the armed services. The assumption is that, between conflicts, the service personnel have more time available. However, in the civilian world, there is often a willingness to play in an evening or at a weekend. Such factors make it appropriate to design small games. People are also better motivated to play well in games of short duration. Boredom becomes less of a problem. If players get knocked out early in one game, there is less difficulty in reinvolving them in the training course when the residue have finished playing. Moreover, the rules of smaller games are usually quicker to learn, and feedback can often be made available more quickly. However, the games may actually be too simple or, perhaps more importantly, may appear to be too simple. Unfortunately, whether they are right in their assessment or not, should the players consider the game frivolous or unrealistic, they are unlikely to be motivated to learn from it.

Real-world problems tend towards complexity so, to aid in under-standing the totality of the problem, most people make simple models of the processes involved. These models will be divided into two parts:

.   the first defining the actors, the situation, the risks, the mechanisms for obtaining information, and the payoffs

.   the second indicating the assumptions as to how other parties will act and react

Gaming can therefore be seen to be a way of testing the behav-ioural assumptions which one has for each set of actual and foreseen circumstances. However, if the gaming scenario lacks an appropriate level of reality, the strategies adopted by the players may be equally unreal.

The designer's problem is therefore to strike a balance for, if the game is too elaborate, the investment of time to understand the model may well be a disincentive to play. Further, the game must always be transparent, i.e. the assumptions behind the game must always be made explicit so that a more constructive appraisal of the learning opportunitites can be made in the post mortem debriefing. This is particularly important if one or more players have failed to optimise their results. This experience tests the maturity of the player and his or her willingness to accept criticism and analyse failure. This reinforces the need to ensure that those initial assumptions are realistic, so that a constructive end-of-game discussion can take place between the players and the designers. One of the other factors to be born in mind is that because the gaming model will be a simplified version of reality, the experienced decision-maker does not immediately know whether real-world solutions can be directly applied to simulated problems. This potential disparity allows players to practice, or experiment with, decision aids and strategies, but the design must retain ultimate plausibility.

One of the more covert aims of any managerial training exercise may also be to test the staff during the play. This will be determined by the type of players and the context of play. Such an exercise can be motivational and can improve attitudes and performance, but it may also be stressful and lead to inhibited performance under supervised conditions. Care is therefore required in properly introducing the aims of the particular game or simulation, so that the gaming session is not unnecessarily stressful. M.A.P Willmer draws an analogy between the Newtonian definition of mechanical force, and the activities of participants in a management game. (8) Hence, Newton stated that every body continues in a state of rest or uniform, straight line motion unless acted on by an external force. The elements of "psychological force" which may act upon a player may be charact-erised as time, the level of mental stress, and the degree of complexity of task. Willmer assumes that complexity is a constant concern whereas the other elements may be variable. So it would be important to measure the rate of change of complexity against time, i.e. as complexity grows, one can expect pressure on the participant to rise and vice versa. Similarly, the rate of change of stress will be a function of changes in complexity. Thus, by adjusting time, or by manipulating uncertainty in the decision-making process, the game designer can directly affect the level of stress inherent in the gaming situation.

If the game or simulation is computer-supported, the opportunity to rerun the model with different input, or to make parallel input to the same game period, can be a most valuable exercise so that rapid comparisons of outcome can be obtained and better forecasting techniques developed. If computer models are to be used as opposed to manual systems, the model itself must always be based on understandable issues. Computer programming depends upon providing the machine with specific values for the variables. In manual gaming, many values can be left vague and approximate, so that the game referee/umpire can adjust the outcome to suit particular circumstances. The fact that computers have precise values within the given model can therefore motivate players to answer correctly, and help to focus the players' attention on the kind of answers that are most desirable for the particular situation, i.e. quantitative and not qualitative estimates. This is not to decry the value of the qualitative approach for many interpersonal decision-making situations require the inclusion of less tangible considerations. It simply indicates one of the limitations in a model that is exclusively computer-based. However, by exploiting the storage capacity of the modern hardware, all the best game runs can be stored whether they be from lowly trainees or experts and, by analysis of this data, the computer can achieve the capacity to advise on strategy optimisation, i.e. the game can become a form of expert system.

The more information concealed within the computer, the more the machine acts like the Delphic oracle, with the programmers acting like a form of High Priest. If all the gaming elements are explicit, the players can get an immediate overview and can quickly determine relevance and assess effectiveness. The attitude of a trainee must therefore be properly receptive and reflective. When a learner sits in front of a computer, judgement must be suspended until the machine has made a number of pronouncements. However, uncertainty can be deliberately exploited if the point of the learning exercise is to force the players to deduce the rules of the game, and to modify their behaviour accordingly. In such gaming, the intellectual commitment of the players must be greater if an adequate analysis is to emerge.

9.5   Conclusions

Most new technologies require the expenditure of time, money and effort if successful implementation is to be ensured. However, commercial organisations see the need to justify their activities in terms of positive rewards from money invested. In the case of CBT, the technology may claim certain manifest advantages. It permits the storage and output of materials to trainees with the time-savings inherent in an individually-paced tuition system because the materials can be more closely matched to the particular trainee's learning needs. It also avoids the need for expensive centralised training facilities, and allows all the materials to be kept up to date without the necessity of continually reprinting the training manuals. The technology also more readily supports the more sophisticated simulations and other advantageous training devices.

However, R.A Avner suggests that success for a new CBT system is not guaranteed, and asserts that, "cost-effectiveness is situation-specific rather than product-specific." (9), i.e. just because twenty organisations have found savings and efficiencies in their computer applications, does not mean that it will be effective in the twenty first. In all cases, educational desi??

expertise is required to ensure that the best use of the medium is made to promote learning. This must reflect a basic truth which is that the subject matter of the training is the primary criterion of effectiveness, while comparative cost analysis between the various possible training methods is merely of importance.

References

(1) published May 1987.

(2) Changes in the Employment of IT Staff. IT Skills Agency and Computer Economics Ltd. 1987.

(3) Software: A Vital Key to UK Competitiveness. An ACARD Report. HMSO, London 1986. p.33.

(4) described in Computer–based training at Barclaycard. A.F.Cook. collected in Computer–Based Learning. A State of the Art Report. pp.3/15.

(5) The Microcomputer in Industry Training. Nguyen Duc Quy and Jon Covington. (1982) (March) T.H.E.Journal 65/68.

(6) Industrial case study – the development of CAVIS. P.Copeland. collected in Computer–Based Learning. A State of the Art Report. pp.17/29.

(7) The Prospects for Operational Gaming: A Summary. Ingolf Stahl collected in Operational Gaming. An International Approach. pp.325/30 at p.325.

(8) The Pursuit of Realism: The Interpretation of Gaming Results Using the Method of Dynamic Similarity. M.A.P.Willmer. collected in Operational Gaming. An International Approach. pp.283/92.

(9) Cost–Effective Applications of Computer Based Education. R.A.Avner. (1978) (April) Educational Technology 24/5.

CHAPTER 10

EXPERT SYSTEMS

Compared to human teachers, the general approach to CAL is limited because:

.   it cannot interact with users in natural language

.   it cannot react to unanticipated questions or responses

.   it has no inherent understanding and cannot learn from the nature of the users' mistakes

.   it cannot experiment with the teaching strategy (1)

The best way forward is therefore to consider to what extent computers can be given expertise in the art of teaching.

10.1 Problem-solving skills, CAL and expert systems

One of the major areas of concern in the modern curriculum is the development of problem-solving skills within each area of domain expertise. Computers can have a dual role to play in this area, both by coaching and helping students to acquire and practice skills, and also by forcing teachers to understand the learning problems involved and thus become better teachers. In general theory, if it is assumed that nothing is interfering with the capacity of an individual to process information and to make choices, there are two main methods of thought which can be used for problem-solving, namely algorithmic and heuristic.

An algorithm is a rule which is capable of providing a definite answer to a given problem. The rule itself will be capable of precise definition and, so long as information relevant to the solution can be specified with sufficient clarity, the user can mechanically produce an answer. If it is not possible to produce sufficient certainty in the information or if, indeed, a genuine solution does not exist, then algorithms are of limited value. Thus, chess is a game of perfect information. It is easy to state the rules for the movement of each type of piece and to predicate the conditions to be fulfilled before such moves may lawfully be made. Moreover, at any moment during the play, one player may examine the board and be presented with exactly the same information as the other player on the physical state of the game. However, in evaluating that visual information, and in planning which of the many possible moves to make, levels of judgement, foresight and tactical ability are required which are outside the capacity of algorithmic rules. The solution to such problems lies in the science of heuristics.

Heuristics is the method of choosing between alternatives. Every person, to a greater of lesser extent, tends to make assumptions based upon past experience. Each person goes through life discriminating patterns of behaviour, acting upon a form of guided trial and error until the implicit and explicit norms of social causality are established, and rules about relationships of all kinds can be placed into a logical, or merely pragmatic, framework. In early life, the learning processes usually depend upon practical experimentation but, as the mind matures, the ability to use symbols grows to permit the actor to investigate issues and concepts at a more abstract level. The reasoning processes involved in both processes are sometimes described as either inductive or deductive.

Logic is said to be deductive because it moves from the general to the particular, i.e. from stated premises to a proper conclusion. The scientific method is said to be inductive because it will move from the particular to the general. However, both processes are really the same, being only distinguishable from each other by the time at which the actor may have recourse to them. Thus, the researcher may make a series of observations or perform a sequence of experiments, and deductively formulate a single hypothesis. By then collecting further samples or specimens, the researcher may inductively seek evidence which will either confirm the original hypothesis as a valid generalisation, or which will suggest new avenues of search. But the whole is the search for knowledge, and knowledge is the science of proof or evidence; it is the drawing of reasonable inferences from things previously known. Whether one terms the system "logical" or "based on the scientific method", the basic aim is to produce an efficient method for the evaluation of information. The conclusions reached will then be stored in the memory and, through the process of recall, will operationalise future decision-making.

In developing problem-solving skills in the student, whether the teaching is performed by a human teacher or a CAL system, or in seeking to model such skills in an expert system, various incremental steps must be taken. Overall, the architecture of the problem-solving process is the application of rules, the manipulation of data structures, and the construction of new rules from old. This breaks down into the following stages:

. Wherever possible, the expertise must be expressed as a series of goals, and a set of rules or strategies for achieving those goals.

. A methodology must be demonstrated for the evolution of these rules and different levels of skill must be defined. This is a historical perspective where links may be perceived between existing rules, and inductive or deductive assumptions made.

. Since a part of the problem-solving skill is the ability to structure and restructure the problem, the student or machine must be shown what data-structures to use. This is a form of epistemology, where the student or machine must be shown the forms in which knowledge may be required at different stages in the problem-solving process.

. The student or machine must be shown which cognitive resources are being used since different skills make different demands on memory and processing power. Here the first step is often to demonstrate the inadequacy of the human learner's existing resources. Little can be communicated until the learner perceives the need to know. This involves teaching the student how to evaluate the degree of complexity in the problem to be solved so that the best solving strategies may be selected. It also involves the recognition by the teacher that certain skills may actually be too difficult for the learner to understand either at all, or unless other skills are first grasped.

Some general research into CAL systems which will advise and coach students in the development of problem-solving skills has already been performed for particular subject specialisms, e.g. in geography (2), medical diagnosis (3), and mathematical games. (4) Equally, research has been on-going into the construction of expert systems which will model human expertise, the most famous of which are MYCIN and PROSPECTOR. MYCIN is a typical AI program which attempts to diagnose bacterial infections in the blood and to suggest appropriate treatment. The system depends upon production rules, i.e. if P then Q, and the whole used to be described as a production system but is now known as an expert system. Each rule consists of a set of preconditions (called the premise) which, if true, justifies the conclusion made in the action part of the rule. By scanning through the rules a chain of reasoning is established for a particular proposition. The system can be run forwards or backwards. Thus, it is possible to use it to specify what symptoms to look for in particular diseases, or it will take symptoms and suggest a diagnosis. Each rule has a certainty factor attached to it to give a degree of probability to the overall diagnosis. It also explains the basis of its conclusions, replacing any rules that were shown to be in error. Within its speciality, MYCIN performs as well as any human expert. For learning purposes, doctors could learn by simply looking over MYCIN's shoulder, but human experts know more than is contained in books. There is a judgemental factor.

As to the issue of user modelling, the best known examples are probably GUIDON and the IMAGE student modeller in GUIDON2. GUIDON tries to teach the medical knowledge in the MYCIN system. This system augments the performance knowledge of the production rules by adding a support level to justify the individual rules, and an abstraction level to organise the rules into patterns. If left at this point of development, the resultant system would be a rather passive tutor. Thus, if the student was going to discover all the reasoning paths through the system, a very large number of questions would have to be asked. By using user modelling, the system can be more active in seeking opportunities to deepen the student user's knowledge. In a GUIDON session, the user role-plays a consultant physician. General details of a patient are described, and lab reports about cultures taken from the site of the infection are provided. The student is then expected to ask for other information. This is a limited goal-directed dialogue, i.e. only the rules relevant to one goal can be discussed at any one time. This imposes a structure on the enquiry and helps the tutor to identify errors. When the student draws each hypothesis for each goal from the collected evidence, GUIDON compares these conclusions to those that MYCIN reached on the same data. The difficulty is that although the MYCIN system provides an strongly algorithmic approach to medical diagnosis, medical problem solving remains an art. While there are some conventions that ensure that all routine evidence is collected, doctors have not agreed an approach to optimise detailed diagnosis.

There are three main parts to the student model which is initialised by asking the student to state the level of existing expertise at the begining. The more advanced GUIDON2, which has more flexibility than the original version, performs the same function for NEOMYCIN. The IMAGE modeller tries to explain a student's behaviour by first considering the choices which NEOMYCIN itself might make in that situation. If a match arises, the student's behaviour is explained. Otherwise, a search is made through the model to see whether the system can identify the rule which the student is using. The point is to try to identify the source of the misconception as opposed to a careless error. The operation of the overlay model is varied given the inherent complexity of the rule which is currently under consideration, the background of the student, and evidence gathered in previous interactions with the student suggesting whether the student knows how to achieve the relevant goals and subgoals. The tutor is therefore given a basis upon which to select component elements for the remediation. If the student has inadvertently selected an option which makes no significant contribution to the solution of the hypothetical patient's case, a different approach will be adopted as against the student who selects that element precisely because more detailed information of that more remote possibility is required.

Both MYCIN and PROSPECTOR have formed the basis of a new generation of expert system shells. (5) By constructing systems for the performance of professional tasks, knowledge similar to that held by the human expert has had to be acquired by the computer. This has led to significant insights into the nature of knowledge and the nature of expertise. However, information or knowledge does not of itself solve problems. It must be capable of application. The general structure of problem-solving which underpins the development of expert systems is three-fold:

. the hypothesise-and-test method

. means-ends analysis

. best-first search (6)

A computer "learns" by being given information which can be processed in accordance with the instructions contained in whichever programming language forms the basis of the system. Because this language is known in advance, it is relatively straightforward to communicate information to the machine in such a way that it can be operationalised. A human may learn by being taught and by self-instruction. It might appear to be easier to be taught by a teacher because the teacher can provide the student with appropriately structured information which the student can simply accept. However, if a student is going to internalise this information in a way which is meaningful for future application, it must be converted for use. Simple rote memorisation gives no more than the ability to repeat the memorised material, and does not guarantee the ability to use that information in the solving of problems. There is therefore no practical difference in the learning process whether it is teacher-led through the oral presentation of material, or student-led through reading or other source exploitation. Both require the student to restructure the information so that usable skills are produced. Thus, the average human being cannot learn to ride a bicycle simply by hearing or reading a description of the skills involved. It is necessary to learn by doing. For most learning activities, practice and experience are an indispensible part of the learning experience. A student is like a theorist who, having obtained partial knowledge, searches for confirmatory evidence in the practice of what is thought correct. At a simplistic operational level therefore, there is little to choose between the problem-solving approach of expert systems, and the adaptive learning strategies of students. However, in comparison with the way in which expert systems acquire and apply knowledge, because the programming language used by human beings is not clearly understood, it is not easy to know how best to present information to the human machine for operationalisation.

If a teacher is to program a computer to present teaching materials in any subject area, there are several levels of understanding required:

.   The teacher must have a good overall grasp of the subject to be taught.

.   There should also be some understanding of the process which is termed "learning", so that information and experience may be given in a way which will optimise that process for the prospective user.

.   It is also necessary to know the various ways in which the "learning" may go wrong. Unless the programmer knows which mistakes are likely to arise in the application or exercise of the knowledge to be presented, the text itself cannot be properly drafted, and either no help will be given where it is required, or even the wrong help may be given.

An American experiment which produced a "student simulator" has proved instructive. Student teachers were exposed to a simulator for elementary arithmetic skills. The results showed that exposure to this simulator significantly improved the student teacher's ability to diagnose procedural errors in a student's behaviour. (7) The primary function of the program was therefore to teach the teachers about the types of mistake which students were likely to make. This helped to compensate for the not infrequent response that, if a particular concept or technique has been easily understood by the teacher, it may not be immediately appreciated that others may not so readily understand.

10.2   What is an expert system?

Expert systems are one of the products of research into Artificial Intelligence. The computer is a machine which has a memory and a processor unit. It stores pieces of information and sets of rules which may be applied either unequivocally, or upon the occurrence of certain pre-defined events. But perhaps more importantly, the computer has the reputation of being a "logic machine". Indeed, gate design is based upon the proposition that the machine can be induced to perform "logical" operations. The consequence is that, if an anthropomophic view is taken, machines may be made human-like, i.e. they can be made to perform many of the functions which could be performed by a man or a woman. In 1961, Marill stated, "At present we have, or are currently developing, machines that prove theorems, play games with sufficient skill to best their inventors, recognise spoken words, translate text from one language to another, speak, read, write music, and learn to improve their own performance when given training." (8)

Although taken within their historical context, these claims were a highly optimistic and somewhat colourful view of the then state of the art, the capacities of the modern machines have been dramatically enhanced, and do begin to demonstrate some of abilities which Marill claimed. Today, as scientists move towards the so-called Fifth Generation computer systems, machine capabilities begin to more closely mirror human abilities. After all, both machines and humans have memory, data manipulation abilities and computational skills. If the consequence of this combination of skills and abilities is intelligence in the human, it is therefore not unreasonable to suppose that a machine may also be persuaded to manifest intelligence.

The improvements in machine performance actually achieved, and the aspirations to emulate that elusive human quality of "intelligence" in a machine, have encouraged a new breed of critics to become more vocal. Amongst the most common assertions are that, "Machines can only do what we tell them to do", or that "Machines are incapable of genuinely original thought", or that "No machine can really be an expert in the human sense of that word". This type of approach tends to suggest either a patronising view of the machine, which consequently confirms the human's innate superiority, or a level of defensiveness which perceives the machine as unfair competition. In the real world, if a human does produce an original result, presumably it is recognised as such. It is interesting to speculate whether, if a computer produced a similarly original result, an objective appraisal would have confirmed the characterisation as original. If so, could that originality be subsequently denied because a computer was then shown to be the source? Is the judgement solely one of performance, or must one consider personality, or the lack of it?

If the reader was to play two games of chess by correspondence, one against a human opponent and the other against a computer, how successfully could the two games be distinguished? Any judgements based upon whether a sequence of moves was "bold", "imaginative" or "foolish" are the form of value judgements which could apply to the human opponent. If the reader nevertheless applies these criteria only to find that the distinction between human and machine is not clear cut, has the computer been invested with a form of perso. lity? Indeed, Turing argued (9) that if a robot could be built so that remote interrogation could not distinguish it from a human being, the interrogator would frequently feel that the other demonstrated human characteristics.

As a practical demonstration of this phenomenon, the various programs which have been designed to conduct psychoanalysis or therapy sessions often produce conversations between patients and machine very comparable to those between patient and human doctor (10). This is not to say that computers have a free-language capacity. There are still substantial and unresolved difficulties preventing the creation of a practical system which will permit an unstructured conversation to take place between a man and a machine. Natural languages use a complex mixture of representations, especially in spoken forms, where stress, intonation, volume and tempo may all interact with each other and with the words selected to provide shades of meaning . However, it does suggest the ability to simulate conversational skills, e.g. the story-telling and responsive capacities of the RACTOR system.

Within the general research field, it seemed a useful step to exploit the memory and computational capacities of the computer by capturing the expertise of human experts, and storing it in computer systems. However, even this proposition is not without difficulty because, before the capture and storage can be accomplished, it requires a clear understanding as to the nature of expertise in human beings. Expertise is clearly something more than the solution of problems by algorithmic means. The knowledge of an expert transcends the formalisable. It has a dynamic quality based upon a series of facts held in memory, an understanding of the relationships which exist between those facts, an ability to formulate short-term and long-term goals, and a grasp of the tactical and strategic implications of seeking to achieve any or all of those goals. Moreover, genuine experts are those who can create new concepts where the old prove inadequate. They can negotiate with other experts, redefine the problem, advance hypotheses, seek consensus and resolve semantic disputes.

In computer terms, one can only begin to model this complex and intangible ability in an expert system. The term has consequently come to be a set of programs which has access to a knowledge base, and which can draw inferences and conclusions from that knowledge in order to satisfy a user query. Then, just as the human expert, the computer should be able to explain how it has arrived at any particular conclusion. Any human expert is, of course, recognised to be capable of error. One of the mechanisms which is used to test the reliability of any advice given by a human, is to ask for an explanation of the thinking processes which led to the particular conclusion. If no explanation can be given, or it does not sound convincing (by whatever criteria the listener makes that judgement) the advice may be ignored. Similarly, a computer which does not explain itself may find its advice ignored, no matter how expert it may be and no matter how right it may actually be in the particular circumstances. This is particularly important if no clear cut answer can given to solve the immediate problem, and the system is merely offering the "best" solution of several possibly relevant solutions, or a range of possible solutions, leaving the choice to the user.

To further clarify the terminology, an expert system shell is an expert system with an empty knowledge base, waiting for a domain expert or a knowledge engineer, acting as an interface between the domain expert and the program, to enter the knowledge and, thus, to realise the system's potential and to make the system functionally expert.

10.3 How does an expert system work?

The core of the knowledge base is an inter-locking system of rules which, when taken together, provide a working model of the particular area of domain expertise. Each rule will be a variation of the type,

> if p, then q

whether stated in this positive way, or negatively,

> if not p, then q

and so on. The machine is therefore programmed with a basic sequence of responses to a variety of situational stimuli. However, such rote responses may not be discriminating enough, for not every "q" will automatically follow upon one particular "p"; either a combination or permutation of circumstances must be seen to exist, or a value judgement of some sort must be made. In the first instance, the giving of the conclusion "q" may be deferred until each of the preconditions has been verified. This may involve using "and" or "or" either singly, in combination, or in permutation both positively and negatively, viz.

> if p1 and p2 and p3, then q

or

> if p1 or p2, then q

or

> if p1 and (p2 or p3), then q

or

> if not p1 and (p2 or p3) then q

and so on.

Value judgements usually depend upon an evaluation of probabilities. Here a great element of intuition, guesswork or other similarly vague mental processes may be detected, and may make any problem-solution strategy less susceptible to mechanical rule-making. It is recognised that not every decision can be broken down into convenient sequences of logical and separable steps. Mathematicians have sought to quantify the resulting uncertainty in theories of fuzzy logic, and this can bring another tier of so-called meta-rules to the knowledge base. This tier will be superior to, but interactive with, the more conventional pattern of rules and will seek to modify rule selection, or the combination of rules in appropriate circumstances. It will also seek to make evaluative judgements in a semi-quantifiable, but nevertheless acceptable manner, e.g.

if p, then to some extent q

where evidential values may be sought and cumulatively lead to a reasoned conclusion.

Thus in British weather forecasting, at a crude level, it may be more likely to snow in December than in July; or given the best satellite pictures, measurements of barometric pressure and other significant factors from ground stations and the historical record, it may be possible to predict snow as more likely than not, given particular combinations of weather system over the Atlantic and continental Europe. In this latter, more scientific approach, meta-rules will be in operation to select the most relevant predictive rules to apply to the new data given the time of year, the immediately prevailing conditions, the overall short-term pattern, historical similarities to the current pattern and, possibly, factors like the state of the carbuncle on the forecaster's nose. The application of the predictive rules will then produce odds that certain results are likely to occur. This is not a process capable of producing certainty, but it enables the forecaster to make predictions with greater confidence.

So far, it has been assumed that either the rules are already written down, or that the expert can be induced to formulate the rules and meta-rules with reasonable clarity. Sadly, this is not always the case. Experts often operate at an unconscious level without every really articulating the precise nature of the decision-making process being engaged in. Indeed, it is this aspect of expertise which the critics of expert systems fasten upon. Thus, Philip Leith argues that rules are simply aides-memoire for the expert who can only handle change and resolve conflicts and complexity within the domain by having a deliberately inchoate, and therefore dynamic, view of the domain. "Sociologists of science are begining to suggest that one of the problems of the rule-based expert system is that, on its own, a rule is a threadbare element indeed. It omits much of what Collins has termed the "tacit" nature of the world, that tacit information which is essential for the non-expert to fully understand the meaning of the rule, for a rule cannot define its own

meaning – that must be given within a certain intellectual context." (11)

The argument therefore runs that to so simplify the human domain
expertise to permit it to be programmed into an expert system, is
to produce a wholly artificial version of the domain which lacks
the essential element that characterised the original expertise.
That element is, more often than not, the ability to understand
the meaning of words in terms of real–world situations and experience. Thus, one may analyse and write down the rules of grammar
but this will not delimit and define style. Experience shows that
wordsmiths like authors and playwrights, poets and gag writers,
often gain an effect by not following the strict rules of language, but by creatively breaking the relevant linguistic conventions. In such a situation, a knowledge engineer may, through a
process of objective questioning, be able to elicit the rationale
for the particular practice. However, no matter how many times
this retrospective process is engaged in, it will not be possible
to program, i.e. quantify literary flair. The result would be a
series of examples where the rules were not followed. If this
list was used to produce a set of meta–rules, indicating situations in which the first tier rules need not be complied with, it
is simply imposing one set of artificial rules upon the backs of
other artificial rules "to bite 'em, and so ad infinitum".

The difficulty with this form of critique is that it often does
not attempt to define the nature of expertise, or to quantify the
proportion of any particular domain which might be the subject of
this problem of definition. Every domain, to some extent, must be
based upon rules, even if such rules are merely imperfectly
understood cause and effect relationships suggested by experience. Thus, before the concept of gravity was mathematically
defined and scientifically evidenced, it was an observable fact
that objects do not usually fall upwards. This odd phenomenon
could be exploited in a variety of different expertises without
actually being understood; e.g. in weaponry, making lead shot by
dropping molten metal from a height into water; in the design of
lifting mechanisms, using counter–balances to bring otherwise
heavy skins of water up from wells, etc. The existence of expert
systems forces domain experts to address the issue, "How functionally rule–based is this particular expertise?"

If the answer is that while all the basic skills are capable of
being reproduced with certainty, higher order skills are not, the
use of machines to undertake the routine tasks frees the expert
to devote more time to the higher order activities. The appraisal
may, however, demythologise the carefully preserved reputation
and, in reality, show the skills to be almost entirely mechanical. The consequences of both extremes may be socially useful in
freeing the expert to perform the expertise more effectively, or
in protecting the public from unjustified fee–paying. In the
middle ground, it is always useful for an expert to think about
the nature of his or her expertise, for all insights gained into

the true nature of the activity engaged in, are potentially valuable.

To entirely dismiss expert systems because of the artificiality of rule-making which, overall, may creep into any particular domain model, is not justifiable. One may cook food "naturally" over a fire, on a gas ring or an electric hob, or in a conventionally heated oven. Microwave ovens do not rely on this "natural" methodology and, for example, will not brown food. That these ovens do not operate in the usual way does not mean that they are not extremely effective in the cooking of many different types of dish. Thus, expert systems may not, either given the present state of the technological development or the state of the human expertise to be modelled, do some of the things which a human mind may be capable of, but this does not mean that machines cannot very efficiently reproduce many of the effects which one would attribute to human expertise.

Indeed, it is possible to use expert systems to derive rules through induction where no rules have previously been consciously expressed. The method is to give a series of examples of a particular phenomenon with the various outcomes achieved in each instance. By classifying the attributes of each such situation, and seeking correlations between them, it is possible to suggest rules for achieving the outcomes specified. The larger and more representative the number of examples given, the more powerful is the computer is identifying relationships between the different elements identified as significant, and suggesting causal links. In this, the machine is capable of learning through examples. It is equally performing the function of teaching through the analysis of examples.

The user accesses the knowledge base through that part of the program known as the inference engine. This part of the system will tend to adopt one of two methodologies. It may reason forwards or backwards. If the analysis is to progress forwards, the initial data is examined, and knowledge is solicited and used to identify and move towards the goal. If the reasoning is backwards, the system starts with the most likely goal and calculates whether it does in fact fit the facts. If the first selected goal proves not to be relevant, the next most likely goal is selected and the process repeated until the goal with the highest likelihood of success is identified.

10.4 Why is an expert system suitable for teaching?

A teacher is an expert at two quite different levels:

.   First, there is an academic and/or practical expertise in the subject-matter to be taught.

.   Second, the teacher is an expert in the art of communication

This art may have been innate, may have been acquired through the practical experience of the teaching activity itself, or suitable skills may have been honed in a formal course. But no matter how acquired, this second expertise imposes constraints upon the first, limiting or reshaping the organisation of knowledge so that it may best be conveyed to the student. Indeed, in the build up of a topic, introductory statements may actually be quite alien in spirit to the overall topic discipline, but be accept-able within the teaching context as a series of signposts to allow students a sense of direction in the study to be under-taken. If a CAL suite for a given topic is to be created, account must be taken of the two interlocking sets of requirements – thus, the computational skills of the full academic expertise must be possible when introductory materials have been assimil-ated, and the flexibility of a teacher's expertise must be possible.

Given a rudimentary understanding of the programming language BASIC, it is possible to construct simple branching programs using the PRINT and INPUT commands, and the conditional GOTO statement. With the addition of file handling and the use of arrays or matrices to store and/or carry forward information, it is possible to produce more complex programs which can present information in a significantly more sophisticated manner. How-ever, the implicit need for the domain expert to have to deal with the mundane mechanics of programming will represent a barrier in terms of the time required to master the relevant part(s) of the programming language(s). It may also be an intellectual skill which has no other relevance to the domain expert and consequently, there may be no real incentive for the expert to invest the time in gaining that skill. If the effort is made, the programming itself may become a substantial distraction from the subject matter to be presented. The expert may become far more interested in the manner and methodology of presentation than in the objective evaluation and analysis of the teaching material. For all these reasons, encouraging lecturing staff to learn how to program in BASIC, PASCAL or one of the other high-level languages, is probably not a constructive step forward, although it may appeal to individual enthusiasts.

The ideal would therefore be to provide a knowledge engineer for each expert willing to donate his or her expertise. This engineer would explore the area of expertise as an intelligent layman and would prompt the expert through a questioning of anything that was not clear. Eventually, the engineer will be able to encapsulate his or her own understanding of the information in such a way that it can be entered into a computer system. The resultant system may then be demonstrated to the expert who can comment upon the machine's performance and thus, ultimately, through an interactive dialogue between domain expert and knowledge engineer, a refined system can be produced. In this way, an expert system can be generated without the necessity for the domain expert to understand anything of the internal workings of a computer.

There are a number of difficulties inherent in this ideal proposal. The first is that there is a chronic shortage of trained knowledge engineers as against the number of apparent domain experts. Thus, even if domain experts were willing to engage in the task, it would take an unreasonably long time before all could be seen. The second problem is that it can take a long time to understand the true nature of another's expertise. Even a clerical task of modest routine can take weeks or months to fully evaluate, program and document. If real decision-making criteria have to be examined, a year or more may be required. This would require considerable commitments of time and patience, both on the part of the knowledge engineer, and on the part of the domain expert; these commitments being made without really knowing in advance, precisely how far the knowledge to be elicited will represent a genuine step forward for the particular trade or profession. Thus, it may later appear that the domain expert was objectively not as expert as had previously been thought the case; or there may be factionalism prevalent within the area of expertise, and many other practitioners may reject that one individual's view; or it may subsequently appear that it is impossible to produce a reliable model of the expertise, and that the resultant system should therefore not be made available for general, and possibly unsupervised, use.

The majority of Higher Education colleges and institutions now have Computer Services Units and other specialist staff who are charged with the responsibility of helping and advising academic staff both in the use of computers, and in the methodology of teaching. For those schools and colleges not large enough to justify in-house expertise, there are both local and national advisory bodies who may be able to offer help. But, as against the overall number of acadmic staff, these specialist support staff represent a tiny proportion of the whole. Consequently, they can do little more than represent a ginger group for the anonymous cohorts, and more active help for the few who are prepared to emerge from the crowd and to show more individual initiative. It is certain in these times of economic stringency, that the education system itself cannot divert the money and human resources from the mainstream of teaching activities in order to produce large expert teaching systems. Similarly, it is doubtful whether industry and commerce would be prepared to fund its own wholesale knowledge engineering exercise, let alone that of the education sector, albeit that major economies and improvements in efficiency would almost certainly result in both sectors.

The more practical short–term solution is for the schools and colleges to better exploit the time available within the academic year. It would be unreasonable for individual establishments to buy in knowledge engineering expertise. The commercial salaries commanded by individuals with these skills far exceeds the salary scales available in the education world. However, it would not be unreasonable for the domain experts to be given software packages which simply ask for information, and which will perform all necessary processing and implementation activities without the need for the expert's intervention. Although there will be consequent piecemeal development, with considerable redundancy and overlap, this is probably a better situation than all waiting for the few knowledge engineers, or the few multi–disciplinary experts, to produce their more professional results. This leaves the question: "What are the best packages to use for this purpose?"

10.5   What is an authoring language?

An authoring language is a set of programs or routines that is designed to minimise the actual amount of programming expertise required by the teacher in the creation of educational software. Some teachers will always seek to write their own software either because the packages will not do what they want, or because they enjoy doing it. But, for the non–expert, these languages can allow the creation of teaching systems without the need to understand in detail how any of the various effects are produced, although the teacher is still going to require good typing skills to enter and edit the subject–matter.

Most high level languages are not attractive to teachers who have no computing expertise, because of the time needed to master and refine programming skills. Such delays impede courseware development. A teacher's primary responsibility and training is to plan and implement teaching strategies. To spend too much time in the activity of programming from scratch in a high level language may not be a proper use of a valuable teacher's time. The ideal would be that the user needs no training to be able to interact with a computer, but such technology is not likely to be available in the immediate future. Teachers must therefore gain some technical expertise. This means that there must be an effective way of evaluating educational courseware available from other sources, or the teacher must use some form of computer assistance.

The theory of an authoring language is that the teacher merely deals with content, and the package takes care of the programming. The teacher must also deal with the motivational side of the design, and select the most appropriate learning strategies for each topic. Because it takes less time to learn, an authoring system can be more popular with teachers. The reason for this popularity is simple efficiency, for the teacher is given the capacity to produce exactly what is required to fit into the given course. The difficulty with commercially available teaching programs is that, to justify their cost, they are sometimes longer and more sophisticated than are required for everyday teaching purposes. A form of policy balancing act must therefore be performed. It must be accepted that the productivity of teachers in producing software will not be as great as that of the professional, and so the real cost of in-house production will be higher than the cost of acquisition; but the level of commitment to the home-produced system is likely to be greater, and so the in-house software may actually be better value for money.

Authoring languages have often been designed with training in mind and, because some designers see training as more CAI than CAL-based, the languages are more frame-based and limited in node switching, i.e. the system depends upon fixed window sizes, and only a limited number of branching options are available at each input point. This lack of true flexibility can be frustrating if the aim is to promote learning rather than to supply simple instructional materials. The education service initially achieved more through the direct application of programming skills but, with the dissemination of interest, more staff now want to create software and, for all their limitations, the use of an authoring language is one of the few ways in which this ambition can be realised. This is not to suggest that software technology is standing still. There have been many improvements made. But, for example, although an increasing number of authoring languages now have the facility to check student input for incorrect or omitted characters, or additional unwanted characters, until a more free language input mode is achieved, CAL input is always likely to be less than friendly. This is because no CAL writer can afford the time to predict and store all the possible permutations of free language answer which might be provided by students at each input point. Human speech is usually syntactically incomplete, and computers have no real basis upon which to comprehend the entirety of meaning which may be included in a group of sentences although, with better data search and retrieval systems, computers are getting better at comparing input with stored text to determine the most likely meaning. However, for all the improvement, this process is still very error prone.

10.5.1 What does an authoring language do?

Essentially, it executes the educational decisions of the teacher as programmer. Thus, it sends the appropriate text and/or a picture to a terminal, moving the cursor on the screen to the appropriate position to signal that student input is required. If appropriate, it can execute calculations either to determine which node to switch to next, or for some other purpose, e.g. verification of the student's answer. It will wait patiently for a user response and then analyse the response, or take action if a pre-set time limit has expired. It will test any specified condition and move to the next relevant unit of informations, or terminate as the designer requires. Some systems are form-driven, some menu-driven, and some macro-based.

To assist in the evaluation of authoring languages, the following points should be born in mind. A good system should allow a preview facility to allow the author to see what the screen will look like when the completed system is running. It should also be possible to drop out of the simplfied world of macros, and to write addenda which will augment the switching capacity or add calculation facilities. The package ought to have good screen editing facilities, not only for creation purposes, but also for later maintenance and updating; and it is also useful if the system provides a facility for the students to record text while working through the program. This latter facility may be to allow the student to make his or her own notes on the materials, or to communicate, albeit indirectly, with the designer. The claimed advantage of some packages is the availability of a graphics package, but purchasers must ensure that the production of reasonable images is not too complicated and time consuming. Proper record keeping capacity is essential, as is an interactive video link; and the buyer must ensure that the package will interface with existing printers and other peripherals.

10.6 What is interactive video?

Don Binsted reports (12) a series of laboratory studies to explore the potential of interactive video (IV). For these purposes, the interaction is between a computer and either a video tape or video disc machine which has prerecorded teaching materials. The purpose of the study was to evaluate the usefulness of IV for generating packages suitable for management training. The term 'management training' covers a wide range of skills, e.g. problem-solving, decision-making, and interpersonal skills, and involves attitudinal learning, planning, etc. Thus, because the development of these skills is equally important in the academic student, the conclusions of his study are considered applicable

251

to education at large. The use of visual images is useful for two reasons. First, problems in the real world often arise either out of dynamic situations or out of conversations. No matter how well written the case study or simulation, it can be difficult to convey the detail of a situation without boring the reader. But, by using a visual medium, the student can literally take in the situation at a glance. By then allowing the computer to take student input at strategic points in the scenario, and allowing the software to select the next visual passage, the student can be shown the effect of each decision.

Secondly, as a facilitation for learning, video has been found to involve the users, and to have greater potential for entertainment and fun than convention presentational techniques. It is not merely that dramatised case studies are more interesting than their written counterparts; they achieve an immediacy of impact which can significantly promote the learning process. However, for all that video tape technology has been available for some years, there has yet to be a significant production of materials exist for evaluation. Graeme Keirle discusses the plans of the Centre for Educational Resouces for the Construction Industry (CERCI) to develop useful systems which can be supplied to prospective clients to assist in identifying the right product, or supplying basic information on health and safety within the construction industry. The advantage of video should be obvious in that pictures of different materials and products can be brought together to test colour or stylistic compatibility, and the dangers of the building site can be more graphically demonstrated. (13) The difficulty lies is the cost of production. The mastering of video discs is still expensive, albeit that high quality images are produced in a robust medium. Even if video tape is used, the time taken to write, act and edit each sequence is substantial.

10.7   How useful are authoring languages and IV systems?

The range instructional packages commercially available such as MICROTEXT, DOMINO and TOP CLASS, potentially represent a modern enhancement of the straightforward branching systems achievable in BASIC, adding facilities such as a graphics package and an inter-active video capacity to make the presentation visually more interesting. But it is almost impossible to make such systems "expert" in any real sense of the word. Their true value lies in the ease with which most may be operated by non-computer specialists. The systems require an undemanding evaluation of domain expertise which is quick to make because most systems will not permit computational intervention to remember what has been asked and what the replies were. The result is a multibranch option unique to each decision node, unless the user has the know-how to drop out of the system and to write supplementary sections in assembler or the support language (usually PROLOG or PASCAL). Although it is also possible to so design the question sequence that there is implicit memorisation of question and answer, such results are always optimisations obtained to some extent against the spirit, and within the limitations, of the authoring system.

However, whatever their faults and limitations, these packages do represent a real option to schools and colleges, both in introducing staff to the teaching capabilities of the computer, and in the actual production of teaching packages. Given the importance of the need to interest and motivate staff, the comparative ease with which reasonable results may be obtained is a crucial factor. Work of a different nature may be required of staff but, if this work is more a part of their own domain expertise rather than connected with the programming of an alien computer, there is less excuse for staff not to undertake the work as an ordinary part of a staff–development exercise.

There are several authoring languages such as PROLOG which have been developed to facilitate the programming of logically based material. Ignoring the problem of the domain expert coming to terms with a more complex programming language, PROLOG borrows a preexisting formalism from classical logic, and shows how relevant it is to the programming of computers. The difficulty with formalism is both that it presupposes that uncertainty has been removed, and that others will have nothing real to contribute. Further, the particular concept of predicate logic which is used by PROLOG, was developed by Frege to assist in the more rigorous proof of mathematical theorems. To apply such an approach to the world of business, law and ordinary social relations, is to ignore the fact that many aspects of life are not based upon formal logic. The result is that PROLOG is ideal for routine administrative work and unambigious tasks, but is dangerous to apply where more subtle tasks are to be undertaken.

For teaching purposes, authoring languages can be used to produce working models of many of the analytical techniques underlying most of the major sciences, and of the more "logical" topics within the humanities. Indeed, within its limitations, PROLOG is a powerful computational tool which may be used to create sophisticated sequences of analysis and calculation. However, if it is intended merely to produce instructional materials, it is less effort to buy one of the existing software packages, based upon one of the authoring languages and specifically designed for that task.

10.8 What are the advantages of expert system shells?

Again, there is an increasing range of expert system shells now available on the commercial market. Most of the shells are supplied in two versions: a larger mainframe system, more suitable for complex tasks, and a smaller version suitable for use on a PC, e.g. SAVOIR and Micro Expert. Although the ideal system for the creation of software would be subject-led, and not software-led, to permit the human expert to structure the information in the most internally consistent and intellectually satisfying way, this presupposes that the experts actually understand their subjects in a way which is suitable for conversion into a knowledge base. It was this problem which could be mitigated by allocating a knowledge engineer to each expert, and giving that engineer the task of both representing a form of external objectivity to the creative process involved, and of tailoring the software to the knowledge.

Without this outside assistance, the expert needs a series of prompts from the software itself to indicate the format requirements of the particular system. The danger in this is, of course, that the software will then represent a form of intellectual strait-jacket, restraining and inhibiting the structuring of the knowledge and the computational range of the processes which are to be performed. Thus, if the domain expert was, when asked, to clearly state that the method adopted to solve a particular problem was a given series of procedures, a knowledge engineer could either select an appropriate piece of software "off the shelf", or create routines which would perform those procedures in their proper context. But if the expert is told from the outset that only a limited number of software procedures are available in the particular shell supplied, it is entirely possible that none of these procedures will match those required within the domain expertise. In such a case, either the expert will be deterred from attempting to create the system, or will distort the real world expertise to meet the constraints of the shell. Neither result is satisfactory, but perhaps some effort is better than none. Even if the ultimate response of the domain expert is negative, if that rejection is upon a rational basis, it will have been as a result of a coherent evaluation of existing methodology in the light of the assistance which might be rendered by the computer. Such constructive appraisals are always potentially useful so long as the expert is prepared to implement any discovered improvements.

The somewhat simplistic modelling which is directly permitted by the authoring packages has little chance of providing the expert with sufficient flexibility and responsiveness. Improvements in performance are possible, but require rather too much initiative from the expert who is likely to be an inexperienced programmer. Thus, for all their individual faults and idiosyncracies, the expert system shells represent a real and valuable stimulus to creative thought by an expert about his or her domain expertise, and once the teaching system has been created, it will give consistent and accurate help to the students. From the point of view of a teacher, not only does such a shell potentially repres- ent a better way of structuring the academic expertise, it also has a built-in system for explaining to the user how and why any particular step has been taken. This focuses the mind of the domain expert who may not lightly make statements if all must be capable of explanation. It also gives an ability to write explan- atory commentaries which may be invaluable to the student user. This is not to argue that the same effect cannot be produced by using the authoring software. It is, for example, possible to buy a standard saloon car and to fit twin carburettors, a better suspension system, more effective brakes, and a range of other gadgets, but this will not make the resultant vehicle as good as a Porsche.

10.9 What is ICAI?

ICAI is the acronym for Intelligent Computer-Aided Instruction. This was preceded by adaptive or generative CAI, i.e. systems which generated problems of an appropriate level of difficulty for the learners to solve. The sophistication lay in the task- selection algorithm, and this is now extended in the modern systems. It goes beyond a simple examination of the answer given by the user and allows the system to examine the methods used by the student to answer the questions, and to experiment on the user and thereby to arrive at a point where student behaviour can be more closely modeled. The end-product is a supportive learning environment where the learner may learn by doing; transforming factual knowledge into experiential knowledge. The problem is to pitch the instructional material at the right level to respond to the student's query or mistake, i.e. the system may assume too much or too little knowledge. The programmer may also start with fixed preconceptions about the sort of errors which the students are likely to make, and thereby provide an inadequate conceptual framework of advice for the students. User interaction is still too limited – student responsiveness and tutor assistance are strait-jacketed.

The problem with ICAI was that it required substantial computing power which was only available on the larger mainframe systems, e.g. SOPHIE. (14) This restricted ICAI to use in limited topic areas. To maximise the investment of resources, bottleneck topics were selected, e.g. basic arithmetic, the solution of algebraic equations which were fundamental to future educational progress. Now that greater computing power is available in smaller and more economical machines, the development of ICAI techniques can rapidly accelerate. A great deal of the knowledge and problem-solving skills implicitly communicated by human teachers has never been articulated. It lives in the minds of the teachers, developed through experience. Computer coaches can only learn in a limited fashion, so the practical knowledge of the teachers will have to be made more explicit before ICAI can really move forward.

Central to any tutorial system is the need to have a detailed, domain-specific knowledge. If an ICAI system is to measure student progress toward instructional goals, it must incorporate some knowledge of the domain to be taught. The nature of the stored knowledge not only determines the content of the tutorial interaction but also the goal structure that governs the tutor's selection of questions and examples, and the way in which student misconceptions are diagnosed and corrected. (15) If knowledge is to be used effectively to explain why a given phenomenon occurs, it must be ordered and, to a greater or lesser extent, linear elements must be linked by temporal or causal connectors.

Such a knowledge structure does not, however, directly assist in diagnosing student misconceptions. It may be better to consider the functional relationships between all the factors involved in the particular process to be described and its result. This is non-linear and interactive, thus functional relationships would work in both directions, e.g. a given variable could both increase and decrease rather than having to be shown as two separate causal chains. The causal linear chains govern the sequencing of major topics within a tutorial, whereas a functional approach describes the dominant features of the interaction microstructure. Tutors discuss topics in a rational order but need the more detailed knowledge to diagnose errors which appear in the dialogue. Much of the teacher's skill in diagnosing error depends on knowledge of the type of errors students are likely to make. A particular conceptual bug is often shared by many students, but may be manifested in a variety of different forms. In most cases, a single bug accounts for each error, but there are cases where bugs interact to produce a single surface error. This interaction may actually produce non-obvious patters of error. It is therefore dangerous always to attribute a given error to a given bug because the error/bug relationship may be quite subtle.

People are able to solve mathematical, mechanical and other problems based upon a reasoning process which they have not seen before – naive problem-solvers tend to make the same kind of mistakes because they make reasonable, though unsuccessful efforts to adapt existing knowledge to the new situations. Given that we are not taught incorrect answers nor solution procedures for every type of problem, this regularity demands an explanation, M. Matz proposes a theory of mathematical competence. (16) Such a theory would explain how new rules are constructed from familiar knowledge, or more particularly, how existing rules are extended (successfully or not) to handle a wider range of problems. Every individual formulates base rules which incorporates knowledge and protocols derived from previous learning experiences. The would-be solver then applies extrapolation techniques that specify the way to bridge the gap between the known and the unknown.

Common errors are therefore caused by:

. having inadequate (but not necessarily incorrect) base knowledge

. by making an inappropriate use of a known rule in a new situation

. by incorrectly modifying a known rule in the hope that it will then solve the new problem

In fact, the known rule may work in other problem areas which are highly comparable to the given problem, and the extrapolation technique may itself be sound but the particular application be in error. Extrapolation is a creative process because the student has to consider how to adapt an existing rule or how to view the new problem as a variant of one more familiar. Initially learners are taught a single correspondence between rule and problem. With experience, meta-knowledge develops and allows a more flexible understanding of the relationships between given rules and general problem-solving in that domain. The formation of general rules by the student from the sample already seen is based on the assumption that particular elements in the sample problems are incidental rather than essential. This assumption is often valid. In addition to conceptual errors, a student may also make execution errors in performance of correctly deduced principles.

Any model of the student must therefore be dynamic to reflect the developing state of the student's knowledge and understanding as the course progresses. Without this capacity to reflect changes in the student's knowledge, inappropriate advice may be offered, viz. advanced techniques may be introduced too early, or may be referred to prematurely. The ICAI system must, however, have some basis upon which to decide whether to intervene, what topic to discuss and how much to say about the topic. The system must therefore know how the learner's knowledge is likely to evolve, i.e. "from simplification to elaboration, deviation to correction, abstraction to refinement, specialisation to generalisation." (17) Implicit in this model is a theory of learning based upon a modelled distinction between a problem-solving specialist and an active learning specialist. For the purposes of the computer coaching system, the problem-solving specialist tries to solve the problem using the information appropriate to the learning specialist at that person's level of attainment. However, the model should not change too quickly. Observation shows that, for example, a student does not always use a skill which has just been explained. This assessment of conservative progress should assist the computer to predict the possible sources of the student's difficulty and to encourage further learning. The modelled learning specialist extends knowledge in line with the human student.

The major problem is that the machine cannot really be told what processes the student may use to draw analogies, recognise deviations, induce generalisations or construct conceptual refinements. All that can be given is the equivalent of a road map showing the various routes by which a student might seek to achieve understanding. If this map has many possible links, it might highlight areas of learning complexity. Goldstein speculates that where there are clusters of linked routes, joined by generalisations and analogies, the repetition of concepts and their mutual reinforcements will tend to make the concepts easier to understand, whereas more sparsely drawn sections of the map may require more effort to explain and understand. (18) The further difficulty in diagnosing student error is the unreliability of the evidence which the computer has to work with. Thus, the cause of the given response may be that the student may have misunderstood the question, or lost interest in formulating the answer, or changed goals entirely. There is a fundamental problem because the computer cannot see the student' expression, understand the language, or respond to a pause at the terminal. This latter case is acute because it is not known whether the student is thinking, or has merely been distracted, or has left altogether without logging off.

In developing a model of a skill, like speaking a language or solving algebra problems, people who are fluent in the skills can overlook both its subtle and its obvious aspects. Errors, as evidence of students' misconceptions and missings conceptions, call attention to the tacit knowledge that fleunt problem solvers automatically apply. This will also provide evidence for possible process-oriented decompositions of procedures, i.e. when a student's effort to carry out a procedure fails or is inadequate, the resultant error can indicate better intermediate stages of the execution of that process. However, given the currently level of technology, the actual level of expertise which can be given to a CAL system is limited. The expertise consists of a set of facts or rules. The student's knowledge is modelled as a subset of this knowledge and the tutoring is restricted to intervention in situations where the missing fact or rule is the critical ingredient.

In 1984, Logica UK began a research and development program which has resulted in the TUTOR system. The proposition is that an intelligent front end is essential for a system which is going to offer good tutorial support to students. Industry's training programs assume a high degree of isomorphism in trainees because it needs to meet operational goals cost effectively so staff need to be matched to tasks. Learning by discovery is said to be inappropriate to industry where a more regimented approach is supposedly required, i.e. minimal trainee initiative but ample opportunity for practice. The aim of TUTOR is to teach rule-based subjects, e.g. legislation, emergency procedures, etc. Such topics are well-organised and susceptible to criterion-referenced testing, i.e. TUTOR is capable of testing whether trainee has grasped all the rules. Because the subject-matter must always be formatted on an algorithmic basis, the TUTOR system is limited in its scope.

There is a natural language interface which is capable of handling 19 sentence types which may originate either from the student or from TUTOR. The interface is limited but has the virtue of ensuring that the dialogue does not become too verbose. Natural language as the communication medium between the user and the machine makes the use of the system more convenient because a totally new system does not have to be learned, and can make the system more flexible through the expressive quality of language. Artificial constraints on language restrict the user's perceptions of machine capability. Similarly, prompt or menu systems are inherently limited and slow down access. The system stores information on the success or failure of each student to answer individual questions requiring knowledge of a concept, and keeps track of an understanding of clusters of inter-related rules. In the example given of training students to understand the traffic lights sequence, the authors admit that TUTOR's general domain knowledge is limited and that it has only the simplest form of inference engines. The system does, however, have the capacity to accept simple student enquiries based upon the facts already posited by the program and to offer explanations on a "what if" basis. (19)

The architecture is as follows:

. The system stores a teaching strategy controlling the frequency and timing of exposition and the presentation of remedial information. The score performance criteria for each rule are also stored. When the trainee's score meets the criterion, no further training is given, unless performance in a dependent rule shows that a refresher course in the original rule is required. In this way, mastery can be measured and confirmed. Decision-making is based on the rules contained in this section of the program and by inter-relating to other parts of the program.

. TUTOR has to be able to remember what a student has done and what decisions TUTOR itself has made. This information permits the teaching strategy to avoid re-presenting a recently given task, determine how long it has taken to train each individual, and determine what degree of initiative the trainee has demonstrated in reaching understanding.

. Central to TUTOR is the knowledge base of the rules and an interpreter of them which are to be communicated to the trainee. Each rule has an internal executable form, which is expressed as a PROLOG clause and contains preconditions, prerequisite actions and an action part. It also has an external form which contains two strings of text,

(a) a description of the rule, and

(b) a justification of the rule.

These are used for expository purposes.

. TUTOR maintains for each student, a model of his knowledge of the subject he or she is learning. This is used to influence tutorial action.

In intelligent teaching it is important for the system to have a model of the user's state of knowledge. If the user is learning some new idea or skill, he or she may not yet be able to explain what is known, and may not understand the point of some of the questions posed by the computer system. The machine therefore needs to be able to make assumptions about the user and to base future action upon them. It is also possible to monitor a user and to prevent the user from taking lines of action which will be wrong. Thus, if a user has just spent an hour typing in a program, it might be disasterous to allow the user to leave the system without first saving the program. In some cases, the system ought to query perfectly legal commands because the context in which they are being used may suggest inaccurate understanding. The problem is that it may be not justifiable to infer that because a trainee has not demonstrated knowledge, that knowledge is not there. If a system makes that assumption and seeks to teach something which is understood, alienation may set in. This is a part of the more general issue of how effectively a computer may guess at a student's intention or motive.

10.10 What is a user model for?

This is the key design issue. If it is to be used for predicting responses and then taking appropriate educational decisions, a procedural model will suffice. However, if the computer is to be used for making factual judgements about a user, should the user be told the function of the program and given an opportunity to comment on the provisional deductions? There are moral issues here. An assumption of total ignorance would require the system to undertake considerable work before a stable picture of the student was built up. If one starts from a single stereotype and measures divergence towards other possible types, or from a range of possible stereotypes in parallel, and tests hypotheses to determine the most likely type of user, this may be efficient so long as the initial stereotype selection is made with some idea of the intended target group.

In this, it must be possible to represent the standard types of faulty knowledge that individuals may have. Equally, the system must be able to cope with mistyping and to make the appropriate judgement, i.e. cannot spell, is dyslexic, is foreign and has not yet learned much English, or cannot use the keyboard well. There may also be factors of boredom, lack of motivation, or haste. If the computer is to make judgements, it must be understood what the aim is, i.e. a competence model that captures an idealised section of an individual's skills and knowledge, or to identify the source of any misconception. (20)

10.11 The construction of expert systems

An expert system is a computer system which possesses a set of facts about a particular domain of human knowledge, and by manipulating these facts intelligently, it is able to make useful inferences for the end user. The concept of intelligence has different dimensions but, at the end of the day, it is not what a system can do that determines whether we think of it as intelligent, but also how it is done. Simple exhaustive searching, if sufficiently fast, may be perceived as intelligent. However, it may be considered more intelligent to avoid the search altogether, or to delimit it by prior enquiries. Perception of intelligence will also be determined by the use to which the computer is put. The paradigm is that an intelligent system is one capable of solving problems which cannot be resolved by using crude computational methods, i.e. there is a distinction between standard data processing techniques and the genuinely "expert" system. The point of expert systems is that they should exhibit expert behaviour. The power of any truly expert system is that some representation of the knowledge used by a human has been achieved in a form which can be used as a basis for computation.

The computer system depends for its effectiveness upon the facts elicited from human experts which then constitute a conceptual representation of the relevant expertise. There are two levels of difference between a human expert and a beginner.

. An expert knows more.

. An expert is likely to use knowledge more effectively.

In the first instance, the actual content of the knowledge base will be unique to each individual and the explanation of the content will be a personal process. However, the notational system of concepts used to explain how that knowledge can be understood, could equally apply to other expert's knowledge, and will also explain the range of questions which can be asked, problems formulated, instructions understood, etc. Knowledge acquisition, i.e. the extraction of the knowledge which forms the underlying base of the expertise from the human expert, or knowledge identification by the expert for entry into a shell are the most difficult aspects when developing an expert system of any size. In some domains where the procedures involved are simple and algorithmic, the knowledge can be made explicit fairly easily. A preliminary survey through basic textbooks, followed by confirmatory interviews or discussions with colleagues, will usually be sufficiently effective to permit the creation of a prototype conceptual model which can then be tested.

Generally, the most effective ways for a knowledge (or software) engineer to acquire information from experts such as observation in the field or in-depth interviewing, are inherently slow, a major problem given that experts' time tends to be limited. It can also be difficult to represent the rules thus obtained because information obtained in this way is often incomplete and inconsistent, and continual reference back to the experts for clarification increases the amount of time involved, and tests patience. The most usual approach is to rely on informal interviews to elicit information which is then converted into empirical rules (usually in a form laid down by the target shell). However, not all expertise is capable of being represented as a rule system, e.g. areas of medical diagnosis may depend upon extensive practical experience and strategic knowledge which is difficult to verbalise, and the informality of the interview may enhance the incompleteness and inexact nature of the information which is acquired.

Any expert's knowledge is likely to be of different types. It is difficult, if not impossible, to taxonomise knowledge but, with due diffidence, Gammack and Young (21) suggest the following broad categories:

. knowledge of concepts and relations, i.e. overview knowledge

. knowledge of routine procedures

. particular facts and heuristics

. classificatory knowledge – making fine distinctions among a number of similar items, knowing about when various tests are best deployed

One way for the expert to gain an insight into knowledge held is to write information down. For the objective outsider, an interview of the expert with these classifications in mind can be helpful. This can quickly generate a lot of information that indicates the terminology and the main components of the domain, and is thus a good start procedure to establish a basic framework. It is also useful to ask the expert to give a one hour lecture which can be followed by later systematic probing interviews where depth is added. But, as indicated above, all interviews have limitations. Although experts have the knowledge, it may not be communicable in the interview situation.

It is possible to combine knowledge extracted from several different experts and thereby overcome the problem of incompleteness, but this may cause severe problems if the experts approach the resolution of problems with different methods. The ideal solution would be to produce systems which could induce rules from all the examples given by the contributing experts. However, the danger with such systems is that there may be a large number of rules generated, or that the one or two rules induced work well with the particular examples given, but do not work well outside the data set.

One of the more recent developments is called Protocol Analysis which records the behaviour (verbal or otherwise) of the expert as a problem is addressed and solved. This protocol is analysed and converted into a set of productions that transform one solution state to the next. Its merit is that it goes beyond what the expert can explicitly tell the knowledge engineer, to permit inference of what knowledge they must be using but either cannot verbalise or are unaware of. By reconstructing the solution using inferred production rules, the expert's knowledge can be modelled. Protocol Analysis is preceded by task analysis, i.e. the constraints imposed by the nature of the task are determined. By taping the expert at work, additional or incidental protocols may be elicited, i.e. informal remarks may provide key insights into the expert's thinking which might not have emerged during a formal interview.

The problem is that this approach is labour-intensive, requiring the transcription and analysis of significant quantities of data and reducing the useful amount of end-product material. A number of multidimensional scaling techniques have been used in psychology to show how a particular set of concepts are structured, viz. repertory grids can elicit finer grain criteria than formal interviews. By identifying clustering on the dimensions, the system designer can give a structure which more clearly differentiates the domain objects. It can also lead to the development of meta-knowledge, which provides the overall structuring of individual elements or concepts. However, such techniques are extremely specialised and demanding, and will not normally be available for the creation of expert teaching systems.

But there are a great many areas in the industrial and commercial world where the development of consultative expert systems would be of considerable benefit. Ready access to knowledge, with the ability to manipulate it, is increasingly important in the post-Big Bang management world. Yet it is not achievable in the standard database systems. Industry can, of course, afford the fees demanded by the knowledge engineers, but the problem is the time taken to develop and refine the final model.

The answer for both the educational and commercial sectors lies in the expert system shell. The concept of the shell has been developed to allow newcomers to develop their own expert systems without the need for specialist knowledge engineering skills. The standard shell will provide a means for encoding the domain knowledge and inferencing mechanisms to make use of the encoded knowledge. Most fact-seeking expert systems elicit findings by interviewing the user in an inflexible way. The user has no control over the course of the interaction, which tends to be lengthy and tiring. This pattern may be acceptable for inter-viewing clients, but for the busy professional it is not completely acceptable. However, whether through interview or through self-generated input, the knowledge database can be constructed. Because it is easy to adjust the knowledge modelled, it is even sometimes better for the knowledge engineer to proto-type by using a shell before building a bigger system from scratch. However, if a shell is used, there are still problems:

. How do you persuade a shell to iterate towards an optimum solution?

. What to be done if the user does not know the answer to a given question?

. How good is the Man-Machine Interface (MMI)? i.e. the system should always permit variable amounts of text to be dis-played, and should not require particular grammatical styles and constructions. To help the user, the shell should be based on existing high level languages to enhance port-ability. The problem is that many of the commercially avail-able shells are very restrictive in the amount of text that can be shown in each frame. This is extremely inhibiting when it comes to the creation of a CAL suite unless the knowledge is capable of being represented in very small chunks. The only ways to avoid this problem are either to acquire shells written with the possibility of CAL in mind, or to modify the shell by accessing the supporting high level language.

. How good are the correction facilities? If the user realises that a mistake has been made, it should not be necessary to scrap the program and to start again. It should be a simple matter of going back to the relevant node and changing the wording of the material displayed or amending the switching comands.

. A.P.White also identifies fundamental difficulties in basing evidential evaluation on a Bayesian odds approach. The difficulty is that the likelihood ratios to obtain the posterior odds of H when two or more pieces of evidence are

264

available are prohibitive in terms of effort. The usual solution is to assume that all pieces of evidence are conditionally independent. However, "where conditional independence does not hold, the posterior odds will be in error. Furthermore, the greater the number of steps in the inference procedure, the greater this error is likely to be." (22) Thus, in trying to assess the degree of fuzziness in the logic, great care should be taken.

10.12 Conclusions

An expert system is not simply a collection of individual rules. Each rule relates to some concept in the domain and it must be consistent with, and complementary to, the other rules relating to the same concept. Rules should therefore be created and revised as a functioning unit. Unfortunately, the elicitation of knowledge from the expert, or formulation of rules by an expert in a piecemeal fashion is likely to result in an unco-ordinated collection of rules, and attempts at modification of a patchwork of rules are likely to fail.

The end-product combination of rules has to be checked comprehensively against the greatest number of possible situations, and any rules that make specific conclusions on the basis of the inability to prove some item should be avoided. It should also be recognised that if there are errors in the rules for proving the item, the system is likely to give the wrong answer. In the prototyping phase, where trial runs are being performed, misdiagnosed cases are useful in diagnosing errors in the rule system. It is also foolhardy to use uncertainty mechanisms if they are not properly understood by the domain expert. The cases on which they operate are likely to be the difficult cases and the precise nature of those difficulties should be brought out into the open. This is because:

.   the ability of the system to give the correct answer needs to be verified

.   the end user of the expert system may need to know that the query has raised a difficult and unusual case

This latter point is particularly important in the medical field, where it is useful to give all the possibilities so that, if the apparently most probable diagnosis proves wrong, the doctor knows where to go next. As a final point about construction, experience suggests that quality control is difficult in large systems, and that knowledge representation using logic suffers from the difficulty that it is essentially propositional.

However, in the comprehensiveness of the end-product lies the advantage of the expert system. Because it represents an interlocking sequence of propositions, each one self-justifying and explained, it becomes a good teaching vehicle. Because it is not only possible to make the system expert in the subject domain, but also as a teacher by creating a user modelling and evaluation system, it may become an ideal teaching system. The greater the degree of expertise created in both parts of the teacher's task, the more effective the learning opportunities created for the students or trainees. It is true that authoring systems have begun to make progress in the direction of expertise and that there are considerable strengths in their ability to interface with other media of presentation. But the best hope for the future must lie in developing "expert" teaching systems.

This will rely upon either the teaching profession itself engaging in considerable introspection to elicit its own knowledge in a form appropriate to become a knowledge database, or the expenditure of considerable time by knowledge engineers to extract the relevant expertise from the teachers. In the short-term, both possibilities are unlikely, but better shells may soon be developed. The situation in industry is more hopeful. Many firms are now actively investigating the possibility of creating expert systems. If funds are committed to that project, it is relatively inexpensive to add an embedded training system for the benefit of the staff. Further, if the system is given the facility of storing examples from real-world problems and the best solutions, the system can achieve considerable expertise which can be passed on to each generation of managers.

References

(1) The some of the exceptions in modern practice are described in A Self-Improving Tutor for Symbolic Integration. Ralph Kimball, and A Self-Improving Quadratic Tutor. Tim O'Shea. collected in Intelligent Tutoring Systems. pp.283/307 and 309/36 respectively where the systems have a limited power to experiment in the presentation of teaching materials.

(2) AI in CAL: An artificial intelligence approach to computer assisted instruction. J.Carbonnell. IEEE Transactions on Man-Machine Systems, December 1970, MMS-11 (4).

(3) Tutoring rules for guiding a case method dialogue. W.B.Clancey. (1979) 11 Int. J. of Man-Machine Studies 25-49.

(4) An investigation of computer coaching for informal learning activities. R Burton & J.S.Brown. (1979) 11 Int. J. of Man-Machine Studies 5-24.

(5) Expert Systems: The Vision and the Reality. M.A.Bramer, Research and Development in Expert Systems, 1984, ed. M.A.Bramer, Cambridge University Press, p.1-12.

(6) The art of artificial intelligence: Themes and case studies of knowledge engineering. E.A.Feigenbaum. Proceedings of the Fifth International Joint Conference on Artificial Intelligence, Pittsburgh. Dept. of Computer Science, Carnegie-Mellon University, 1977.

(7) Diagnostic Models for procedural bugs in basic mathematical skills. J.S.Brown & R.Burton. (1978) 2 Cognitive Science 155 at pp.170/1.

(8) T.Marill (Inst. Radio Engineers) Trans. Human Factors Electron. II (1961) 2.

(9) Computing Machinery and Intelligence. A.H.Turing. (1950) MIND.

(10) A Computer Model of Psychotherapy. Colby, Watt & Gilbert. (1966) Journal of Nervous and Mental Diseases 142.

(11) Artificial Intelligence and the Legal Rule. Philip Leith. Paper presented at: Technology in Legal Education. University of Warwick, April 1986. The reference to H.M.Collins being, "The Concept of Explanation in Expert Systems" presented at Explanation in Expert Systems, March 1986, University of Surrey.

(12) Don Binsted. Interactive Video: Research into its Potential for Management Education. collected in Trends in Computer Aided Education. pp. 47/54.

(13) Graeme Keirle. What Can Higher Education Do For Industry? collected in Trends in Computer Aided Education. pp. 64/74.

(14) A model-driven question-answering system for mixed initiative Computer-Assisted Instruction. J. S. Brown, R. Burton & F. Zdybel. IEEE Transactions on Systems, Man and Cybernetics. SMC-3(3), 248/57.

(15) Misconceptions in students' understanding. Albert Stevens, Allan Collins and Sarah E Goldin. collected in Intelligent Tutoring Systems. pp.13/24.

(16) Towards a process model for high school algebra errors. M. Matz collected in Intelligent Tutoring Systems. pp. 25/50.

(17) The genetic graph: a representation for thge evolution of procedural knowledge. Ira P. Goldstein. collected in Intelligent Tutoring Systems. pp.51/77 at p.68.

(18) ibid at p.74.

(19) TUTOR – A Prototype ICAI System. N.G. Davies, S.L.Dickens, L.Ford. collected in, Research and Development in Expert Systems. (ed) M.Bramer. Cambridge University Press, Cambridge. 1985.

(20) For a fuller explanation see, User Modelling in Intelligent Teaching and Tutoring. Peter Ross, John Jones and Mark Millington. collected in Trends in Computer Aided Education. pp.32/44.

(21) Psychological Techniques for Eliciting Expert Knowledge. John G. Gammack and Richard M. Young, collected in Research and Development in Expert Systems. 105/12 at pp.106/7.

(22) Inference Deficiencies in Rule-Based Expert Systems. A.P. White collected in Research and Development in Expert Systems pp.39/50 at p.41.

CHAPTER 11

THE BROAD POLICY ISSUES

In this final chapter, it is necessary to consider the more practical political issues. Most schools and colleges are still under Local Authority control, and so it is expedient to consider what policy-making function Local Education Authorities have at a time when Government is adopting a centralist stance. Further, the British Government must be seen in the context of membership of the European Economic Community which has also developed policies to promote the use of IT technology.

11.1 What is the role of the Local Education Authority?

The education system is, to a greater or lesser extent, controlled by Local Education Authorities (LEAs) which, in turn, are controlled by locally elected politicians. Even though they have found their national negotiating role diminished, LEAs are still responsible for paying the salaries of the teaching staff, and for maintaining day-to-day control of expenditure on supplies and maintenance for primary, junior, secondary and some tertiary institutions. They are also primarily responsible for in-service training within the system. It is a part of their function to create policies for the use of computers in education in the institutions for which they are responsible. For these purposes, a "policy" is a formal statement that attempts to co-ordinate activity.

The interactive process which may lead to policy implementation or change within LEAs is notionally between the advisers, the officers and the elected members who jointly and severally respond to local, regional and national pressures. The way in which these groups actually operate inevitably depends upon the flow of information within the system. Sadly, it is often the case that the innovative suggestions from the advisers who are, after all, the supposed specialists in curriculum and teaching methods, never reach the lay members who have to sanction the consequential expenditure. This is because the officers, who should facilitate communication in the hierarchy, do not pass the information on. Alternatively, the advice of the more expert may be made available for consideration, but is ignored in the face of short-term political expediency. There is also the difficulty that many advisers already carry a heavy workload, and cannot afford the time to go through the full consultation and discussion phase. Thus, for a variety of reasons, many important decisions are taken on a second-best basis.

Yin suggests that policy innovation passes through three stages (1), namely:

.   The initiation and adoption stage where the idea is discussed and leads to the decision to create a policy.

.   The implementation stage follows in which support for the policy is canvassed so that proper provision can be made available to support the scheme. There will also be a monitoring element in these initial phase to measure the effectiveness of the policy in practice.

.   The Routinisation stage where the innovative quality of the policy disappears as the activities and staff connected with it become a part of the ordinary serice of the authority.

In each of these stages, major responsibility is assumed by the officers for maintaining continuity of effort, and if the more senior officers are hostile or indifferent to the policy issue, progress is likely to be slow. Indeed, even under the best of circumstances, "delays of 2 or more years were experienced, even in the leading authorities, between initiation and routinization of a formal policy for the use of microcomputers in education." (2) Given that the formulation of positive policies in support of computerisation are an essential precondition of progress, for those authorities where the priorities lie elsewhere, little real activity is likely in the schools and colleges. LEAs also find themselves much under pressure from the Government on a series of issues, and even the best authorities may find it difficult to co-ordinate future developments.

Hence, the Education Bill 1987 is also to include a requirment to pass some degree of financial control to headmasters and school governors. This will involve major amendments to the in-house financial software to enable each LEA to produce detailed financial information for individual schools. Micros linked into local authority systems to exchange information will therefore become an essential part of school administration. Like any business, a school or college needs financial management. It has to deal with inventory control of all assets and it has to match student needs in much the same way as customer needs. This radical amendment is to be made at a time when data processor managers in Local Government are facing one of their biggest challenges in the need to create new software to support the proposed poll tax system.

11.2 What has the Government actually done?

The attitude of the Local Education Authorities could have been entirely negative and, with the implicit support of a conservative teaching profession, could have denied the additional burden of hardware and software expenditure, and of staff development on already overstretched budgets. Indeed, within the public authorities at large, a 1987 Computer Weekly/Romtec survey (3) shows that, of the organisations surveyed in the public sector, 85% were cutting back on computer purchases and were finding increasing difficulty in recruiting appropriately qualified staff. It should not therefore be considered surprising if many education authorities have not made significant progress in developing a suitable strategy for the introduction of the new technology, or in implementing that strategy. Governments must recognise that, in the current financial climate, simple exhortations to computerise the education sector are likely to be wholly ineffective, and that mere capital grants will be considered inadequate in the face of the longer-term revenue implications.

The direct responsibility for monitoring progress in the education sector falls upon the Department of Education and Science (DES), which is supposed to ensure that sufficient financial support is provided for all approved activities in schools and both Further and Higher Education. The DES should also provide both tangible and intangible support for curriculum development groups and other similar nationally-based bodies, overseeing the entire system through the inspectorate. In a world of increasing complexity, any Government, no matter what its political persuasion, has to establish a style of leadership. Some Governments prefer to adopt a low profile and, in the classical laissez faire mould, tinker gently with the status quo. Others adopt a more radical and interventionist approach, and force through major changes of policy by exploiting the in-built parliamentary majority. Thus in the commercial sector, the role of the Department of Trade and Industry and of the

Treasury could be the direct supervision of the business world in general, and of the city in particular. Alternatively, some form of retrospective regulatory function might be considered politically more acceptable, given that the response can be tempered by the immediate practical political need. By way of analogy, in health terms, it is the substantive difference between preventative medicine and curative medicine.

Because the various Governments which have held office from 1970 onwards have had some commitment to the concept of computerisation in the education sector, it has been necessary for the various central departments to devise, and then to seek to maintain if not co-ordinate, suitable policies. One of the first positive initiatives to promote computer-based education was the Computers in the Curriculum Project (CIC), which was initially based in Chelsea College. It began in 1973 with funding from the Schools Council, but subsequently drew upon a diverse funding base. Its aim was to research and develop CAL materials for schools across a wide range of subject areas and, to that end, it has maintained a strong central team which has liased between active groups of practising teachers. (On a smaller scale, the activities of Investigations on Teaching with Microcomputers as an Aid (ITMA) based at Plymouth are also of interest.) This was followed by the National Development Programme in Computer-Assisted Learning (NDPCAL) which arose from a report of the National Council for Educational Technology and ran from 1973 to 1977 with the declared aim of encouraging curriculum development, teacher training, and resource organisation and support. The real impact of this otherwise useful body was restricted to Further and Higher Education which had access to the then largely mainframe technology which was to host the software.

The NDPCAL represented a centralised approach whereas the Microelectronics Education Programme (MEP) was decentralised, setting up a national network of fourteen regional information centres, with additional funding for special education called SEMERCs. It was the Labour Government which promoted the introduction of microtechnology through the MEP, and £12.5m was the sum proposed in 1979 to increase levels of awareness in schools. Sadly, this initial enthusiasm was not maintained and, in 1980, the programme's budget was cut to £8m over a three year period, i.e. 0.02% of the overall education budget, by the newly elected Conservative Government. This is a direct reflection of the sense of priority which the programme attracted in Government thinking, and there was considerable public reluctance on the part of Government to actively support the scheme which further reduced levels of staff morale. Indeed, apart from some mild gimmickry on the part of some Government departments, viz. in 1979, the DOI sponsored a competition among schools to win a micro, followed by a scheme to pay half the cost of a micro in every secondary school, this period is one of marked centralised inactivity.

In 1981, the DES published The Micro-Electronics Education Programme (The Strategy), which stated the aims of the programme as:

. encouraging schools to amend the content and method of teaching the curriculum

. enriching the study of individual subjects by using the computer and fostering a better teacher/pupil relationship

. developing the individual pupil's capacity for independent learning and information retrieval

This was supplemented by the Micros in Schools Scheme funded by the Department of Industry which was designed to assist in the placement of a micro in every school by the end of 1982. In addition to this broad specturm initiative, some more special- ised assistance was offered. Hence, in July 1982, the DOI intro- duced the Primary School Scheme which would provide half the cost for the purchase of a micro by primary schools if two teachers from the purchasing school agreed to attend a short awareness course.

This was followed by the British School Technology (BST) programme, a three year project begun in 1984 with a £2m yearly budget to retrain existing teachers and to get expensive equipment into schools in the most cost-effective way. Under the chairmanship of Sir Henry Chilver, training courses have been run at Bedford and Nottingham, and the mountain has come to the schools through the conversion of fifty buses into mobile laboratories which have been supplied to local authorities. The primary advantage of the buses is that it solves the problem of in-service training without disrupting the schools in the process. The normal retraining system would involve the teacher in taking time from work to attend a course. Moreover, when the bus comes to school, both staff and students can benefit from exposure to the latest CAL techniques. However, following the inevitable logic of Conservative philosophy, as from 1987, BST is to become a charitable trust and, consequently, it will only survive if it is capable of being self-funding.

In 1986/7, a further £3m a year was made available by the DTI to fund the Microelectronics in Schools Support Unit. In the Further Education market, the Government is also currently helping colleges to respond to employer demand by enabling them to buy the latest equipment, e.g. through the Computer Numerically- Controlled Machine Tools Scheme. In other subjects, non-advanced further education (NAFE) colleges are being helped by a major Education Support Grant (ESG) programme to extend the use of IT across the curriculum. By early 1988, it is estimated that over four hundred colleges will have purchased at least £40,000 worth hardware, and funding for the training of staff in its use is also made available. To assist in the staff retraining effort, thirty new IT Staff Training Centres have been created.

In October 1986, the Government announced plans to create a new generation of computer literate children by launching the City Technology Colleges scheme. This scheme calls for the creation of twenty colleges to cater for the 11 to 18 age range, and the intention is to provide a curriculum rich in computer sciences and technology. One of the more interesting aspects of the plan, which could provide a welcome boost in the number of technologically aware people, is that industry and commerce is invited to provide £1m to establish each college. It seems that the only benefit offered in return for this investment is that when each cohort of students emerges on to the job market, employers will have better trained individuals to recruit.

The result is that many of the larger hardware companies like IBM and DEC are not enthusiastic. The main theme of the attack from industry at large is that the Government policy should be to encourage a closer link between commerce and the state sector. To invite the private sector to overtly support a selective and elitist college system is politically difficult. By backing such colleges, companies could damage their existing links with state schools and LEAs in as much as the new colleges will be outside the control of the LEAs, will be taking the better students and staff from the state system, and could be run more to the demands of the individual sponsors rather than to objectively satisfactory educational standards. The scheme further asks commerce for a substantial financial input for a nebulous reward. Teachers are also hostile because, by creating centres of excellence, an elitist approach will be developed that will drain the few experienced teachers away from the ordinary state school and therefore prejudice the already disadvantaged pupils.

For any set of initiatives to succeed, the active support of the education system is required. The degree of support will partly be determined by the level of information available to schools and colleges on the range of opportunities which are available for exploitation. The National Education Resource Information Service (NERIS) is an initiative by the Industry Education Unit of the Department of Trade and Industry which initiated a direct technology input by providing a modem for twelve hundred schools. Although no subsidy for increased telephone charges has been provided, most of the important information sources about education have now been made available via a local telephone call. This is because NERIS is available on The Times Network System (TTNS) which in turn operates on Prestel Education and British Telecom's national Packet Switch Stream (PPS), so there is also access to the general mail box and message board system. In February 1987, NERIS was launched as an electronic mail and database delivery service. It is on the same mainframe (Sperry 1100 at the Open University) as the Educational Counselling and Credit Transfer Information Service (ECCTIS) database which provides students and careers officers with information about Further Education courses available in Britain. The Resource Service has been given an initial £1m grant but, naturally, thereafter it is expected to become self-financing and to find its own annual running costs which have been estimated at about £450,000. NERIS holds information about learning materials. It permits searching on the standard subject domain key words, and responds with data matching as to age of students and level. The core of the data base is a list of available materials (i.e. books, film, video, sound tapes, multi media resource packs and computer programs), and copies of teaching materials and software in the public domain can be down-loaded to schools.

Independently of these, and other similar, projects, the DES has now issued a set of strict guidelines to LEAs, telling them how best to exploit IT, and demanding five year development policies and information strategies from each of them by the end of 1987. This is a response to the uneven performance of LEAs in implementing proper computing provision in schools. The letter identifies the key concerns as:

. establishing a small student to computer (terminal) ratio

. better training for teachers

. continuing development of education software

The intention is to ensure that the £19m Education Support Grant for 1988/9 to back education computing (£8.5m set aside for purchasing hardware, and £10.5m for employing advisory teachers trained in IT applications) will be best spent, i.e. it will be targeted where there has been least activity.

11.3 What should Government policy be?

The Government has the capacity to influence the development of computer technology not only through the setting of national policies and targets which can stimulate national awareness and attitudes, but also through purchasing and procurement, sponsorship and research. The Advisory Council for Applied Research and Development (ACARD), now to be replaced by the Advisory Council on Science and Technology (ACOST) have recommended TYPSSEA – the Ten Year Pipeline Strategy for Software Engineering and Applications, (4) which would have four main elements:

. The use of public purchasing power to exercise demand-side leadership by pulling through new ideas in the pipeline. Such a principle is, of course, incompatible with the lowest cost tender system which the Government has been seeking to introduce, and ACARD suggests the adoption of the more flexible cost-plus system with adequate safeguards built in, whereby innovative specifications can be implemented (i.e. those which go beyond current need and perhaps represent quality standards that would facilitate export). Without this positive support, ACARD predicts that the slide of British industry into uncompetitiveness will accelerate.

. Given that this would amount to a form of publicly funded research and development scheme, the Government has a direct role to play in preserving the continuity of the research effort. Once the principle of funding is accepted, the confidence of the researchers must be maintained. Any form of stop/go policy is demoralising and should therefore be avoided.

. The Government should also accept responsibility for accelerating technology transfer. At the very least the Government should act as a form of clearing house for information, where appropriate, demonstrating and accepting state of the art technology. The acceptance and implementation of new ideas should also be encouraged by tax allowances for private sector in-service training, and by Government sponsored training and distance learning schemes, improving the standards of professional certifying bodies, etc.

. The final element reflects the fact that the IT skills shortage is particularly acute in the public sector and, if good advice and support is to be offered by Government, an effective public sector in-service training programme is essential.

A further issue is that, at present, responsibility for the development of computer-based skills is divided among many different Government departments. This inhibits the development of coherent policies. The need is therefore for a better co-ordinated approach where common issues are studied, and if necessary, funded together. In this way, joint targets can be maintained over a reasonable period of time.

There is an inevitable conflict between a "Value for Money" approach which looks for the apparently efficient use of resources, and the issue of "accountability" in education. Industry has the somewhat jaundiced view that the curriculum and the knowledge of relevant staff are not geared up to meet employers' needs. This is said to result in a shortage of well-qualified individuals entering the employment market place. One possible response to this criticism would be for the Government to invest heavily for the future by giving tax allowances to encourage industry and commerce to engage in research and development. This is strongly recommended in The IT Skills Crisis - a Prescription for Action, published by the National Computing Centre in September 1987.

At present, organisations appear to be trying to solve their problems by recruitment. If firms also had the incentive to train and develop their own staff who, in turn, would become more creative, then the deficiencies of the formal education system could be circumvented. The problem here is one of accountability in both the literal and the metaphorical sense. Many firms could claim the allowance but, subjectively, the results might not be felt a genuine improvement. A form of stand-off would emerge whereby employers would not invest in training because, according to conventional accounting principles, there is no discernable return. Similarly, the Government would not give the tax allowances because of the ideological view that anything that industry is unwilling to pay for is not worth investing in.

Alternatively, the Government could directly fund research and make the benefits of this research available to all those who might be able to exploit the new technology. If such a strategy were to be adopted, work undertaken could be more closely monitored and controlled. However, this can generate a claustrophobic and bureaucracy-ridden atmosphere which inhibits the more creative minds, and it leaves the responsibility of inspiring the research to a Government which may not have an appropriate level of technical expertise to commission the most constructive projects.

In general, there are two possible strategies for funding research:

.   the diffusion-oriented approach

.   the mission-oriented approach

The diffusion-oriented approach requires that resources are put into education, co-operative research and product standardisation in order to upgrade the capacity of firms to use the new tech-nologies. The emphasis is on technology transfer and the innovative use of the best of the new ideas. The natural tendency is that research which is done by industry is more related to industries' and the market's needs, whereas research in the academic environment or Government research establishments tends to be more abstract. The policy would therefore be to encourage Higher Education to aim at more practical projects, perhaps by changing the basis of funding from deficit to incentive.

There is also the possibility that where industry and commerce have not kept up, there should be incentives given to import foreign technology, whether through capital goods or licensing. This will represent a holding action until indigenous skills are built up. But information technology is central not just to industry, but to public administration, the utilities and defence. The more overseas technology that is imported, the greater the potential to influence strategic aspcts of the UK economy, defence and administration by manipulating the price or availabilty of both software and hardware. "The availability of software may be restricted in at least three ways to influence the UK strategically: temporally, totally or partially:

(a) Temporal restrictions refer to the potential for foreign suppliers to only sell last year's model in the UK. This could ensure that the UK had a reduced competitive ability in important fields and markets.

(b) Total restrictions refer to deliberate decisions to prevent the UK purchasing essential software. For example, the USA's recent technology embargo has demonstrated that this tactic could be used to gain commercial advantage.

(c) Partial availability, such as supplying programs in binary but not source forms, is a common commercial practice. Strategically it means that, should a foreign supplier withdraw support and service from the UK, then the UK would not be able to maintain or develop the software on its own." (5)

When existing resources are used more effectively, then a research and development campaign is likely to be successful. But there is every sign that the UK companies do not have the international muscle to maintain growth and present market share (6). This suggests that the alternative strategy, the mission-oriented approach, might be more effective. This would allocate resources to projects of national significance, often connected with national defence. In fact, a very high proportion of national resources is already spent on research and development for defence and nuclear energy. However, to optimise results, it is necessary either to attempt to align national research efforts with the needs of industry, or otherwise to ensure that all spin-off developments of relevance are declassified and transferred to the private sector for evaluation and development with the minimum of delay, hence the Pipeline proposal.

Perhaps the Government in some way ought to encourage the mobility of experts so that both industry and academia can import expertise to plug gaps where the British research effort is weak. This country has been experiencing the so-called brain drain for many years, whereby a significant proportion of our better researchers have been tempted abroad by higher salaries and more positively supported research facilities. Both at a national and a company level, reform of the attitude towards research as reflected in status, pay levels and equipment availability could retain more graduates in the British environment. It might even bring home some of the expatriate workers. However, given the existing shortage of good research workers and the increasing activities of recruitment agencies which persuade trained staff to leave, there is an emerging practice for firms to bid against each other for experienced staff, combined with a trend to tie key employees to their firm by contractual means.

Thus, for example, a top researcher may be offered a mortgage subsidy to permit the purchase of a house in the London commuter belt, but the employer takes an interest in the house as a joint tenant, thereby limiting the employee's freedom to sell up and move to another area. This is particularly likely where large financial rewards may accrue to the firm from the commercial exploitation of the research. In such a situation, the company would require such a high figure of compensation, and such rigorous guarantees as to commercial confidentiality that a mobility scheme might be unworkable as between firms in the private sector. But exchange schemes as between the private sector and academia might be feasible. In the public sector, so great is the skills shortage that local authorities have begun to recruit staff on the basis that they repay any training costs if they leave within two years, (cf. the services firm Electronic Data Systems which has applied this principle in the private sector. (7)) This reflects the consensus view that the pay-back period for training is between two and three years.

But this does beg the question of whether academics can genuinely relate to industry. Those who research tend to be most interested in the research activity itself rather than the more pedestrian development of a marketable end product. This can lead to misunderstandings through a lack of awareness of commercial reality. However, if the academic researcher can learn some of the discipline of industry, this may focus attention and produce better results. Indeed, both sides may find their perspectives increased and, given the serendipity of academic research, there can often be unexpected benefits through the diversity of approach.

One of the major problems in the current relationship between academia and the commercial world is that often industry only offers short-term research contracts. From an organisational point of view, it is inefficient to put together a team for a project if it is only going to have an active life of, say, one year. This is particularly so because it is largely continuity of staffing, and the relationship between people who form a team, that is most conducive to productive research. Moreover, because the academic environment does not command the same level of salary as industry, academic consultancy can be a cheaper form of research investment for industry than the recruitment of in-house staff. There is the further indirect advantage that this form of experience can give academics an insight into the needs of commercial management, and may produce more realistic curricula in the planning for the training of the next generation of technologists. However, it may also produce both a brain and an entrepreneurial drain away from the academic environment if the educators leave the universities and polytechnics to attempt the commercial exploitation of good ideas. It also begs the question whether, without proper training, the educators can be the managers of innovation in this new area of computer applications.

As a result of Government pressure, more of the industrial and commercial world has acknowledged the need to properly train its work force so that it may become more competitive in a less protected market place. Indeed, the Government's skills shortage committee, chaired by John Butcher, has strongly advocated that industry and academia collaborate, and the trade union ASTMS has launched a campaign to argue that it should be every employee's contractual right to be trained, and to have skills upgraded. Further, the technical demands inherent in the information to be communicated, call for more subject-based expertise than the non-specialist human resources staff can provide in-house. A positive role for consultancy and collaboration has therefore arisen, and the academic community has responded with a number of projects.

The Cranfield Information Technology Institute has now been created with directors seconded from DEC, Cable & Wireless and British Telecom, and it intends to offer a range of short courses and modular post-graduate degrees to support management training aspirations. Similarly, Salford University has launched an IT Institute, while Strathclyde University has a £1.5m Information Technology Associate Scheme with ten major Scottish manufacturing companies each making a regular contribution. The commitment implicit in taking the step to become a mixed-funded institution, forces the educational side to keep in tune with the customers' needs. This may be left to the discretion of individual institutions, or it may be formalised. Thus, IBM UK have set up a joint industry and academic group called JUPITER (Joint University and Polytechnics Industrial Technology Education and Research). In the first instance, this will publish and maintain a guide to over ninety vetted and approved short management courses covering the planning, buying, introduction and support of computer systems in industry. The group will also seek to better define industry's training needs, so that better management education may be produced. (8) Their final aspiration is to develop a technology management degree course to be run at several different educational institutions, each of which would contribute its own speciality course module to the whole.

Naturally, IBM is not acting in a wholly philanthropic manner, for it hopes to foster a more favourable attitude among students towards IBM. But the end product is likely to be better educational standards upon entry to industry. IBM have also announced a joint educational effort with Portsmouth Polytechnic. This is paralleled by Nixdorf which is to set up an apprenticeship scheme to supply itself with the young skilled workforce which it needs. The company is currently negotiating with the DES and the DTI to secure recognition that its scheme will lead to a qualification similar to those awarded by FE. This scheme will be in substitution for any support of the City Technology Colleges which are considered of little relevance.

The Government could also review the substantive law on monopolies within the general ambit of directly effective Articles 85 and 86 of the Treaty of Rome to allow the formation

of larger commercial organisations which might be able to fund
major research projects, or which might achieve sufficient
diversity of commercial mix that significant cross-fertilisation
of ideas could arise. The law on both horizontal and vertical
technology transfer is reasonably well established, but the
exploitation of new ideas can lead to undesirable distortions in
the market place. If larger organisations are created which
achieve a dominant position in the market, the enforcement
agencies at both a national and a supranation level, must retain
the right to intervene to reassert the values of fair competition
and to curb abuse for the protection of the consumers.

Finally, in restricting attention to the immediate concerns of
this book, this leaves the question as to the nature of the
academic research which both Government and industry can best
promote to ensure improvement in the technology of learning. It
should be apparent that research into the way in which people
read might enable designers to optimise screen layout, while
research into learning theory would help the design of new aids
to learning, and give an insight into the best way of monitoring
any given student's progress. It is possible that synthetic
speech could be further refined to produce more effective automated delivery systems, and any move towards a natural language
interface would improve performance. Indeed, in a sense, there is
no shortage of work which academics could do in order to improve
the technology of the teaching/learning situation.

11.4   What is the European policy approach?

In February 1976, the Council of the European Communities adopted
an Action Programme to increase and improve the circulation of
information about educational policy. EURYDICE was set up to meet
that need. It is first of all a clearing house for information.
In addition to responding to specific requests, EURYDICE units
exploit their growing stock of comparative information on
educational policy issues by selective dissemination of processed
data in the form of overviews, analyses and thematic dossiers. It
also operates a specific enquiry system for policy makers. The
primary purpose is to improve co-operation between Member States
and to enhance the collective capacity to learn about and from
each other. This pooling of information is essential since the
historic connections of some members states individually have not
always been with those who are now their partners in the EEC.

One of the major themes identified by the policy makers has been
co-operation in Higher Education, leading to the COMETT programme
(Community Programme for Education and Training for Technology)
which is designed to encourage links between Higher Education and

industry in new technology. It entered its operational phase in January 1987 and consists of four elements:

.   the development of University–enterprise training partner-ships

.   the transnational exchange of students and personnel between universities and enterprises

.   the design and testing of joint University–Enterprise projects in the field of continuing education in new tech-nology

.   the development of multi–media systems for the new tech-nology

The programme funding is 45m ECUs for four years, with 13m ECUs for the first years.

In September 1983, the Council adopted a Resolution (OJ No C256, 24.9.1983) incorporating a series of measures to promote the introduction of new information technologies (NITs) in education. This Resolution was, and continues to be, the basis for a series of measures at Community level aimed at supplementing and supporting action taken by the different Member States. The measures to be taken in the educational field are but a part of an overall strategy designed to develop the human resources necessary to meet the challenges posed by the modernisation of industry. (9) The plan is to reinforce the competitiveness of industry and to ensure that these technologies are merely supportive and not dominant in society.

The Community announced general support in May 1987 for a general four year action programme (1988/91) to promote the integration of the handicapped into the education system. It is estimated that approximately 30m citizens, i.e. 10% of the current population of the Community, could benefit. The use of the new technologies is accorded a high priority for this purpose.

EuroTecneT is further part of the EEC's Action Programme on IT and training. It is a network of demonstration projects to build up and adapt training skills in relation to the new technologies. Although considerable progress has been made within the Community to eradicate the more overt barriers to the free movement of goods and labour, there are still problems in the movement of trained personnel. One of the more obvious starting points for reform is in the hallowed halls of the professional accreditation bodies to require a redefinition, and thereby a harmonisation, of professional qualification standards and practitioner require-ments. "The main resource of the European Community is its human resources, its people. Giving them proper training at all levels and thereby enabling them to master the technical, social and cultural changes of the end of this century is the major challenge of today." (10) The 1987 goals are:

- a valorisation goal, i.e. improving and developing past achievements

- a transfer goal, representing both a geographic transfer between countries and a sectoral transfer between training institutions and companies,

- a multiplying and opening goal, emphasising the external influence of the network and the possible influence of pilot experiments on ther vocational training systems of the Member States.

At a purely domestic level, the report of the Alvey Committee entitled A Programme for Advanced Information Technology was published in 1982. (11) The Government's response was to create the Alvey Directorate to supervise a collaborative research programme for the UK. All the research projects were to be carried out by at least two industrial parties and it was hoped that academic and Government research establishments would be included in the collaborations. By this means, it was hoped that the sponsored research would be more effectively exploited. At the time the Alvey Directorate was being established, Japan was investing US$500 million on the Fifth Generation Computer Programme. In the USA, President Reagan's August 1981 Economic Legislation provided incentives which were expected to encourage an additional US$3 billion spent in collaborative research and development over the subsequent five years. Perhaps it is indicative of the attitude of the United Kingdom to such schemes that, on the 25th June 1987, Plessey announced that it was to abandon one of the most prestigious and heavily-funded projects in the entire Alvey Programme. This was due to their inability to raise adequate venture capital to keep their part of the project going. At the time of writing, GEC may take over the project. Plessey is the fourth biggest recipient of Alvey funds in the UK, and it is disturbing that such a company should take public money and then decline to follow up the growing project with its own money. This shows a lack of commitment both on the part of Plessey and on the part of the City which failed to come up with the money for such a well-publicised project.

The comparable European initiative has been Esprit which made 750m ECUs available. Now Esprit 2 will offer 1,600m ECUs (£1.12b) over five years – a figure which assumes that Britain will pay its assessed share of the budget). Alvey's potential successor was originally dubbed the IT86 Committee under the chairmanship of Sir Austin Bide but there are funding problems because the Government has not wanted to commit itself until decisions were taken within the ambit of the EEC plan which is to produce a "Framework" project on Esprit funding. The primary concern of the IT86 committee has been to improve the exploitation of existing technology and to generally promote a better understanding of the uses of IT technology. Their report entitled Information Technology – A Plan for Concerted Action, identifies a number of

obstacles which may slow down, or even prevent, improvement.
These include:

- the fact that British industry has consistently shown itself
  unable to follow through research effort and to produce a
  good product for the market place

- that the attitude of banks and venture capitalists is short-
  term and thus not supportive of research efforts

- that even when money is made available, the interest rates
  are often high to reflect the speculative and high risk
  nature of the exercise from the perspective of the finance
  house; this lack of confidence provides a direct disincentive to creativity and innovation which is reinforced
  through the general lack of Government support.

Yet, the world market itself is distorted by both direct and
indirect government subsidies, and a failure at both a national
and international level to address the issue of competitiveness
in the exploitation of IT technologies will only accelerate home-
based uncompetitiveness. This is likely to become more acute as
the rate of technological change creates problems of obsolescence
and replacement. International restraints such as those imposed
by the United States which may limit access to the new technology
will further exacerbate the problem. If the response of the UK
Government is deregulation of the British home market, then this
may open up our market to unfair competition from suppliers who
work within a subsidised and protected home market. The Bide
Report calls for a £1b programme with a £425m contribution from
Government. The Government's response has been to confirm the
creation of a steering committee to be known as IT92, but its
funding and scope have yet to be confirmed. This resistance to
domestic funding also emperils the Esprit funding of projects,
and confidence in the research arena is low in the face of
Government reluctance to commit itself to support even existing
projects. This is matched by the Government's decision to close
the UK's national think-tank on IT. The IT Working Group is one
of twenty groups run under the aegis of the National Economic
Development Council, which is to be closed. Further, the
Government has not appointed a replacement for Sir Geoffrey
Pattie as IT Minister, thereby signalling a demotion in the level
of significance accorded to IT.

11.5 Conclusions

Whether the stimulus for innovation comes from within the
Government, from industry, or from the educational hierarchy, the

political decision which is to be taken is as to whether funding can be made available to support IT implementation; and, if so, what is the amount of that support to be, and is it to be payable as a result of a co-ordinated policy or will it be made available on an ad hoc or piecemeal basis? Budgetary considerations will obviously predominate, with the growing skill shortages important among the other factors which will affect the decision. Because of their accountability, Governments are often influenced by factors like cost-effectiveness, hence the suggestions which emerge from both the DES and the DTI that CAL/CBT will improve the quality of education and training which can be made available. If the Government is going to overcome the problem of development, it should probably look for the creation of, "a critical mass, that is, that the project should be of such a scale as to make a fundamental contribution to the teaching of the subject rather than merely providing enrichment material. This idea of critical mass also implied that the project should involve a large number of students and staff, thus demonstrating its relevance in a wide variety of educational environments." (12) To play with a number of limited projects is not satisfactory.

Another factor is that national Governments often choose to support national manufacturers through a now modified system of preferential procurement - the modification being necessary to conform to EEC principles of reduced or eliminated discrimination on the ground of nationality as between Member States. Hence, some public or private sector users may be forced into a situation where CAL or CBT is to be implemented using non-ideal equipment. Indeed, unsuitable computers can be placed in classroom almost by Government decree (e.g. the MEP) although, subject to pronouncements to be included in the National Curriculum, their use is not yet mandatory. The private sector is no more immune from error in acquiring hardware. Unthinking patriotism or simple lack of objective advice will frequently lead to the installation of an inappropriate system.

A neutral stance is the most usual public response of large organisations when confronted with the need to consider whether to make a change. By then filtering the decision-making through a large committee structure, it can become easier to do nothing. The difficulty is that if supposed decision makers actually do nothing in the short-term, enthusiasts may try to fill the gap, say, by buying computers as "lab equipment" or as some other justifiable item in the budget. Although this stop-gap measure may be thought to show laudable initiative, it often results in piecemeal systems which, in turn, makes any software produced less portable; and it does not provide for the situation of the activists moving to other jobs, leaving capital equipment unacknowledged and unused.

Wells concluded a comparative review of the effectiveness of a variety of technologies and instructional methods with the observation that, "given favourable conditions pupils can learn from any instructional medium now available." (13) But in practical experiments, students tend to concentrate on details of the practicality, e.g. what step to perform next, what continuing state of affairs to maintain, etc., and do not directly address the causes of the changes which are occuring or not, as the case may be. Where CAL is used, there is greater likelihood of the student asking, "What would happen if..?" or "Why did that happen?", i.e. they are led to question the reason behind the facts and to develop a feel for the principles involved. With CAL support, there is also a greater willingness, "on the part of the teacher to use questions which are more open-ended and which also place a greater intellectual demand on the pupil... The increased demand of the questions does not appear to produce a corresponding increase in the number of incorrect responses from the pupils; it does, however, seem to generate longer responses." (14) This permits the teacher a better insight into the students' thinking processes and can improve error correction. It should also enhance student/student dialogue and teacher/student dialogue.

There is little doubt as our society approaches the 1990s, that the computer will become more common in the education sector. In accepting the advent of the computer, education is responding to four allied, but distinct, pressures:

. The students themselves have become more aware of the power of machines from their experience in the real world, and now begin to expect some form of computer-based instruction.

. The Government wishes to make the education system more efficient, and to stabilise or reduce the overall budgetary contribution made from public funds. The new technology is seen as one possible mechanism for achieving this aim. The Government also has a formal policy of encouraging the spread of Information Technology in order to maintain Britain's position as a technologically-efficient country.

. The computer hardware and software producers see the schools, colleges and universities as a shop window for their wares. The next generation of commercial users and managers are now undertaking training in Higher Education, and habits obtained in this formative phase will stand the producers in good stead when such people begin to influence the decision-making in the real world.

. Prospective employers require adequately trained students who are familiar with standard applications packages and who can begin to make use of IT within industry and commerce.

The more widespread use of computers depends upon their effectiveness and their low cost. In many academic areas almost no effective CAL teaching materials exist; in all areas, the existing materials are fragmentary and only employed extensively in a few locations. There are three main reasons for this shortage of materials:

- Firstly, because there is a limited commercial market, there have been few incentives for entrepreneurial staff to prepare computer-based materials. Few of the aids which support more conventional authors are available to support computer authors. Educational software remains a cottage industry, yet if an author wishes to publish a book, a publisher offers an editorial and advisory service which is backed up by advertising and reviews in general and specialist publications.

- Secondly, up to this point in time, there have been few useful shells, and it has been left to the more specialist member of staff to struggle with an ordinary high-level language or a more specialised authoring language. Thus, the educationalist has had to be a programmer as well as a domain expert. Now with the development of more appropriate shells and friendly front-ends, non-computer specialists can more easily produce useful material.

- Thirdly, problems of portability have made it uneconomic to develop mass-market software. Now, with increasing standard-isation, e.g. in the IBM/clone/look-alike market, there are greater commercial opportunities to exploit.

In the longer-term, the structure and organisation of the education sector may change and assume more of the characteristics of distance learning. Each home may have its own terminals and work stations connected to a national grid where instructional materials may be found on all the major subject disciplines at a variety of different educational levels. Actual class contact in tutorials may become unnecessary if telephone-based conferencing facilities (with or without televisual backup) are made more cheaply available. Actual face-to-face contact may only be considered appropriate for physical skills training or for psychological reasons to prevent society from devolving into a hive culture such as that described by E.M. Forster in "The Machine Stops", or by Michael Frayn in "A Very Private Life". Until such "science fictional" albeit dystopic, advances become reality, there will continue to be a need for schools and colleges, and the day-to-day practice of instruction. This is not to argue, however, that there is no need for change today. Indeed, the use of CAL/CBT techniques is seen to be educationally sound from a theoretical point of view, and it has been shown to be as effective as other teaching methods in all the major practical research which has been undertaken. It is therefore reasonable to argue that the most constructive method of developing the currently available educational resource within education, is to invest financial and intellectual resources in the development and dissemination of coherent CAL suites.

It is freely admitted that although the title to this book appears to limit the debate to the education environment in the academic sense, some attention has been paid to the implications for industry in their training function. In fact, it is intended that everything said about CAL should be considered applicable to CBT although no reference was made at each point to CBT work. There are two reasons for this view:

.   It was felt necessary to address the general issue of the place and the role of the computer in the education sector. If a case could be made out for the adoption of CAL generally, and expert systems in particular, then it would follow that it should be applied to training in the commercial sector. Equally, if no case could be argued for CAL and/or expert systems, there was no single educational feature inherent in the needs of CBT that would rescue the lost argument.

.   In any event, the general view is taken that if there is any educational difference between the approach required to teach the purely academic, rather than more practical skills of the employment market place, it is perhaps rather more in degree than in substance. Thus, it is probable that a more explicit and expository style in the presentation of concepts and ideas is required for non-advanced work, with a greater likelihood of curriculum emphasis on the development of practical skills. There will also tend to be a greater need both for some remedial work, and for the more general implicit aim of influencing the processes of socialisation and intellectual development in the student. CAL may there- fore be more particularly suited to supporting this educa- tional area because the more complete the introductory and computer-based tutorial materials, the more the teacher may devote precious class contact time to helping individuals or small groups. In advanced work, it may be possible to argue that the learning activity is, or should be, more student- centered, but whether this is "true", in reality depends upon how the teacher proposes to communicate basic concepts and to consolidate the students' understanding of the practical or academic gloss. In this process, the greater the freedom of the teacher to leave the introductory and general teaching to machine-based, machine-supported or machine-reinforced systems, the more time may be spent on developing detailed understanding in the student, no matter what the academic level one seeks to achieve.

It cannot be denied that there are problems associated with the introduction of CAL but it is submitted that, overall, the advantages outweigh the disadvantages. This is particularly because the major disadvantages are of a more administrative than educational nature and only require a shift in policy and an allocation of resources for the educational and professional advantages to stand clear. The initial problem is two-fold:

.   Firstly, CAL packages have to be produced.

.   Secondly, teachers have to be persuaded to incorporate those
        packages into their teaching strategies.

While the programming of computers remained an arcane science,
teaching staff could legitimately avoid CAL's true implications.
The development of delivery systems and shells removes the excuse
which has for so long insulated staff from the power of the
computer. Now, the only real question is whether staff should
start with systems like MICROTEXT, TOP CLASS or DOMINO, or
whether expert system shells should be used.

On a straight cost-comparison, expert system shells are more
expensive to buy than the conventional authoring packages, and
the licensing situation is less clearly and coherently worked out
by the software producers. This is mainly a function of the
market place where demand for expert system shells is, as yet,
not well-established. However, schools and colleges are already
confronted by the need to acquire samples of both expert system
shells and completed expert systems for use in Information Technology modules. Given that many schools and colleges must make
the expenditure if a comprehensive training in IT is to be
offered, it is only sensible that the institutions maximise the
utility in that capital investment and adopt one or more shells
as the basis of a standardised approach to CAL either within an
individual school or college, or within an LEA if economies of
scale in development terms are to be achieved. In any event, as
the market develops, the price of the shells should become more
competitive, and make their acquisition and development more
economically feasible.

It is admitted that greater educational skill and care is
required to get the best out of an expert system, and that there
are considerable problems to be overcome both in training and in
motivating the ordinary member of staff to invest the requisite
time and effort in the programming of teaching materials from
scratch. Indeed, some staff will experience feelings of resent-
ment merely when asked to define or redefine the learning
objectives to be fulfilled by each element in the course taught.
It is sometimes felt to be unprofessional to query the teaching
methodology of colleagues.   But, for all the reasons previously
given, it is submitted that the educational rewards are so
significantly superior, that all staff should be encouraged to
learn the use of CAL, and to adopt one or more expert system
shells, rather than the more simple multi-branching systems. If
individuals are encouraged to start at a level where the end
results achievable are less open to criticism on both academic
and educational terms, they may be encouraged to go on. If
individuals start on a low level, they may be confirmed in their
worst fears and abandon the effort, or they may too easily
satisfied and not progress to the more educationally satisfactory
systems. If expert system shells are used, students may gain
access to superior teaching methodology. If teach staff are to
create knowledge databases, a better understanding of both the

domain expertise and of the art of teaching is likely to be gained.

This book has both implicitly and explicitly addressed a number of major policy issues:

.   How constructively do schools and colleges, and the industrial and commercial firms exploit the expensive resource represented by the teaching or training staff if CAL is currently not used, or used only sporadically?

.   How organisationally and financially can schools and colleges, and the indutrial and commercial firms implement the detailed educational appraisal work necessary to determine whether CAL could directly benefit individual courses offered within the institution or firm?

.   Should decisions about the implementation of CAL be left to individual institions, or should there be a nationally co-ordinated effort to avoid or minimise problems of parochialism or the duplication of effort?

.   What are the implications for the training and retraining of teaching staff in the use of CAL techniques?

It is not the purpose of this book to attempt an answer for all these questions directly, but any interim decisions made on the strength of this book must be taken against the broader pattern which those issues represent. The overall resolution of the debate can only occur after the proper consideration of input from the Government and national co-ordinating bodies, from trades unions and the National Students Union, from the LEAs and representatives of school, college and university management, and all other interested parties. Education has become a more significant part of every individual's life, and it is therefore incumbent upon the policy and decision-makers to engage in constructive consultation with a view to improving the provision of learning opportunities.

These opportunities should be offered at both ends of the age spectrum. It is not simply a matter of making provision for the young. In general, society perceives older people in negative terms. Old age is seen to be a period of inevitable decline, ill health and decrepitude. This image of the old is reinforced through much advertising which pitches computer hardware at the young. Education also tends to fall into the trap of age-prejudice, but in a society where retirement is either compulsory or strongly encouraged at 55, there is in fact an increasing need to service this growing sector of the community. (15) In addition to ageism is the continuing sexism, and the combination tends to pose significant barriers in the way of older women in the retraining or continuing education environment. In fact, there are many computer application in the areas of health education, diet, exercise and leisure which could be beneficial and interesting to the older person but which have not been written with the old person in mind. Similarly, greater access to information on welfare rights, consumer advice, etc., could significantly improve quality of life. It becomes all the more important to encourage greater awareness because the national policy is to encourage much greater self-reliance and self-care by the elderly in the community.

However, whether the example of the Lamplighter School in using LOGO with three year old children, or the vision of post-retirement courses inspires the move in the direction of CAL, there is perhaps one slight modification to the terminology which should be made to emphasise that, at the end of the day, no matter what decisions are taken, the heart of the matter is the human process of learning. Therefore, for all that computers are involved, the decision-makers should be concerned with the application of teachnology and not mere technology.

References

(1) Changing Urban Bureaucracies: How New Practices Become Routinized. R.K.Yin. Lexington, Massachusetts. 1979.

(2) Local Education Authority policies for computers in education. F.J.Burdett. (1987) 3 Jo. of Computer Assisted Learning 30/9 at p.37.

(3) Computer Weekly, July 2nd, 1987. pp.24.5

(4) Software: A Vital Key to UK Competitiveness. An ACARD Report. HMSO, London. 1986.

(5) ibid at p.11.

(6) A Competitive Assessment of the United States Software Industry. T.Miles and R.Ahlberg. US Dept of Commerce. GPO Stock Number 003 009 004364. 1985. Focus on Innovation, published by the Technology Requirements Board, July 1987.

(7) Computer Weekly, Thursday, July 9th, 1987. p.1.

(8) Computer Weekly, Thursday, June 18, 1987.

(9) see OJ No C166, 25.6.1983 vocational training and new technologies, COM(83)6 final and V/1523/84-F/EN co-operation between industry and universities on advanced training.

(10) Marin, speech to People and Technology Conference, London November 1986. quoted in EuroTecnet, No:3 Feb. 1987, produced by European Centre for Work and Society, Holland.

(11) HMSO ref. ISBN 0 11 5136533.

(12) Teaching Applied Statistics by Computer. F.R.Abbott and J.R.Hartley. collected in Selected Readings in Computer-Based Learning. pp.188/94 at .p188/9.

(13) Evaluation Criteria and the Effectiveness of Instructional Technology in Higher Education. S.Wells. (1976) 5 Higher Education 253-75.

(14) Evaluating CAL for the classroom. John L. Chatterton. collected in Teachers, computers and the classroom. pp.88/95 at p.94.

(15) Computers and Older People. Mirian Bernard. collected in Microcomputers in Adult Education. pp.36/52.

Bibliography

Alessi, Stephen M. and Trollip, Stanley R. **Computer-Based Instruction. Methods and Development.** Prentice-Hall Inc., New Jersey. 1985.

Atkinson, Richard C. and Wilson, H. A. (ed) **Computer-Assisted Instruction. A Book of Readings.** Academic Press, New York. 1969.

Bell, Robert; Fowler, Gerald and Little, Ken. (ed) **Education in Great Britain and Ireland. A Source Book.** Routledge & Kegan Paul, London. 1973.

Bostock, Stephen J. and Seifert, Roger V. **Micro Computers in Adult Education.** Croom Helm, Beckenham. 1986.

Bramer, M.A. **Research and Development in Expert Systems. Proceedings of the Fourth Technical Conference of the BCS Specialist Group on Expert Systems.** Cambridge University Press, Cambridge. 1985.

Cline, Hugh F.; Bennett, Randy Elliot; Kershaw, Roger C.; Schneiderman, Martin B.; Stecher, Brian; Wilson, Susan. **The Electronic Schoolhouse: The IBM Secondary School Computer Education Program.** Lawrence Erlbaum Associates, New Jersey. 1986.

Gagne, Robert M. and Briggs, Leslie J. **Principles of Instructional Design.** Holt, Rinehart and Winston, New York. 1979.

Goldenberg, E. Paul; Russell, Susan Jo and Carter, Cynthia J. with Stokes, Shari; Sylvester, Mary Jane and Kelman, Peter. **Computers, Education and Special Needs.** Addison-Wesley Publishing Co, Massachusetts. 1984.

Hudson, Keith. **Introducing CAL. A Practical Guide to Writing Computer-Assisted Learning Programs.** Chapman and Hall, London. 1984.

Lawrence, John Shelton. **The Electronic Scholar.** Ablex Publishing Corp., New Jersey. 1984.

Lewis, Robert and Tagg, E.D. (ed) **Trends in Computer Assisted Education.** Blackwell Scientific Publications, Oxford. 1987.

Margolin, Joseph B., and Mirsch, Marion R. (ed) **Computers in the Classroom. An interdisciplinary view of trends and alternatives.** Spartan Books, New York. 1970.

293

Martin, C. Dianne, and Heller, Rachelle S. (ed) **Capitol—izing on Computers in Education.** Proceedings of the 1984 Association for Educational Data Systems Annual Conference. Computer Science Press, Rockville, Maryland. 1984.

O'Shea, Tim, and Self, John. **Learning and Teaching with Computers. Artificial Intelligence in Education.** Harvester Press, Brighton. 1983.

Reid, William A., and Walker, Decker F. (ed) **Case Studies in Curriculum Change.** Routledge & Kegan Paul, London. 1975.

Rushby, N.J. (ed) **Computer—Based Learning. A State of the Art Report.** Pergamon, Oxford. 1983.

Rushby, N.J. (ed) **Selected Readings in Computer—Based Learning.** Kogan Page, London. 1981.

Sleeman, D. and Brown, J.S. (ed) **Intelligent Tutoring Systems.** Academic Press, London. 1982.

Smith, Christopher (ed). **Microcomputers in Education.** Ellis Horwood Ltd, Chichester. 1982.

Stahl, Ingolf. **Operational Gaming. An International Approach.** Pergamon Press, Oxford, 1983.

Traub, Joseph F. (ed). **Cohabiting with Computers.** William Kaufman Inc, Los Altos, California. 1985.

Woodhouse, David and McDougall, Anne. **Computers: Promise and Challenge in Education.** Blackwell Scientific Publication. Carlton, Victoria, Australia. 1986.

Yazdani, Masoud. (ed). **New Horizons in Educational Computing.** Ellis Horwood Ltd, Chichester, 1984.

Index

295

CB Student Text Series

Hardware

Computer Systems Organisation

Software